Finding O
Educati...

a Guide to Sources of Information
by
Peter B. Clarke

Published by Longman Industry and Public Service Management, Longman Group UK Ltd, Westgate House, The High, Harlow, Essex CM20 1YR, UK.
Telephone: (0279) 442601
Fax: (0279) 444501

First published 1990

British Library Cataloguing in Publication Data
Clarke, Peter
    Finding out in education: a guide to sources of information
    1. Great Britain. Education. Information sources
    I. Title
    370.7041

    ISBN 0-582-06754-5

Printed and bound in Great Britain by
Biddles Ltd, Guildford and King's Lynn

Contents

Note. Throughout the book the term 'Latest edn.' has been used rather than, say '3rd edn.' or '5th edn.' to indicate works which have been appearing regularly in new editions.

Preface

He had a dream, a vision splendid,
Of a library building open-ended
Where information grew and grew
Spreading ideas old and new
Not only in book and encyclopaedia
But in all the audio-visual media:
A store of knowledge so complete
That it made lectures obsolete.

Teachers no longer spouted truths
To doubting maids and doubtful youths
Who sat all day in silent rows
Praying for the day to close,
But sent them to the library shelves
To find the answers for themselves,
And all the students in the college

Were filled with a new desire for knowledge
And studied in ways much more exploratory
Within the library laboratory,
Striving to achieve perfection
Under their lecturers' direction.

No one will be too surprised
His dream has not been realised
But there are signs to minds discerning
Of a move towards resource based learning,
A movement that needs no apology
In this age of new technology,
For libraries will change and grow
In ways that none of us yet know.

(Peter B. Clarke)

Acknowledgements [   ]

I have enjoyed writing this book but it has also been very demanding. It would not have been completed without the help of many people.

I am grateful to Sir Henry Wood, former Principal at Jordanhill College, for giving me the opportunity to work there, and to start building up the kind of resources which made the book possible; and also to his successor, Dr Tom Bone, C.B.E, for his continued support. I owe a debt to Anne Williamson, my Deputy Librarian for many years, whose knowledge of the literature of education was a boon to a generation of students and teaching staff, and also to me.

Fortunately I was also able to draw on the expertise of the Systems Librarian, George Geddes, who created the Media Library in the College and has already made a name for himself in his chosen field. He is certainly not responsible for any shortcomings of chapter 20. Other members of the Jordanhill staff have helped me on numerous occasions, particularly David Alcock, Ian Allan, Linda Emery, Gina Hamilton, Anne Macdonald, Maureen O'Hara, Jean Smith and Irene Stirling. I am grateful to them all.

Among the libraries which I used to my advantage were Bearsden and Milngavie District Libraries, Glasgow College Library, Glasgow University Library, the Glasgow Mitchell Library, the Heriot Watt University Library, the National Library of Scotland, Newcastle Polytechnic Library, Paisley College Library, and St Andrews College Library in Bearsden. I much appreciate the opportunities which they provided, and the help which I received.

A number of other people responded promptly and professionally to my requests for information and advice, in particular John Birch, Deputy Librarian of the DES Library; Dr Ronnie Carr, Staff Tutor in the School of Education at the Open University in Scotland; John Dyer of the SCFL; Avril Johnston of SCET; Carol Stewart and Anita Goodall of NERIS (Scotland); and Tegwen Wallace of the SCCC. I also received courteous attention and very useful material from the Advisory Centre for Education, MARIS On-Line, and the National Council for Educational Technology. Again, they bear no responsibility for the final result.

Being involved in a work of this kind inevitably impinges on family life. I am very grateful to my wife Sylvia and my daughters Jennifer and Rachel for their patience, forbearance and support during my endless hours at the word processor and elsewhere. They will be pleased that their ordeal is over.

Patrick B. Clarke,
June 1990.

1 Introduction

Education as a subject is studied by all intending teachers and should be of continuing interest to teachers in service as well as to lecturers in colleges and universities. A guide to the literature of education geared to their immediate and long-term needs should therefore be useful to students and teachers alike, indeed to anyone who has a general or particular interest in education.

This is not a subject guide. In other words it is not arranged by topics or under different aspects of education. Nor is it concerned with standard textbooks, monographs, etc. within the educational field. My aim has been to indicate the different *types* of reference material available for the study of education, and to describe the sources which could be helpful to those who wish to explore the literature for themselves.

There is a strong emphasis on British sources and, where relevant, on Scottish sources, but no apologies are made for this. Most of the other sources included are American, and these have been clearly indicated by adding the letters: 'USA' to the entries. There is also an emphasis on contemporary sources since most of the material included has been published within the last ten years.

The term 'education' has had to be strictly defined. Briefly, it covers all aspects of the subject included in the divisions of the Dewey Decimal Classification 370–379 (see chapter 4). It therefore excludes subjects related to education, e.g. philosophy, psychology, sociology and the social sciences, except for a few relevant examples. More significantly it excludes the teaching of particular subjects such as history.

There are of course many general works which will yield information on education, e.g. general encyclopaedias, directories, handbooks of statistics, biographical dictionaries, periodical indexes and bibliographies. Because of pressure on space, references to such works have been kept to an essential minimum and full descriptions have not always been given. However, their inclusion will be welcomed by those who do not have access to a specialised education library, and by those who wish to obtain general information on education quickly.

Some readers may feel that the two chapters on educational research have little relevance for them. This is understandable. They are intended primarily for students, teachers and lecturers who are undertaking a more serious investigation into some limited aspect of education, possibly for a higher degree. Even so, they contain information which would be useful to any reader, e.g. the notes on how to make bibliographical references, and the specimen bibliography.

Research, perhaps unfortunately, tends to be given an elevated status. Research in some form takes place at all levels. Anyone who investigates an educational topic for an essay, assignment or project is involved in educational research of a kind, and will have to use some of the sources mentioned in the following pages if the work is to be completed successfully.

There are several checklists which have been included to meet particular needs, i.e. 'Some books on how to study' (pp.7–8): 'Official reports on education' (pp.37–40); 'Guides for governors' (pp.51–2); and 'Open University course readers' (pp. 106–7). These lists are quite long and it has not been possible to provide annotations, but some readers may be grateful for them.

I have been fortunate during the preparation of this guide in having access to the resources of the largest college of education library in Britain, one which I know intimately since I was closely involved in its development over a period of almost twenty years. This means that I have been able to examine personally, and in many cases to use, the majority of the works described here.

I hope that the guide will be a reliable source of reference for students who wish to explore the literature of education beyond the limited world of their text books and lecture notes; for teachers and lecturers who are trying to keep themselves up to date; for those who, either full-time or part-time, are undertaking educational research of some kind; and for any others who are endeavouring for whatever reason to be more fully informed about educational developments.

It may also be welcomed by librarians (and students of librarianship) in this country and abroad who have been trying to meet the demands of their readers without an up-to-date guide to mainly British sources of information to help them. The standard guide by Michael Humby (see p.126) has long held a respected place and will still have to be consulted for older material not included here. However, a new text is needed for new times, and this must be the justification for the present work.

Although teacher training until recently has been contracting in this country the literature of education has continued to grow apace and trying to keep abreast of it is not an easy task. There is a formidable amount of detail in this guide. I should be most grateful therefore to have any errors or omissions pointed out and to receive any suggestions for its future improvement.

2 The information explosion

The tremendous explosion in the output of knowledge and information is a phenomenon of the twentieth century and more particularly of the last few decades. It creates special problems of identification and digestion for those people in our society who need access to it, and who must be familiar not only with what has been written already but also with new publications as they make their appearance. This is certainly true of students and teachers who now find it increasingly difficult to isolate from this wealth of printed information the material which is relevant to their needs.

Teachers and students in the final decade of this century are still to a large extent dependent on the printed word for their understanding of most subjects taught in our educational institutions. However, the information and ideas which they derive from printed sources are increasingly being supplemented by those they obtain from non-print sources as more and more material is produced in this form.

To the remarkable output of books and periodical literature must now be added the flood of non-book materials, from filmstrips to computer packages, which are now being produced to meet the demands of the new approaches to teaching and learning in schools, colleges and universities in this country and elsewhere.

Now important new resources are available which are adding another dimension to the search for information. Sophisticated information retrieval systems, provided they are accessed efficiently, are making the researcher's task less labour-intensive and are producing impressive results. These on-line systems and the rapidly developing CD–ROM facilities which can now be found in many academic, public and special libraries are already becoming indispensable for educational research. They are also being used more readily by the student and general reader to obtain bibliographical and directory-type information.

It is essential therefore that those who require access to the world's accumulated store of knowledge and information should develop the ability to 'tap the memory' of libraries in general and their own library in particular as quickly and efficiently as possible. Teachers, students and pupils in all types of educational institutions are now being encouraged to acquire library skills for information retrieval purposes. One of the main functions of professional librarians is to help them whenever they encounter difficulties.

3 Guides to libraries

The guides mentioned below should enable you to identify the libraries in your area which have potentially useful resources, and also those further afield which it may be worth writing or travelling to for particular purposes. Although much of the information presented in these guides is in a concise form, they should help you to estimate the strengths and weaknesses of individual libraries and how useful they are likely to be in meeting your requirements.

Aslib Directory of Information Sources in the United Kingdom. **Latest edn.**
Aslib. 2 vols. Vol. 2: *Social Sciences, Medicine and the Humanities.*

> This is a standard work and much the largest of the British guides. A Shorter Aslib Directory was published in 1986.

Libraries Year Book. **Latest edn. J. Clarke & Co.**

> A detailed list of all types of libraries. Formerly the *Libraries, Museums and Art Galleries Year Book.*

Libraries in the United Kingdom and the Republic of Ireland:
> A Complete List of Public Library Services and a Select List of Academic and other Library Addresses. Library Association, annual.

Scottish Library and Information Resources.
Latest edn. Scottish Library Association.

There are several more specialised guides:

Guide to Government Department and Other Libraries. **British Library:** Science Reference and Information Service, 2-yearly.

Directory of Polytechnic and Other Libraries.
Latest edn. Council of Polytechnic Librarians.

Libraries in Colleges of Further and Higher Education in the UK. **Latest edn. Library Association.**

Directory of Rare Book and Special Collections in the UK and the Republic of Ireland. Library Association, 1985.

> A much more substantial guide intended for researchers rather than the general reader.

General information on national, academic, public and special libraries in this country will be found in *Libraries and Information in Britain* (British Council, 1987).

For libraries in the USA and Canada there are two established guides, both published by Bowker: the *American Libraries Directory.* (Latest edn. Bowker: USA, 2 vols.); and Subject Collections (Latest edn. Bowker: USA, 2 vols.).

There is also a more specialised *National Directory of Education Libraries and Collections* (Meckler: USA, 1990).

For libraries worldwide you could refer to the latest editions of the *World Guide to Libraries* and the *World Guide to Special Libraries* (W. Germany), both published by K.G. Saur

4 The Dewey Decimal Classification

As most readers are aware, the Dewey Decimal Classification is used by the majority of libraries in this country for the arrangement of their bookstocks and often for the arrangement of non-book materials as well. There are other systems in use, particularly in university libraries, e.g. the Universal Decimal Classification (UDC), a modification of Dewey; the Bibliographic Classification of Bliss (BC); and the Library of Congress Classification (LC). These all have their advantages and disadvantages, but Dewey is still the system most likely to be encountered by students, teachers and the general reader. It divides the whole of knowledge, as it is found in books, into ten main classes, and each class is assigned a number as follows:

000 General works
100 Philosophy, psychology
200 Religion
300 Social sciences
400 Language
500 Pure sciences, mathematics
600 Technology
700 The arts
800 Literature
900 Geography, history.

Each of these is further subdivided, for example:

300 Social sciences
310 Statistics
320 Political science
330 Economics
340 Law
350 Public administration
360 Social services
370 Education
380 Commerce, communications
390 Customs

Education (370) is subdivided as follows:

370 Education
371 School organisation, special education
372 Primary education
373 Secondary education
374 Further education
375 Curriculum
376 Education of women
377 Schools and religion
378 Higher education
379 Education and the state.

Each of these sections is then subdivided using the decimal point, for example:

371 School organisation and management; special education
371.1 Teaching and teaching personnel
371.2 School administration and management
371.3 Methods of instruction and study
371.4 Guidance and counselling
371.5 School discipline
371.6 Physical plant
371.7 School health and safety
371.8 The student
371.9 Special education.

Further subdivision is carried out as necessary, for example:

371.271 Tests and examinations
371.3358 Educational television
371.95 Gifted students.

The following example illustrates the whole process:

300 Social sciences
370 Education
371 School organisation, etc.
371.3 Methods of instructions
371.3358 Educational television.

An outline of the complete Dewey Decimal Classification will normally be displayed in your library, with individual tier and shelf guides as required. The full classification schedules are much more detailed, and in the 20th edition they fill four very substantial volumes.

The classification and cataloguing sytems in a library are complementary. The classification system arranges the books on the shelves in a convenient order. The library's catalogue, which may be on cards, on microfiche, or online provides a complete record of all the books in the library, usually by author and subject, and sometimes by title. Since the class number is added to each entry, the catalogue also enables you to locate a particular book on the shelves.

5 Some books on how to study ☐

It may be helpful to provide beginners or mature students, and possibly some more experienced ones, with a select list of books on how to study efficiently. More books of this type are being published nowadays because of the growing emphasis on student centred learning.

Those listed here are essentially practical books and they have not been annotated. A number of older books which have proved their worth have been included, but none was published before 1980. A few of the titles are concerned particularly with writing and examination techniques. There are two books listed below which are designed primarily for students from overseas: by F.X. Asibong and S. Sambilene.

A fuller bibliography of books and periodical articles could have been compiled on the theoretical aspects of study techniques for the benefit of teachers and tutors. However, this would have extended the list unduly.

ACRES, D. *How to Pass Exams Without Anxiety.* 2nd edn, Northcote House, 1987.

ASHMAN, S. and GEORGE A. *Study and Learn: A Self-Help Guide for Students.* Heinemann, 1982.

ASIBONG, F.X. *A Guide to Practical Study Skills.* Arnold, 1983. (Primarily for overseas students).

BARRASS, R. *Students Must Write: a Guide to Better Writing in Course Work and Examinations.* Methuen, 1982.

BARRASS, R. *Study! a Guide to Effective Study, Revision and Examination Techniques.* Chapman & Hall, 1984.

BEDDOES, C. *Returning to Study.* Hutchinson, 1989.

BURGEN, A.D. *How to Study: a Practical Guide.* New edn., Nelson, 1985.

CARMAN, R. A. and ADAMS, W.R. *Study Skills: a Student's Guide for Survival.* 2nd edn, Wiley, 1984.

CASEY, F. *How to Study: a Practical Guide.* Macmillan, 1985.

CASSIE, W.F. and CONSTANTINE, T. *Student's Guide to Success.* Macmillan, 1985.

CLOUGH, E. *Study and Examination Techniques.* Hodder, 1986. (Teach Yourself Books).

COCKER, D. *Successful Exam Technique.* Northcote House, 1987.

COLES, M. and WHITE, C. *Strategies for Studying.* Collins, 1985.

DUNLEAVY, P. *Study for a Degree in the Humanities and Social Sciences.* Macmillan, 1986.

ELLIS, R. and HOPKINS, K. *How to Succeed in Written Work and Study: a Handbook for Students.* Collins, 1985.

FREEMAN, C. *Mastering Study Skills.* Macmillan, 1982.

GOOD, M. and SMITH, C. *In the Know: 8 Keys to Successful Learning.* BBC Books, 1988.

HOWE, A. *How to study: a Student's Guide to Effective Learning Skills.* Kogan Page, 1986.

HUMPHRIES, D. *Improve your Study Skills.* CRAC: Hobsons, 1985.

MADDOX, H. *How to Study.* Revised edn., Pan Books, 1988.

MARSHALL, L. A. and ROWLAND, F. *A Guide to Learning Independently.* Open University Press, 1983.

MEREDEEN, S. *Study for Survival and Success: Guidenotes for College Students.* Paul Chapman Publishing, 1988.

PALMER, R. and POPE, C. *Brain Train: Study for Success*. E & F. N. Spon Ltd, 1984.

ROBERTSON, S. and SMITH, D. *Effective Study*. Longman, 1987.

ROWNTREE, D. *Learn how to Study: A Guide for Students of All Ages*. 3rd edn., Macdonald Orbis, 1988.

SAMBILENE, S. *Strengthening your Study Skills: A Guide for Overseas Students*. London University Institute of Education, 1982.

SELMES, I. *Improving Study Skills*. Hodder, 1987.

WILLIAMS, K. *Study Skills*. Macmillan, 1989.

6 Signposts to educational information

The purpose of this brief chapter is to draw attention to several publications which are particularly useful for locating general educational information. The first is a compact paperbound handbook which will provide answers to many enquiries:

Education A–Z: Where to Look Things Up, by E. **Wallis. Latest edn. Advisory Centre for Education.**

The function of the Advisory Centre for Education (ACE) is 'to provide essential information and advice for those involved in the maintained education service' and more particularly for parents. Its free advice service deals with about 200 enquiries per week. The ACE is a registered charity and is doing very worthwhile work with limited resources. There is no equivalent in Scotland.

This handbook is a signpost to relevant sources of information. There are alphabetical subject headings ranging from the pre-school years to adult education. Under each heading there is a brief article followed by notes about organisations, official reports, reference works, and important books on the topic. There is a separate index of organisations mentioned in the text. The handbook is always worth trying as a first source for basic educational information. It may not contain what you are looking for, but it will often point you in the right direction. There is much here that you will not find so readily elsewhere. One of the virtues of *Education A–Z* is that it continues to be revised and updated as necessary. Meantime, more recent information will be found in the:

ACE Bulletin. **Monthly. Advisory Centre for Education**

This well established periodical was called simply Where from 1961–79 and *Where to Find Out About Education* from 1980–84. Intended primarily for the educational consumer, it contains lively and practical articles and has a valuable section called the *ACE Digest*. This is a selective guide to recent pamphlets, books, reports, journals, newsletters, official publications, etc., all briefly annotated, with the addresses from which they are obtainable. HMI and Ombudsman reports are listed. Regular reference to the *ACE Digest* is one of the best ways of keeping up to date with new publications and is strongly recommended.

The ACE issues many other publications which are designed to be helpful to schools, teachers, parents, governors, etc. in a practical way. Some of them are mentioned elsewhere in this guide. Worth noting here are the information sheets on specific topics, e.g. 'Framework for school government'; 'Primary schools today'; 'The Race Relations Act and education'; 'School closure'; and 'Sex education and the curriculum'. These information sheets appear as inserts in the *ACE Bulletin* (above) and multiple copies are obtainable if required.

The last publication is another handbook but it has a different function and arrangement from the one above:

The Education Fact File: A Handbook of Education Information in the UK, **by J. Statham and D. Mackinnon. Hodder in association with the Open University, 1989.**

It was produced as a set book for the Open University course *Exploring Educational Issues (E208)* but could be very useful to others. It aims to provide basic factual information in words, diagrams and figures about education in the UK today and succeeds in being readable as well as informative. Sections are: (1) Background; (2) The system; (3) Curriculum, achievement and equality; and (4) Educational terms and abbreviations. Worth noting are chapter 3, which summarises the principal official reports on education and related subjects since 1944, and chapter 4 which outlines the most important educational legislation from the Education Act of 1870 to the Education Reform Act of 1988.

II   General reference sources

7 Guides to reference books

As explained in the introduction it has not been possible to give full descriptions of general reference books or to include many references to works in areas related to education. As a possible alternative you are encouraged to consult the following guides which should be available in any fair-sized reference library:

HIGGENS, G. *Printed Reference Material.* **2nd edn. Library Association, 1984.**
> An excellent survey of the different types of reference books with advice on how to use them, but with only limited reference to education. There is a good chapter on online information retrieval systems.

The standard guide by A.J. Walford is much more detailed in particular subject areas and has a valuable section devoted to education:

WALFORD, A.J. *Guide to Reference Material. Vol. 2: Social and Historical Sciences, Philosophy and Religion.* **Latest edn. Library Association.**
> You may also wish to refer to Vol. 3: *Generalia, Language and Literature, The Arts* (Latest edn.) which describes general encyclopaedias, bibliographies, dictionaries, etc. There is also a *Walford's Concise Guide to Reference Material* (1981). Although it is more selective and less recent it includes essential sources on education.

The American equivalent of A.J. Walford is:

SHEEHY, E.P. *et al. Guide to Reference Books.* **Latest edn. American Library Association.**
> It contains what is probably the best short guide to American education reference sources. Supplements are issued between editions.

Useful lists or descriptions of reference books on education will be found in other types of publication, as described for example in 18.7 'Guides to the literature of education' pp.126-9 and 25.3 'Organising the literature' pp.170-1. There is one short British publication which may be mentioned here:

British Educational Reference Books: An Annotated Bibliography. **2nd edn.,1981 British Council.**
> Note the date. This slim booklet claimed to be a 'comprehensive annotated guide to reference books on all aspects of education in Britain' but is much more limited in scope. It provides a list of publications which are concerned with careers, course entry requirements, grants and awards, etc., and with primary, secondary and higher education in this country. The British Council planned to revise and re-issue it on a regular basis.

8 Dictionaries

Dictionaries, like encyclopaedias, may be multi-volume or single volume. They may be comprehensive or abridged. They may also be up to date or out of date. You may look in vain, even in some of the better known dictionaries, for very new or recent words.

Some dictionaries are almost like small-scale encyclopaedias in the range of information they contain. However, for fuller accounts of any topic and more detailed information you will normally have to turn to the standard general or educational encyclopaedias (see 9.1 and 9.2).

Several excellent dictionaries of education have been published in recent years (see 8.2). They are not always the quickest source for educational terms in common use, e.g. 'teach-in', but they will be preferred by those who require more precise definitions of specialised educational terms.

Education, like most subjects nowadays, has its fair share of acronyms and abbreviations. Some general and specialised dictionaries of abbreviations have been included in 8.3.

If you are engaged in educational research, you may wish to use a dictionary-type publication called a thesaurus. Some of the better known educational thesauri are described in 8.4.

8.1 General dictionaries

The largest and best known British dictionary is the:

Oxford English Dictionary, 2nd edn. Prepared by J. A. Simpson and E. S. C. Weiner. Oxford University Press, 1989. 20 vols.
This is the first new edition since its completion 60 years ago. Its sheer size and remarkable detail make it difficult to use for quick reference. Moreover, it was designed on 'historical principles' and the most recent meanings are given last in each

entry. However, it is still the ultimate authority, and there are plans to reproduce it in machine-readable form. There is a whole family of Oxfords. They have traditionally been literary dictionaries, and not as up to date as they might be. They include the:

Shorter Oxford Dictionary. 3rd edn. 1973. 2 vols.
Concise Oxford Dictionary of Current English. 8th edn, 1990.
Oxford Reference Dictionary. 1986.
Oxford Paperback Dictionary. 3rd edn, 1988.

This seems to be the age of reliable one-volume dictionaries. Outstanding examples are: *Chambers English Dictionary* (Latest edn., formerly *Chambers 20th Century Dictionary*), one of the best general purpose dictionaries; *Collins English Dictionary* (Latest edn.) which has clear definitions; and the *Longman Dictionary of the English Language* (Longman, 1984) which is very good on usage. All three have numerous offspring in the form of concise versions.

Penguin have published two dictionaries, both compiled from the Longman database. The larger and fuller one is the *Penguin Reference Dictionary* which is good value. The smaller *New Penguin English Dictionary* has no etymologies.

One of the most attractive dictionaries of all is the *World Book Dictionary* (revised annually. World Book Inc: USA, 2 vols) a stable companion of the *World Book Encyclopedia* (see p.22) which has a year book containing a supplement of very recent words.

A more compact one-volume American work is *Webster's New Collegiate Dictionary* (9th edn. Merriam: USA, 1983) an offspring of the standard, unabridged but now rather dated *Webster's Third New International Dictionary of the English Language*. More generally accessible to British readers is yet another Oxford production: the *Oxford American Dictionary* (Oxford University Press, 1981).

Two other works of American origin deserve a place in British libraries: BARNHART, C. L. *et al. A Dictionary of New English 1963–1972* (Longman, 1973), and *A Second Dictionary of New English* (Longman, 1982). They contain many words and phrases not often found in more conventional dictionaries. One example is 'megaversity: a very large university with an enrolment of many thousands of students'.

There are smaller works which contain definitions of words you may not find elsewhere: GREEN, J. *A Dictionary of Jargon* (Routledge, 1987), and *Longman Guardian New Words;* ed. S. Mort (Longman, 1986) which has been extended by the *Longman Register of New Words;* ed. J. Ayter (Longman, 1989).

Those with a general interest in education would enjoy browsing in: DE BONO: *Wordpower: an Illustrated Dictionary of Vital Words.* (Penguin, 1983.) It deals with words used every day without a precise knowledge of their meaning. 'Parameter' is a good example.

There is an excellent short account of general dictionaries in *British Book News* (July 1984, pp.519–21). A. J. Walford (see p.00) has a good section on dictionaries. For fuller comparisons of general dictionaries in use on both sides of the Atlantic consult WALSH, J. P. *English Language Dictionaries in Print: a Comparative Analysis.* (Latest edn. Bowker: USA.)

Some idea of the tremendous range and variety of dictionaries published throughout the world may be obtained from *World Dictionaries in Print: a Guide to General and Subject Dictionaries in World Languages.* (Latest edn., Bowker: USA.)

8.2 Dictionaries of education

There are numerous excellent dictionaries of education which you can use to check definitions of specialised terms with which

you are unfamiliar. Several of them have supplementary information, e.g. lists of abbreviations or official reports. Some less recent examples have been included since they contain a number of terms which are less familiar now.

BARNARD, H.C. and LAUWERYS, J.A. *A Handbook of British Educational Terms.* **Harrap, 1963.**
A short book now rather dated, but useful for brief definitions of terms then current. Names of official reports are included and there is a list of educational abbreviations at the end.

COLLINS, K.T. et al. *Key Words in Education.* **Longman, 1975.**
More recent than H.C. Barnard (above) but follows the same pattern. It includes some references to further reading and has four appendices: (1) The educational system of Great Britain; (2) The more important Education Acts in England and Wales; (3) The more important educational reports published since 1926; (4) Educational journals.

GOOD G.V. *Dictionary of Education,* **3rd edn. McGraw-Hill: USA, 1973.**
This is an American publication but it is the most detailed and scholarly of all these dictionaries although its definitions are fairly brief. Unlike K.T. Collins (above) it excludes the names of persons, institutions, school systems and organisations. Its main concern is with technical terms over the whole area of education. There are separate sections of terms used in Canada, and in England and Wales.

GORDON, P. and LAWTON, D. *A Guide to English Educational Terms.* **Batsford, 1984.**
Sets out 'to provide concise definitions of those terms most likely to be encountered in current discussion of educational matters'. It is designed for parents, teachers, school governors, educational administrators, and students on teacher training courses. It does not attempt to be comprehensive. There are only a few Scottish terms, and terms used in America but not familiar over here are excluded. There is one alphabetical sequence of words and phrases such as computer assisted learning, Down's syndrome, Duke of Edinburgh's Award, and the *Dunning Report.* In many cases a book or article is recommended for further reading. Also included are: a brief guide to the educational system of England and Wales; a chronological list of landmarks in the development of English education since 1900; a brief list of acronyms such as

QUANGO and STOPP; a random collection of useful reference books; and chronological lists of Ministers of Education, etc.

HAWES, G.R. and L.S. *The Concise Dictionary of Education.* **Van Nostrand: USA, 1982.**
This very American dictionary covers economic, administrative, sociological, psychological and other aspects of education, 'spanning the range from pre-school years to postdoctoral studies and adult education'. Here you will find terms such as Pell grants, latchkey children, creationism, CEU, and preppy. Not all the definitions are easily digestible.

HILLS, P.J. *A Dictionary of Education.* **Routledge, 1983.**
This unusual work is described as a 'conceptual dictionary' for students, teachers, administrators and general readers. Part 1 is devoted to Areas of Education and consists of brief articles by specialists on topics such as curriculum development and educational research with references for further reading. At the end of each article is a list of terms related to the topic. These are fully explained in Part 2 which is the dictionary proper. Serious students will use both the inter-related parts. Others will turn to the dictionary section only.

KOEPPE, R. and SHAFRITZ, J. *Dictionary of Education.* **Facts on File: USA, 1989.**
Contains about 5,000 current terms, concepts and processes used in 'the academic study and professional practice of teaching'. Slang terms are included. There is information on 'notable people, unions, laws and organisations specific to the North American system' and on educational administration from pre-primary to tertiary level.

PAGE G.T. and THOMAS, J.B. *An International Dictionary of Education.* **Kogan Page, 1977.**
This attempts to provide comprehensive coverage on all levels and to be 'truly international in its terminology'. It includes entries for educational organisations and for famous educationists. A new edition is needed.

ROWNTREE, D. *A Dictionary of Education.* **Harper & Row, 1981.**
This was a welcome addition to the number of available guides to educational terms. Entries vary from a paragraph to a few lines. Brief descriptions of important educational reports are included and there are commonsense definitions of terms in current use. There are also short entries on educationists, psychologists and sociologists. A new edition would help it to retain its place as a handy source of reference for students and teachers in this country.

WALKER, W.G. et al. *A Glossary of Educational Terms: Usage in Five English-Speaking Countries.* **University of Queensland Press Australia, 1973.**
Although it was designed primarily for educational administrators this could be more generally useful because it helps readers to distinguish between terms which have different meanings in different countries, e.g. 'supervision' (in Britain and America), but note the date.

There is a dictionary with a rather different purpose from those already mentioned except perhaps the one by P. J. Hills:

BARROW, R. and MILBURN, J. *A Critical Dictionary of Educational Concepts: an Appraisal of Selected Ideas and Issues in Educational Theory and Practice.* **Wheatsheaf Books, 1986.**
Compiled by two Canadian professors, it is 'a critical analysis of central concepts'. The kinds of questions it asks are: 'Can educational success be assessed, and if so, in what way? Is there any reason to care about creativity testing? What is the status of value judgements? What distinct types of understanding, if any, are there? How do language and thought relate to one another?... The essay length entries analyse such major subjects as assessment, culture, emotional development, teacher effectiveness, development theory, knowledge, the learning curriculum, and critical thinking'. The compilers of the dictionary did not set themselves an easy task, but some readers may find it helpful.

Some of the dictionaries mentioned above are more like miniature encyclopaedias since they give fuller explanations of topics rather than simply the meaning or usage of a word. Other dictionary-type publications take the process a little further:

A. PATES et al. *Education Fact Book: an A–Z Guide to Education and Training in Britain* **Macmillan, 1983.**
This describes itself as a 'consumer's guide to the complexities of the education and training system'. If you want concise information on topics such as autism or distance learning, the Youth Training Scheme or the Business Education Council, or would like to know if the MSC was a quango or not, you are likely to find it in this fact book. However in its efforts to be up to date and all-embracing it bears evidence of hurried compilation, e.g. there is an entry for student-centred learning but not for individualised learning or resource-based learning, although there is one for private study.

IZBICKI. *Daily Telegraph Education A–Z.* Collins, 1978.
A less recent book which includes over 400 topics from the world of education: type of school, teaching methods, key reports and papers, pressure groups, teachers' organisations and so on. There are also entries for topics such as violence, streaming and truancy.

Remember also the invaluable *Education A–Z* (see p.9). Although it is not a dictionary its alphabetical arrangement and treatment make it readily comparable with the works described above.

It is regrettable that there are not more dictionaries devoted to particular aspects of education. Only a few examples can be given here. The first three are concerned with special education:

WILLIAMS, P. *A Glossary of Special Education.* Open University Press, 1987.
Intended for teachers, administrators and parents. It provides brief explanations of 'the terminology of education, psychology, medicine and social work used in special education... It also covers the more important psychological and educational tests, influential reports, and Acts which affect special education'. There is a list of special needs organisations. There is a comparable American work:

MOORE, B.C. et al. *A Dictionary of Special Education Terms.* Thomas: USA, 1980.
It gives brief definitions and pronunciation. The major areas dealt with include mental retardation, emotional handicap, hearing, vision and learning disability, speech, physical handicaps, and giftedness. However, there is another American work which is much more ambitious:

DAVIS W.E. *Resource Guide to Special Education: Terms, Laws, Assessment, Procedures, Organizations.* 2nd edn. Allyn & Bacon: USA, 1986.
This is not just another dictionary. It was designed as 'a complete special education reference system'. It defines terms in special education and related areas, lists commonly used acronyms and abbreviations, describes educational and psychological tests, summarises key pieces of legislation, and lists relevant organisations and agencies. Previously entitled *Educator's Resource Guide to Special Education.*

An international Dictionary of Adult and Continuing Education was announced for publication by Routledge in 1990. The remaining example is on a more specific topic:

ELLINGTON, H. and HARRIS, D. *Dictionary of Instructional Technology.* Kogan Page, 1986.
The terms come not only from mainline instructional technology but also from the fields and disciplines impinging on it, e.g. educational psychology, statistics, film and TV production, photography, reprography, computing and information technology. British and US terms are covered, with some from other English speaking countries. This is a dictionary with an unusual mixture of terms such as 'refresher course' and 'special effects generator'.

One other dictionary should be mentioned since it impinges on many subject areas including education:

Fontana Dictionary of Modern Thought, eds. A. Bullock and O. Stallybrass, 2nd edn. Fontana, 1987.
If you want to know the difference between vertical and lateral thinking, or the names associated with de-schooling, or about educational priority areas and other such matters you will find this dictionary helpful. There is a separate *Fontana Dictionary of Modern Thinkers* (see p.98).

8.3 Educational acronyms and abbreviations

As the introduction to *Everyman's Dictionary* (below) observes: 'The manufacture of abbreviations remains one of the largest and fastest growing industries in the world today'. The education industry spawns more abbreviations than most but there are surprisingly few dictionaries devoted specifically to them. Both general and educational sources must therefore be used. Standard British works are:

Everyman's Dictionary of Abbreviations, by J. Paxton. 2nd edn. Dent, 1986. (Re-issued as the *Penguin Dictionary of Abbreviations.* Penguin, 1989.)

World Guide to Abbreviations of Organizations, by F.A. Buttress, revised by H.J. Heaney. Latest edn. Blackie.

There are American general lists on a much larger scale:

DE SOLA, R. *Abbreviations Dictionary.* Latest edn. Elsevier: USA.
Acronyms, Initialisms and Abbreviations Dictionary. Gale Research Co: USA, annual. 3 vols. (For terms outside the US there is a companion volume: *International Acronyms, Initialisms and Abbreviations Dictionary.*)

Obviously you will find many educational abbreviations in all these lists, but your library may have more specialised works:

MARDER J. V. *Acronyms and Initialisms in Education: a Handlist.* Latest edn. LISE.
Issued by the Librarians of Institutes and School of Educations, this is 'a guide to the terms in current or recent use in the field of education in Great Britain and Ireland. Additional examples from international organisations and some American terms in common use have also been included'. Occasionally notes of explanation have been added to the entries, but addresses of societies, etc. are not given – the reader is referred to standard directories, e.g. the *Education Year Book* (see p.57). If you do not know what OPUS and SCALA stand for, this is your guide.

LOCATE: *List of Common Abbreviations in Training and Education,* by L. Roberts. Newpoint, 1986.
A clearly presented booklet which provides explanations of over 600 acronyms and abbreviations in current use. It also gives brief descriptions of qualifications available in four areas: general; pre-vocational; vocational; and professional. It deserves to be updated.

For mainly American abbreviations we have:

PALMER, J. C. and COLBY, A. Y. *Dictionary of Educational Acronyms, Abbreviations and*

Initialisms. 2nd edn. Oryx Press: USA 1985.
Based largely on information supplied by the ERIC (see p.190) Clearing House in America. Part 1 lists over 4,000 acronyms, etc. in one alphabetical sequence. Part 2 is a 'reverse list' of acronyms in their unabbreviated forms. As the editors admit, no list of short forms is ever complete, but there are few British entries.

There is another work which is worth mentioning:

MONTGOMERY, A. C. *Acronyms and Abbreviations in Library and Information Work: a Reference Handbook of British Usage.* 3rd edn Library Association, 1986.
Although designed for librarians this could be more generally useful. It includes educational acronyms. There are more than 6,000 entries.

It should be remembered that lists of abbreviations can also be found in many general and subject dictionaries, encyclopaedias, directories and other reference works. See for example some of the sources described in 14.14 'Educational qualifications.'

8.4 Educational thesauri

Closely related to dictionaries of education are educational thesauri, or lists of terms used mainly in educational research. They are normally designed for use with an information retrieval system (see 26.7). They can be particularly helpful to researchers who wish to identify or define the specific terms to be employed in the course of a literature search, either manual or more usually online. The best known example in education is the:

THESAURUS of ERIC Descriptors. Latest edn. Oryx Press: USA.
New editions appear every few years. The latest one is essential for searching new files of ERIC (Educational Resources Information Centre) in America (see 26.7). The thesaurus contains an alphabetical list of terms, or rather descriptors, used in the

ERIC indexes and also therefore, for searching in the ERIC system either manually or by computer. This will be the thesaurus most used by those involved in serious educational research. New descriptors added to the system since the previous edition was published are listed in the current issues of *Resources in Education* (see 26.6) under the heading 'New Thesaurus Terms'.

A new British thesaurus became available online in October 1988, and there is also a printed version:

British Education Thesaurus (BET) ed. J.V. Marder, Leeds University Press, 1988.
It owes 'a massive debt' to the *ERIC Thesaurus* (above). It is designed to serve as a key to the indexing terms used in the *British Education Index (BEI)* (see p.156) and *British Education Theses Index (BETI)* (see p.184). It contains over 8,000 terms in current academic and professional use, and particular attention has been paid to the needs of British terminology. There are two main parts: an Alphabetical Descriptor Display of terms used for searching in the merged BEI/BETI and MESU/NERIS databases (see below); and a Rotated Descriptor Display, which provides an alphabetical index to all the words found in the descriptors.
    BET should be especially helpful to those who are using the printed or online versions of the *British Education Index*. It is significant that both MESU (Microelectronics Support Unit) and NERIS (National Educational Resources Information Service) (see p.86) have chosen to take the educational vocabulary for their databases from BET. If it proves to be as flexible as the *ERIC Thesaurus* and is updated just as frequently it will be a boon to researchers.

There is also a *Canadian Education Thesaurus (CET)* (Council of Education Ministers and Canadian Education Index, 1988). Efforts are currently being made on both sides of the Atlantic to ensure basic compatibility between these three thesauri (ERIC, BET and CET) in the interests of freer worldwide use of educational information.
    Some readers may be familiar with the *London Education Classification: a Thesaurus/Classification of British Educational Terms* (2nd edn. Longman, 1974 (Education libra-

ries bulletin, supplement 6)). Devised by D.J. Foskett, it has been used notably in the classification of the University of London Institute of Education Library (see p.121) and in the arrangement of the NFER's *Register of Educational Research* (see p.186).
    MARIS On-Line (Materials and Resources Information Service) has developed a thesaurus to help its subscribers to retrieve information from the database (see p.87).
    There is a European thesaurus for education:

EUDISED: *Multilingual Thesaurus for Information Processing in the Field of Education.* English version. EUDISED, 1984.
This was designed by the European Documentation and Information System for Education (EUDISED) to meet the same kinds of needs as the IBETA series (below). It uses a documentary language specially devised for the processing of information in the member states.

The IBETA series of reference books are issued by the International Bureau of Education under the auspices of Unesco. They are intended for use by 'educational documentation centres, educational institutions, administrators, and educationalists'. A particularly relevant example is the:

UNESCO: IBE *Education Thesaurus: A Faceted List of Terms for Indexing and Retrieving Documents and Data in the Field of Education, with French Equivalents.* Latest edn. Unesco Press.
The introduction is careful to point out that this thesaurus is intended for international use in indexing, 'hence it is different from the national directories or word-lists based on usage in countries with English or French as native languages. The choice of terms and fixing of meanings have therefore a somewhat arbitrary character'. Also in the IBETA series are the:

Glossary of Educational Technology Terms (English, French). 2nd edn. Unesco Press, 1987.

Terminology of Adult Education (English, French, Spanish). Unesco Press, 1979. Reprinted in 1985.

Terminology of Science and Technology Education (Arabic, English, French, Russian, Spanish). Unesco Press, 1984.

Terminology of Special Education (English, French, Russian, Spanish). 2nd edn. Unesco Press, 1983.

Terminology of Technical and Vocational Education (Arabic, English, French, Russian, Spanish). Unesco Press, 1984.

Note also the *Thesaurus of Vocational Training*. 2nd edn. HMSO, 1988, produced by CEDEFOP (Centre for the Development of European Vocational Training).

There is an older thesaurus published by Unesco which is not confined to educational terms:

Unesco Thesaurus. Unesco Press, 2 vols, 1977.

It is described as 'a structured list of descriptors fo indexing literature in the fields of education, science, social science, culture and communication' It seems likely that it will eventually be merged with *Unesco: IBE Education Thesaurus (above)*.

An example of a modest attempt to com pile a thesaurus in one specific area o education, which could be of interest t some readers is:

STONE, M. *et al. In-Service Education: ¿ Research Vocabulary.* Durham Universit Institute of Education, 1980.

Finally mention must be made of a well known thesaurus in an area closely relatec to education:

Thesaurus of Psychological Index Terms. Lates edn. American Psychological Association USA.

'A compilation of the vocabulary used in psychology and related disciplines as generated from the files of *Psychological Abstracts*' (see p.160).

9 Encyclopaedias

Encyclopaedias are among the most familiar and frequently used of all reference books. Normally they are concerned with subjects, not words. They can be invaluable for a first view of a topic before you investigate it further. Often they will provide sufficient information for your purpose.

General encyclopaedias are sometimes the most convenient source for basic educational information. Brief notes are therefore provided on the major multi-volume general encyclopaedias and the better known single 7 volume encyclopaedias which should be available in most reasonable sized reference collections (9.1).

However, more space has been given to the encyclopaedias of education, both multi-volume and single-volume, which have become more numerous in recent years (9.2). In total they now provide a very wide range of educational information which is readily accessible to the student, the researcher and the general reader.

There are of course encyclopaedias of education in foreign languages. They can be expected to provide fuller accounts of education in their native countries than those which are given in their British or American counterparts. They will also represent their national point of view and should therefore be useful to students of the language and country concerned. However for practical reasons they have had to be omitted from this survey.

9.1 General encyclopaedias

The major general encyclopaedias contain much information on education and educational systems, and on people important in the history of education. Perhaps the best way to compare their respective merits is to take a few specific topics and check their treatment in each encyclopaedia for comprehensiveness, accuracy, up-to-dateness, readability, and relevance (in terms of national bias, etc.). It is also useful to check the bibliographies appended to the articles to see if they are adequate and contain references to recent publications. The longest established and best known of all encyclopaedias is the:

New Encyclopaedia Britannica. **Continuous revision. Encyclopaedia Britannica Inc.: USA, 32 vols.**

The reputation of the *Britannica* (now in American hands) was firmly based on the older editions. The restructured *New Encyclopaedia Britannica*, first published in 1974, was not entirely new by any means but it was reorganised into three parts: a Propaedia (1 vol.), a Micropaedia (12 vols) and a Macropaedia (17 vols). It remains a scholarly conspectus of contemporary knowledge but it has become more difficult to use, and some perseverance is required to find the information you need despite the very detailed index (2 vols). There is a year book called the *Britannica Book of the Year* (see p. 27) with an important statistical section: Britannica World Data.

Colliers Encyclopedia. **Annual revision. Macmillan Educational Corporation: USA, 24 vols.**

Has a shorter life history than the other major encyclopaedias and consequently less dated material. It is more attractively produced than the *Britannica* and is more uniformly readable though no less scholarly. It has strong claims to be the best encyclopaedia in the world at the present time at university and college level. Its usefulness for educational topics is limited by its American emphasis. The bibliographies are in a separate volume. There is a year book.

Encyclopedia Americana. **Annual revision. Americana Corporation: USA, 30 vols.**

This has a much longer history than *Colliers*. Articles are shorter and more specific, making it more suitable for quick reference, but it is less attractive and contemporary in its presentation and not always as up to date as it might be, though it has a year book.

Everyman's Encyclopaedia. **6th edn. Dent, 1978.**

A more compact but well-established British encyclopaedia on traditional lines. It manages to include a surprising amount of information and many of its articles are first rate brief accounts of their subjects. The British emphasis is an advantage, not least in the bibliographies, but a new edition is very much needed. Meantime there is an abbreviated and updated *New Illustrated Everyman's Encyclopaedia* (Octopus Books, 1986. 2 vols).

Another once familiar British work: *Chambers's Encyclopaedia* (New revised edn. Pergamon, 1967. 15 vols) is no longer published and it is now very dated in appearance and content. Even a cursory comparison with any of the encyclopaedias mentioned below will reveal the advances which have been made in the attractive presentation of material and general readability in recent years. Outstanding in these respects is the:

World Book Encyclopedia. **Annual revision. World Book Inc: USA, 24 vols.**

It is the standard encyclopaedia in American schools and colleges and is deservedly becoming so in Britain despite its American emphasis. (In recent years two supplementary volumes on the British Isles have been available). Although aimed at a lower academic level than the *Britannica* or *Colliers* for example, it is just as reliable. Moreover, it is meticulously planned, efficiently organised, superbly illustrated, and always lucid. The index forms part of the Research Guide, which is an invaluable aid to exploiting the full resources of the encyclopaedia. There is a *World Book Year Book,* which has all the qualities of its present encyclopaedia.

Macmillan Family Encyclopedia. **Annual revision. Macmillan, 21 vols.**

This attractive work originates in America, where it is known as the *Academic American Encyclopaedia* (Arête Publishing Co.). It was first published in 1980. Entries are short, but the information seems accurate and up to date, and it is well illustrated. There is a year book.

New Caxton Encyclopaedia. **5th edn. Caxton Publications Ltd, 1979.**

Distinguished mainly by its pleasant format, coloured illustrations, and readable text, but the articles are very short and detailed information is not to be expected. Note the date. There used to be a *New Caxton Year Book* but it is now published independently as the *International Year Book* (see p.28).

These are the main multi-volume encyclopaedias which may be found in British libraries. However, there are several excellent one-volume encyclopaedias which should be known and used, since they have definite value for quick reference purposes

The Hutchinson Encyclopedia. **Latest edn. Hutchinson.**

Familiar for many years as the *Hutchinson 20th Century Encyclopedia* but re-named in 1988. Frequently revised and updated, it is an ideal general purpose encyclopaedia.

The Macmillan Encyclopedia. **Latest edn. Macmillan.**

Hutchinson has a rival in this new encyclopaedia which first appeared in 1981, with several editions since. It has already proved its worth. The two works are very similar and may be used to complement each other.

The Longman Encyclopedia. **Longman, 1989.**

The most recent of these British one volume encyclopaedias maintains a comparable standard. It is based on the *Concise Columbia Encyclopedia* (below). They all succeed in presenting the minimum essential information on each subject or topic in a clear and readable way.

An outstanding American example is the:

New Columbia Encyclopedia. **Latest edn. Columbia University Press: USA.**

This massive compendium dwarfs its British counterparts but is less frequently revised and less up to date. It contains a remarkable amount of accurate information in condensed form but still manages to be readable and interesting. There is a *Concise Columbia Encyclopedia* which is equally dependable. A British version of this has been published as the *Penguin Concise Columbia Encyclopedia* (Penguin, 1987). Most readers would find it excellent for everyday use.

9.2 Encyclopaedias of education

Education in general: multi-volume

The large-scale general encyclopaedias described in the last section are authoritative, convenient and readily available sources of information and ideas, and if they have a continuous revision policy and a year book they can at least give the impression that they are very up to date.

The major encyclopaedias of education are of course fewer in number and their compilation is a very specialised undertaking. Once published they have seldom been revised or updated, and none of them has had a continuous revision policy. Only one produced a year book (see below) and this had a very short life. However, it is encouraging to note that one publisher at least is aware of these limitations and is doing something positive about it (see below).

The three largest encyclopaedias of education in current use are as authoritative and reliable as any of the general encyclopaedias. Unfortunately there is no wholly British work among them. Two are American and the third and most recent is mainly American although it includes the word 'international' in its title. However, it has definite plans for keeping itself up-to-date:

International Encyclopedia of Education: Research and Studies, eds. T. Husen and T.N. Postlethwaite. Pergamon, 1985. 10 vols. Supplementary vol. 1, 1989.

This ambitious work was published simultaneously in Britain and America. According to the introduction 'the time has come to take stock of dynamic developments in the field of scholarly studies in education that have taken place all over the world since 1960' for the benefit of educators, social scientists and the inquiring public'. Education is seen as 'a lifelong process, involving both formal and informal efforts at all levels'.

The encyclopaedia covers the major areas of education, e.g. adult education; counselling; curriculum; economics; administration; policy; educational technology; evaluation; higher education; national systems; pre-school education; education research; special education; teaching; vocational education; and industrial education. There are also summaries of related developments in philosophy, psychology, sociology, anthropology and law.

Apart from the 160 entries on individual countries there are 'state of the art' accounts of the different aspects of education mentioned above, gathered from world-wide sources. If there appears to be a strong American emphasis it is because much of the most relevant research on which the articles were based was carried out in America, and the bibliographies appended to the articles reflect this.

The main arrangement of the encyclopaedia is alphabetical but there is a separate volume which contains a 'multi-level subject index with 45,000 entries'. There is also an author index, and a classified list of entries which provides a schematic overview of major areas covered. This index volume is a valuable reference guide for the reader who wants to make maximum use of the encyclopaedia.

A major work of this kind, on a subject changing as rapidly as education, is bound to go out of date in many respects fairly quickly. However, computer technology was used for processing the articles, and the entire contents are stored on computer disc for future updating. Moreover Pergamon have planned a series of supplementary volumes which will extend and update the main work with appropriate cross-references. The first was published in 1989. They are also issuing a number of one-volume encyclopaedias based on the parent work (see below).

Encyclopedia of Education, ed. L.C. Deighton. Collier-Macmillan: USA, 1970. 10 vols.

A well-organised and reliable encyclopaedia with a strong emphasis on American aspects. Although it is arranged alphabetically by main topics there is a detailed index to which users will need to refer. The articles are quite long and give good accounts of their subjects. Initially an *Education Year Book* was issued as a supplement, but regrettably this ceased publication with the 1973–74 volume.

International Encyclopedia of Higher Education, ed. A.S. Knowles. Jossey-Bass: USA, 1977, 10 vols.

This covers a more limited field but is equally ambitious with again a marked American emphasis. There are lengthy articles about systems of education in many different countries, essays on contemporary topics in education, and entries on

142 fields of study. The general arrangement is alphabetical. Educational associations are included but there are no biographical entries. Vol.1 has a list of acronyms and a glossary of terms used in higher education. It is a valuable but now partially dated encyclopaedia which needs a new edition. Note also the:

World Education Encyclopedia, ed. G.T. Kurian. Facts on file: USA, 1988. 3 vols.
On a smaller scale than the encyclopaedias already mentioned but more up to date. Part 1 provides global educational statistics; Part 2,3 and 4 have in-depth descriptions of the educational systems of virtually every country in the world 'from pre-primary education in Argentina to tertiary levels in Zimbabwe'; Part 5 consists of appendices, bibliography and index. (Cf. *the Encyclopedia of Comparative Education and National Systems of Education* on p.25).

There are two much older multi-volume encyclopaedias which give good coverage of the history of education and of earlier educationists but have little contemporary relevance. They are mentioned because they may still be useful for occasional reference. The first is British, the second American:

WATSON, F. *The Encyclopaedia and Dictionary of Education.* **Pitman, 1921-2. 4 vols.**

MONROE, P. *A Cyclopedia of Education.* **Macmillan: USA. 1911-13. 5 vols.**
These encyclopaedias are briefly described in Humby, M.'s guide (see p.126) along with other early works such as: the *Teacher's Encyclopaedia of the Theory, Method, Practice, History and Development of Education at Home and Abroad,* (ed. A.P. Lowrie. Pitman, 1922. 4 vols). The first edition was published just before the First World War in seven vols. and may still be found in some libraries. It was a brave enterprise for its time. Humby, M., also has notes on several French and German encyclopaedias of education.

Education in general: single-volume

There is a real need for a good one-volume encyclopaedia with comprehensive and up-to-date coverage of education today. Meanwhile there are two works which should be included here although neither of them is recent:

Blond's Encyclopaedia of Education; ed. E. Blishen. Blond Educational, 1969.
A compact British work which could more accurately be described as an encyclopaedic dictionary. It has very short entries and its coverage is uneven. However, it is sometimes a handy source for straightforward enquiries if its date of publication is kept in mind.

RIVLIN, H.N. *Encyclopaedia of Modern Education.* **Philosophical Library: USA. 1943.**
Again, note the date. Despite its title this encyclopaedia is not contemporary and its coverage outside America is very limited. Despite these drawbacks, it is a useful encyclopaedia for its period.

Particular aspects of education

We have a number of well-produced encyclopaedias of recent origin on particular aspects of education. The most substantial of these is in three volumes:

Encyclopedia of Special Education: a Reference for the Education of the Handicapped and Other Exceptional Children and Adults, eds. C.R. Reynolds and L. Mann. Wiley: USA, 1987. 3 vols.
It is 'designed to present a comprehensive vision of what special education is about in a readable, understandable, usable and summative form' with contributions from 300 experts. It is aimed at professionals working in special education, lawyers, physicians, psychologists, social workers, etc. and provides information about developments worldwide. Although the main arrangement is alphabetical the various entries can be grouped conceptually into seven major categories: (1) Biographies, (2) Educational and psychological tests, (3) Interventions and service delivery, (4) Handicapping conditions, (5) Related services, (6) Legal, and (7) Miscellaneous entries. The biographical entries include key contemporary and historical figures and many have portraits. The articles have references for further reading.

The others are all single-volume encyclopaedias. Pergamon are to be commended for producing an ongoing series of volumes based on the contents of the *International Encyclopedia of Education* (see p.23) with revisions, new material and updated bibliographies. Each encyclopaedia is themati-

ally organised and aims to be comprehen-
ive. Titles so far are:

Encyclopedia of Comparative Education and
National Systems of Education, ed. T.N.
Postlethwaite. Pergamon, 1988.
This is in two parts. The first has articles outlining
major aspects of education viewed comparatively,
including a valuable one on documentation by M.
Debeauvais (pp. 41–8). The second has detailed
descriptions of the education systems of 159
countries (cf. The *World Education Encyclopedia* on
p.24). Short bibliographies are appended to the
articles but these and the statistics are not always
recent.

Encyclopedia of Human Development and
Education: Theory, Research and Studies; ed.
R.M. Thomas. Pergamon, 1987.
Contains over 100 articles written by international
authorities. Designed for specialists and also for
professionals in related fields, e.g. counselling.
Outlines theories of human development, learning
and personality, and also covers selected topics such
as child abuse, drug abuse, delinquency,
homosexuality, multi culturalism and one-parent
families. Supporting bibliographies are provided
throughout.

International Encyclopedia of Teaching and
Teacher Education, ed. M.J. Dunkin.
Pergamon, 1987.
Aimed at students, teachers and researchers with
coverage of both theoretical and practical aspects.
Again it is arranged by broad themes, with six
sections: (1) Concepts and models, (2) Methods and
paradigms for research, (3) Teaching methods and
techniques, (4) Classroom processes, (5)
Contextual factors, and (6) Teacher education.
There is a subject index and a name index. Like the
other volumes in the series it reflects the American
emphasis of its parent but presents a valuable view
of teaching and teacher education in the 1980s.

International Encyclopedia of Curriculum, ed.
A. Lewy. Pergamon, 1990.
Covers curriculum processes, theories, approaches
and methods, as well as curriculum evaluation. It
also includes articles on specific curricular areas,
e.g. the arts, humanities, social studies, foreign
languages, science education and mathematics.

International Encyclopedia of Educational Evalu-
ation, ed. H.J. Walberg and G.D. Haertel.
Pergamon, 1990.
Provides a survey of evaluation theories and
practices, focusing on educational needs

assessment, measurement, evaluation design,
decision making and educational policy. It also
covers tests and examinations and research
methodology. New material covers recent
developments in educational evaluation research.

International Encyclopedia of Educational
Technology, ed. M. Eraut. Pergamon, 1989.
Planned as a comprehensive collection of 'state of
the art' reports covering the whole field of
educational technology throughout the world. It is
thematically organised within five inter-related
sections. 'Coverage is given to conceptual
frameworks, technical developments, design and
distribution of instructional resources, the
organisation of educational technology, and
practical problems of classroom use.' Future
directions are also considered.

The above encyclopaedia appeared about
the same time as a long-awaited new edition of another on the same subject:

Encyclopedia of Educational Media Communi-
cations and Technology, ed. D. Unwin and R.
McAleese. 2nd edn. Greenwood Press: USA,
1988.
The first edition was published by Macmillan in
1978. 'EEMCAT 2' has a more international
approach. The contributors are experienced
specialists in their particular fields. There are
'macro' entries on all the main aspects of
educational technology and 'micro' entries giving
short definitions of terms likely to be encountered
in an educational context. The emphasis throughout is on 'ideas rather than equipment'. The work
has been some time in preparation and a few of the
articles on recent developments such as CD–ROM
are inadequate. The absence of a detailed index is
also to be regretted. However, it is a notable achievement in a difficult area. The references appended
to the main articles are an important feature.

Finally mention should be made of an
older one-volume encyclopaedia on a more
specific topic:

Encyclopedia of Educational Evaluation:
Techniques of Evaluation in Education and
Training Programmes, S.B. Anderson *et al.*
Jossey Bass: USA, 1975.
The objective of this encyclopaedia is 'not so much
to say more' about educational evaluation, as 'to
make some order out of the field and to bring its
major concepts and techniques together in one
place'. The arrangement is alphabetical by topic

and most articles are only a few pages in length. The bibliographies are a very minor feature. The reader is encouraged to approach the work through the eleven major concept areas listed at the beginning. Note the date.

10 Year books

One of the disadvantages of the major encyclopaedias is that even with continuous revision they cannot be relied upon to provide recent information. As we have seen they usually try to offset this by publishing year books to update their contents. These may be used without reference to their parent encyclopaedias by readers who wish to keep abreast of current developments. The best known examples are briefly described in 10.1

The term year book is often applied to directory-type publications, many of which also appear annually. However, these are concerned less with reviewing developments than with providing basic information and statistics which are updated from one year to the next. A good example is the *Commonwealth Universities Yearbook* (see p.59). Directories of this type are described in chapter 14.

As already indicated the major encyclopaedias of education with one or two exceptions have not issued year books. However, there are several excellent independently published works of a similar kind which review developments in education, or specific aspects of it, on an annual basis. These should be used by anyone who wishes to keep abreast of current trends or is specialising in a particular field, e.g. educational technology. They are described in 10.2

10.1 General year books

Several general encyclopaedia year books have already been mentioned in connection with their parent encyclopaedias (see 9.1). It is not really possible for a year book to update all the contents of a major encyclopaedia. Its main purpose is to give a detailed survey of developments and events in a particular year. It is normally arranged under broad subject headings to cover significant trends in all fields including education. The contents of the year book usually relate to the year preceding the one which is indicated on the cover.

***Britannica Book of the Year.* Encyclopaedia Britannica Inc.: USA, annual.**
The fullest and most detailed of these year books and the best known. The cover title is *Britannica World Data Annual* since there is now a large statistical section covering each country's people, society and economy. This means that 'volatile statistical data' have largely been removed from the Macropaedia volumes of the *Britannica* itself. There is a useful biographical section on people of the year.

The encyclopaedia year books tend to complement each other in a variety of ways. Other well-known examples, similar in many respects to the *Britannica Book of the Year* are:

***Colliers Year Book.* Macmillan Educational Corporation: USA, annual.**

***Americana Year Book.* Americana Corporation: USA, annual.**

Another American encyclopaedia year book which is particularly suitable for secondary schools and colleges and for general reading is the:

***World Book Year Book.* World Book Inc.: USA, annual.**
Like its parent encyclopaedia it is very clearly written and presented. Sections headed 'The year in brief' and 'The year in focus' are followed by a series of special reports on subjects of current interest and importance, which may include aspects of education. The main part of the book: 'The year on file' covers the year's events in alphabetically arranged articles. This is undoubtedly the most readable of the American year books.

A British year book whose function is rather different from those already mentioned is the:

International Year Book: a Year of Your Life.
**Caxton and English Educational
Programmes International, annual.**

This used to be linked with the *New Caxton
Encyclopaedia* (see p.22) and was called the *New
Caxton Year Book* until the 1975 issue. It is a
copiously illustrated account of the year's events,
and the photographs are really the main feature.
The volumes as they accumulate provide a lively
conspectus of recent history, but the index could be
more detailed.

The last general year book has no
connection with any encyclopaedia, but
deserves to be included because of its long-
standing reputation and continuing usefulness:

Annual Register: a Register of World Events.
Longman, annual.

It gives 'the story of the year' recorded by experts,
covering every country in the world, international
bodies, social and economic trends, and so on. It
includes a six-year statistical section of economic
and social data and texts of the year's key
documents. Although densely packed with factual
information it still contrives to be readable if taken
in reasonable portions. There are usually incidental
references to education. First published in 1758.

10.2 Education year books

As we have seen, the American *Encyclopedia
of Education* (see p.23) published an
Education Year Book which ceased to appear
after the 1973–74 volume. None of the
other major encyclopaedias has followed
the practice, although the much more
recent *International Encyclopedia of Education*
(see p.23) has issued the first of a series of
supplementary volumes to update the main
work.

However, there are several well-established education year books which are not
linked to encyclopaedias. Another difference is that they tend to concentrate on one
particular field or aspect of education
instead of covering educational develop-

ments generally. Outstanding is the:

World Year Book of Education. **Kogan Page,
annual.**

This is the best known of the British education year
books if we except directories such as the *Education
Year Book* (see p.57) and it is international in scope.
Each issue deals with a specific theme or topic in a
series of chapters which cover developments in
different parts of the world, with very useful
bibliographies.

It was first published almost sixty years ago.
From 1931 to 1964 it was known simply as the *Year
Book of Education* and some of these earlier volumes
still have relevance and interest. Publication was
suspended with the 1974 volume but taken over by
a different publisher after a four-year interval. The
topics covered since 1965, when the title was
changed, are:

1965	The education explosion.
1966	Church and state in education.
1967	Educational planning.
1968	Education within industry.
1969	Examinations.
1970	Education in crisis.
1971–2	Higher education in a changing world.
1972–3	Universities facing the future.
1974	Education and rural development
1975–8	Not published.
1979	Recurrent education and lifelong learning.
1980	Professional development of teachers.
1981	Education of minorities.
1982–3	Computers and education.
1984	Women and education.
1985	Research, policy and practice.
1986	The management of schools.
1987	Vocational education.
1988	Education for the new technologies.
1989	Health education.
1990	Assessment and evaluation.

Another year book with a long and
interrupted history is the:

International Year Book of Education. **Unesco,
annual.**

This has followed a rather different pattern. First
published in English in 1948 it contained
descriptions of national education systems with
statistical appendices. Publication stopped in 1969
but was revived with Vol. XXXIII in 1980. The
content was then based on the biennial International Conference on Education held in Geneva.
Following each conference two editions of the year
book were produced: the first on educational

systems, the second on educational trends. For example, after the 1981 conference vols. XXXIV (1982) and XXXV (1983) were published.

However, the 1985 year book, written by Edmund King, combined both approaches. Its title is 'Technological and occupational challenge, social transformation and educational response' and it is particularly concerned with 'young adults living and working in a context of boundless technological expansion, who are liable to experience a lifetime of uncertainty and relearning'. The statistical tables in Appendix 1 provide data on education for the 161 member states of Unesco, extracted from the 1985 *Unesco Statistical Digest*. Those who wish fuller statistics are referred to the *Unesco Statistical Yearbook* (see p.92).

The 1986 year book entitled 'Primary education on the threshold of the twenty-first century' began a series of thematic year books, still based on the biennial International Conference on Education. Again, two volumes are published on each conference, one dealing in depth with its main theme, the other (published the following year) adopting a comparative approach to education systems throughout the world. Thus the 1987 yearbook 'Secondary education in the world today' was followed by the 1988 year book 'Education in the world'.

Information for the year books is drawn largely from the national reports and replies to questionnaires presented by the member states of Unesco. These documents are listed at the end of the appropriate year book. Details of the documentation for some of the conferences have been published in *Documents of The International Conferences on Education 1979–1986: Cumulative Catalogue*. Unesco, 1988 (See also under *International Conference on Education* on p.35).

There is an important American year book which has a national rather than an international focus, but it has long been familiar over here and should be found in most education libraries:

National Society for the Study of Education Yearbook. Chicago University Press: USA. 2 vols.

The *NSSE Yearbook*, as it is known, is in two parts, each volume being devoted to a separate topic. Although the viewpoint is American, it is not obtrusively so. The year books issued since 1975 are listed below. This should give some idea of the range of educational topics covered. Some of them

are very general, e.g. Policy making in education (1982:1), others are much more specific, e.g. Staff development (1983:2). A few deal with individual subjects, e.g. The teaching of English (1977:1), others with areas related to education, e.g. The social studies (1981:2).

1975:	1	Youth.
	2	Teacher education.
1976:	1	The psychology of teaching methods.
	2	Issues in secondary education.
1977:	1	The teaching of English.
	2	The politics of education.
1978:	1	The courts and education.
	2	Education and the brain.
1979:	1	The gifted and the talented.
	2	Classroom management.
1980:	1	Towards adolescence: the middle years.
	2	Learning a second language.
1981:	1	Philosophy and education.
	2	The social studies.
1982:	1	Policy making in education.
	2	Education and work.
1983:	1	Individual differences and the common curriculum.
	2	Staff development.
1984:	1	Becoming readers in a complex society.
	2	The humanities in pre-collegiate education.
1985:	1	Education in school and non-school settings.
	2	Learning and teaching the ways of knowing.
1986:	1	Microcomputers and education.
	2	The teaching of writing.
1987:	1	The ecology of school renewal.
	2	Society as educator in an age of transition.
1988:	1	Critical issues in curriculum.
	2	Cultural literacy and the idea of general education.
1989:	1	From Socrates to software.
	2	Schooling and disability.

An important European year book which was published regularly from the mid-1960s to the late 1970s has since been transformed into a quarterly periodical:

Paedagogica Europeia: a Review of Education in Europe. Westermann, annual, 1965–78.

It covered new developments in European education, and again each volume was concerned with a particular theme. The earlier volumes were more general in scope but the research aspect was always prominent. From 1974 publication was in two parts (in 1977 there were three). Details from 1975:

1975: 1 The diversification of tertiary education.
      2 Community and youth education in Europe.
1976: 1 New developments in educational research.
      2 Higher education and regional development.
1977: 1 New trends in post-European secondary education.
      2 Zero growth in higher education.
      3 Drop out in European higher education.
1978: 1 Recession and retrenchment: new trends in European higher education.
      2 European universities: 10 years after 1968.

After 1978 the year book became the *European Journal of Education: Research, Development and Policies*, starting with vol. 14 No. 1, 1979. However, each quarterly issue of the periodical still deals with a particular theme. In vol. 14 No. 4, there is a complete contents list of vols 1–18 which covers all the year books issued.

A long-established Australian year book deserves notice. It is rather different from those already mentioned, since each volume consists of special studies on a variety of topics which are not necessarily concerned with current developments:

Melbourne Studies in Education. **Melbourne University Press: Aus, annual.**

This has been appearing regularly since 1957. The emphasis is certainly on Australian education but there are articles of wider interest. In the 1979 volume there are subject indexes covering the year books from 1957 onwards. An interesting and readable year book.

All the year books described so far are devoted to different topics each year. There are several year books which deal with the same subject or topic each year, or with different aspects of it. Three of them are concerned with educational technology:

Aspects of Educational and Training Technology. **Kogan Page, annual.**

Formerly *Aspects of Educational Technology*. This is a record of the proceedings of the Annual Conference of the Association for Educational and Training Technology (AETT) and could have been described in 11.1. However, it is now generally regarded as a year book. Each conference, and therefore each year book, has dealt with a different aspect of educational technology. There is no directory-type information (see below) but there are some useful bibliographies appended to the articles. Titles since 1975 are:

1975: Educational technology for continuous education.
1976: Educational technology for individualised learning.
1977: The spread of educational technology.
1978: Educational technology in a changing world.
1979: Educational technology twenty years on.
1980: Educational technology in the year 2000.
1981: Distance learning and evaluation.
1982: Not published.
1983: Improving efficiency in education and training.
1984: Staff development and career updating.
1985: New directions in education and training technology.
1986: Educational, training and information technologies: economics and other realities.
1987: Flexible learning systems.
1988: Designing new systems and technologies for learning.
1989: Promoting learning.
1990: Making learning systems work.

A classified list of the contents of the earlier volumes was included in the 1984– 85 issue of a year book (pp. 139–75) which comes from the same publisher:

International Yearbook of Educational and Training Technology. Kogan Page, 2– yearly

Despite its title this appears in alternate years. Until 1988 it was the *International Yearbook of Educational and Instructional Technology*. It is really a hybrid since it is both a year book and a directory. it provides an overview of educational technology worldwide, reviewing trends and developments in the field. It also provides lists of sources for those who would like further information about the theory and practice of educational technology. For example the 1990 yearbook has a directory of centres of activity in the UK, USA and elsewhere. There is a comparable American work:

Educational Media and Technology Yearbook. Littleton Libraries Unlimited, Inc.: USA, annual.

There are two sections: for example the first part of the 1986–87 year book has essays on different aspects of educational technology: topics include interactive video, educational computing, satellite TV and distance learning; the second part is a list of media-related organisations throughout the world. There is also a 'mediagraphy' (with a strong American emphasis) which includes a classified list of periodicals and recent books. Producers and publishers are also listed. The essays in the first section provide the main interest for British readers. It was formerly *The Education Media Yearbook*.

Other American year books worth noting are the:

Year Book of Special Education. Marquis Academic Media: USA, annual.

The emphasis in this well-produced year book is very much on current American developments, and some of the chapters may seem only marginally relevant to British readers. Nevertheless there is no equivalent in this country. The same publisher also produces a *Yearbook of Higher Education* and a *Yearbook of Adult and Continuing Education* but these are directory-type publications giving details of relevant institutions and statistical information drawn largely from official sources.

Yearbook of American Universities and Colleges. Garland: USA, annual.

This provides 'an annual review of major developments in US higher education, a list of academic highlights for the academic historian, and a summary of notable documents illustrating the progress and performance of US universities and colleges'. It aims to preserve the most meaningful data and events and is organised under subject headings. It includes a bibliographic guide to publications on US higher education and a 'complete statistical profile'. The first year covered was 1986.

11 Annual reports; conference proceedings

This chapter is concerned with two different types of publication which have much in common: annual reports and conference proceedings. Their function is to describe developments and activities usually in a particular field. Both are normally short, clearly arranged and reasonably digestible. Both appear regularly though not always promptly every year (if we except the proceedings of occasional conferences). Both can be useful to those who wish to keep up to date but they can be difficult to identify and locate, and they usually lack indexes. It is for these latter reasons that they tend to be unjustly neglected as sources of educational information. They are dealt with separately in the next two sections.

11.1 Annual reports

Annual reports or surveys have a different purpose from the year books described in chapter 10. They are normally issued by government departments, official and other bodies, organisations and institutions, and they attempt to provide a formal record, in narrative form, of the year's developments and achievements.

Successive annual reports usually cover much the same ground in much the same way. They are good sources for recent information and often for up-to-date statistics. Earlier reports may prove valuable in retrospective searching. However, very few annual reports have indexes and this can be a real disadvantage if you are searching for specific details.

Some examples of annual reports in the field of education are provided below. Special attention is given to those of the Department of Education and Science and the Scottish Education Department, although they are no longer issued. A few reports which are not primarily educational have also been included since they have relevance for education.

Although annual reports are invariably much shorter than year books it cannot be said that they always make exciting reading, but those who wish to keep up with current developments or follow trends in education over a period will find it helpful to examine them.

DEPARTMENT OF EDUCATION AND SCIENCE. Annual report. HMSO. (Ceased publication.)

Before 1977 this was called *Education and Science in 19—*. The whole series of annual reports stretches back to those of the Committee of Council on Education (CCE) starting in 1839. They were interrupted by the Second World War but the report for 1950 gave a retrospective survey of educational developments from 1900. Fuller details about these older reports will be found in Humby M. (see p. 126), pp. 84–5.

The more recent reports contained an interesting range of information presented in a standard way. The last one (for 1985) runs to over 100 detailed pages and covers general educational developments; the schools; post–16 education in colleges and universities; teachers; staffing; Her Majesty's Inspectorate; statistics and computing services; educational building; civil science; international relations in education; and finance.

The Education (No. 2) Act 1986 removed the requirement for the DES to produce an annual report. 'The Government decided to seek this change in the law because the upsurge of official publications on education, especially in the 1980s, meant that the annual report was little read.' The decision can only be regretted since there is no other source for a succinct review of the year's activities and developments. The annual report has been replaced by the *DES Publications* list (see p. 134) which, useful though it is, has a different function.

This may be a suitable place to mention the *Reports on Education* also issued by the DES. They were not annual reports like the other reports in this section, since they appeared at irregular intervals. Moreover they were only a few pages in length and they could be overlooked for this reason. Nevertheless they contained valuable information and statistics on different areas of education. Each dealt with a specific topic, e.g. the 'Demand for Higher Education in Britain (1983:100)'. They appear to have ceased publication soon after that date. Part of their function has been taken over by the *DES Statistical Bulletins* (see p. 90).

The SED's annual report has not been issued since 1979, but the whole series of reports is invaluable for information on past developments in Scottish education:

SCOTTISH EDUCATION DEPARTMENT. *Education in Scotland in 19—*. HMSO. **(Ceased publication)**
The report was issued regularly from 1873–74 except during the war years from 1939–45 and in 1946 when summary reports only were published. Before the Scottish Education Act of 1872 reports by HMIs on education in Scotland were included in the Committee of Council on Education (CCE) reports for England and Wales, starting in 1839.
The SED reports up to 1938 were much fuller than in more recent years and included much supplementary information, e. g. lists of publications, the texts of circulars, Leaving Certificate Examination papers, etc. which makes them a mine of information on education during the period. The earlier reports have therefore considerable value for historical purposes. Those issued during the nineteenth century particularly have more character and individuality than the impersonal ones of recent years.
From about 1976 the SED annual reports became simply brief factual statements about new developments. The statistical appendices were dropped and so were the lists of circulars, memoranda and other publications. Fortunately there are now other sources for information of this kind (see 19.3). The last report was the one for 1979.

Examples of current annual reports on education are:

ADVISORY COUNCIL FOR ADULT AND CONTINUING EDUCATION (ACACE). **Annual report. HMSO.**

CENTRAL REGISTER AND CLEARING HOUSE (CRCH). **Annual report (See p. 69).**

CITY AND GUILDS OF LONDON INSTITUTE. **Annual report.**

COUNCIL FOR NATIONAL ACADEMIC AWARDS (CNAA). **Annual report.**

FURTHER EDUCATION UNIT (FEU). **Annual report (Before 1982 the FEU was the Further Education Review and Development Unit)**

NATIONAL COUNCIL FOR EDUCATIONAL TECHNOLOGY (NCET). **Annual report.**

NATIONAL CURRICULUM COUNCIL (NCC). **Annual report.**
The NCC replaced the School Curriculum Development Committee (SCDC) following the Education Reform Act 1988. The SCDC issued reports from 1984–85. Its predecessor was the Schools Council, which was responsible for both curriculum and examinations. Its annual reports should still be available in education libraries. There is also a Curriculum Council for Wales.

OPEN UNIVERSITY (OU). **Report of the Vice-Chancellor, annual.**

POLYTECHNICS AND COLLEGES FUNDING COUNCIL (PCFC) **Annual report.**
The PCFC was established by the Education Reform Act 1988, replacing the National Advisory Body for Public Sector Higher Education.

POLYTECHNICS CENTRAL ADMISSIONS SYSTEM (PCAS). **Annual report.**

SCHOOL EXAMINATIONS AND ASSESSMENT COUNCIL (SEAC). **Annual report.**
The SEAC replaced the Secondary Examinations Council after the Education Reform Act 1988. The SEC issued annual reports from 1983–84. Its predecessor was the Schools Council (see above under National Curriculum Council).

SOCIETY FOR RESEARCH INTO HIGHER EDUCATION (SRHE). **Annual report.**

TECHNICAL AND VOCATIONAL EDUCATION INITIATIVE (TVEI). **Review.**
Training Agency, annual. (Formerly issued by the Manpower Services Commission.)

Training Agency (TA). **HMSO Annual report. The TA succeeded the MSC.**

UNIVERSITIES CENTRAL COUNCIL ON ADMISSIONS (UCCA). Report, annual.
UCCA also issues statistical supplements which give statistics and acceptances for each subject.

Universities Funding Council (UFC). Annual report.
The UFC replaced the University Grants Committee following the Education Reform Act 1988. The UGC issued an annual survey, and also a series of quinquennial reviews under the title *University Development.*

The Association for University Teachers published a *British Universities Annual* from 1962–1969. It did not deserve such a brief life. It contained short readable reports from local correspondents on the year's developments by region, including Scotland. A few more general articles were included and, except in the first few issues, some book reviews. There were also statistical tables.

The best known Scottish annual reports are:

CONSULTATIVE COMMITTEE ON THE CURRICULUM (CCC). Report, irregular:
1st 1965–68; 2nd 1968–71; 3rd 1971–74; 4th 1974–80; 5th 1980–83; 6th 1983–87.
The CCC has since been incorporated in the Scottish Consultative Council on the Curriculum (SCCC) (see p.174) which will presumably issue reports on a similar basis.

SCOTTISH EXAMINATION BOARD (SEB). Annual report.
This includes examiners' reports on individual subject areas in the Scottish Certificate of Education (SCE) and the Certificate of Sixth Year Studies (CSYS). The SEB issues two other annual publications which are essential guides for Scottish schools and colleges:

Scottish Certificate of Education: Conditions and Arrangements. Annual.

Certificate of Sixth Year Studies. Annual.
Before 1982 the SEB was called the Scottish Certificate of Education Examination Board.

SCOTTISH VOCATIONAL EDUCATIONAL COUNCIL (SCOTVEC). Annual report (see p. 68).

SCOTTISH COUNCIL FOR EDUCATIONAL TECHNOLOGY (SCET). Annual review. (See p. 174).

Occasionally there are reports which cover longer periods. The quinquennial reports of the UGC and the CCC report (above) were good examples. An even longer span was covered by the *International Extension College* ten-year report 1971–1981. Its annual report is now incorporated in *News About IEC*, 2 per annum.

Annual reports issued by bodies not solely concerned with education will often contain relevant information e. g.
British Council
Economic and Social Research Council
Equal Opportunities Commission
National Association of Citizens' Advice Bureaux.

An example of a report of international interest is:

UNESCO. *Report of the Director-General on the Activities of the Organisation.* **HMSO, annual.**
This contains a section on educational developments worldwide in which Unesco has been involved.

11.2 Conference proceedings

Even the most enthusiastic conference attender might surprised by a brief examination of the following work:

***Index of Conference Proceedings Received;* ed. by the Document Supply Centre of the British Library. Monthly, with annual, 5-yearly, 10-yearly, and longer cumulations.**
It lists accessions to one of the most comprehensive collections of proceedings of conferences, symposia and seminars in the world. About 250,000 proceedings are already available, and about 18,000 are added each year, covering every subject field. All types of conference proceedings are recorded including those appearing in periodical form, those reporting individual conferences and published separately, and those published as part of ordinary periodicals.

As the preface indicates, conference proceedings are notoriously difficult to identify since references

to them may appear in many forms. Arrangement of the index is by subject keywords taken from the title, e. g. education. Within each subject keyword the titles are arranged in chronological order of the date of the meeting. The place where the conference was held is given in bold type. All the conference proceedings listed are available on loan to libraries in the UK which are registered as users of the Document Supply Centre.
A cumulated *Index of Conference Proceedings Received 1964–1988* was published by K. G. Saur in 1989. The main index is also available online as the *Conference Proceedings Index*, through Blaise-Line.

There are two comparable American lists:

Bibliographic Guide to Conference Publications, **G.K. Hall: USA, annual. 2 vols.**

Directory of Published Proceedings: Series SSH–Social Science/Humanities. **Inter-Dok Corporation: USA, quarterly.**

Some examples of proceedings of annual conferences on education are given below:

British Educational Administration Society. **Annual conference. Papers.**

Comparative Education Society. **Conference. Papers (in English, French and German). 2 parts.**

Forum on Educational Research in Scotland. **Proceedings SCRE, annual. (see p.176)**

History of Education Society of Great Britain. **Annual conference. Papers.**

Philosophy of Education Society of Great Britain. **Proceedings of the annual conference.**

Society for Research into Higher Education. **Papers presented to the annual conference. Open University Press.**

    1980: Higher education at the crossroads.
    1981: Is higher education fair?
    1982: Innovation through recession.
    1983: The future for higher education.
    1984: Education for the professions.
    1985: Continuing education.
    1986: Standards and criteria in higher education.

    1987: Restructuring higher education.

Examples of conference proceedings in more specialised areas are:

Association for Educational and Training Technology (AETT). **The proceedings are published in the series** *Aspects of Educational Technology* (see 10.2: Education year books).

Computers in Higher Education. **Annual conference proceedings. Blackwell Scientific.**

Society for Academic Gaming and Simulation in Education and Training (SAGSET). **Annual conference. Papers.**

United Kingdom Reading Association (UKRA). **Proceedings of the Annual Course and Conference. Macmillan.**

European annual conferences include:

Association for Teacher Education in Europe (ATEE). **Annual conference proceedings.**

EURIT. Proceedings of the European Conference on Education and Information Technology. **Pergamon.**

European Association for Research and Development in Higher Education (EARDHE). **Congress proceedings. Pergamon.**

European Association for Research on Learning and Instruction (EARLI). **Conference proceedings. Pergamon.**

European Conference on Computers in Education (ECCI). **Proceedings. North-Holland, Netherlands.**

The longest established international conference is the:

International Conference on Education. **Report. IBE: Unesco, 2-yearly.**
This important conference is held every second year in Geneva. The *International Year Book of Education* (see p.28) is based on it. Microfiches of documents emanating from the conferences have been issued by the International Bureau of

Education. Since 1980 these have been listed in appendices to the year book. There is a handy compendium of recommendations made at the conferences over a long period: *International Conference on Education: Recommendations 1934–1977* (IBE: Unesco). Those adopted since 1977 have been issued in pamphlet form by the IBE. More recently established is the:

Higher Education International. Conference. Annual.

1984:   Forward from U-2000.
1985:   Greater opportunities for international mobility and co-operation in higher education.
1986:   Quality assurance in first degree courses.

The conference was set up in 1983 to provide an international forum for discussing issues of common concern and to encourage international co-operation. The founding organisations were the CNAA, the Committee of Directors of Polytechnics,

and the Standing Committee of Principals and Directors of Colleges and Institutes of Higher Education. For universities we have the:

Congress of the Universities of the Commonwealth. Proceedings. Association of Commonwealth Universities, annual.

The 14th Congress in 1988 was entitled: What can we do for our countries?: the contribution of universities to national development. Two examples of an international conferences in more specialised areas are:

International Simulation and Gaming Association. Conference proceedings. Pergamon, annual.

World Conference of Computers in Education. Proceedings.

12 Educational reports and documents

From time to time you may have to study or consult some of the very large number of educational reports and documents which have emanated from official sources over the years. Not all of them have proved to be of educational significance, but some at least have continued to influence educational policy or methods and have therefore been 'agents of change'.

This chapter starts with a representative selection of reports on education which should be useful for reference purposes (12.1). It is followed by some guidance on how to find out about new or recent reports which are not mentioned in the list (12.2). There is a section describing some of the books which have been written to summarise or evaluate the reports (12.3). Another section (12.4) describes collections of extracts from reports and documents for those who do not have access to, or feel disinclined to read, the originals. The last section (12.5) describes the many guides to the parliamentary reports and papers published during the last two centuries. It should be particularly helpful to the serious student or researcher.

The chapter should be read in conjunction with chapter 19 which contains further information on official publications.

12.1 Official reports on education: a select list

It would be impossible to list here all the educational reports and documents which the reader might have occasion to consult. However, you may find it helpful to have a select list of the more important official reports produced by committees in this country over the last thirty years or more which are known by their chairmen's names.

Starting with the *Crowther Report* in 1959–60 they cover the whole spectrum of education north and south of the border. However, no attempt has been made to include reports on the teaching of particular subjects. One exception is the *Bullock Report* which has relevance for the whole curriculum.

The majority of the reports listed emanate from the Department of Education and Science and the Scottish Education Department. (The Scottish reports have been clearly indicated.) Obviously many could have been added from other sources, e.g. advisory bodies, universities, local authorities, etc. but this would have extended the list unreasonably. You will therefore look in vain for the *Venables Report: Continuing Education* (1976) issued by the Open University, or the *Hargreaves Report: Improving Secondary Schools* (1984) which came from the Inner London Education Authority.

Full details of the reports and documents are not given for lack of space but sub-titles have been added where this would be helpful. In multi-volume reports the titles of individual volumes have been indicated. Further information may be obtained from your library's catalogue or from some of the indexes mentioned in 12.5. It is appreciated that a chronological arrangement would have been equally useful but for ready reference an alphabetical arrangement has been preferred.

ALEXANDER: *The Challenge of Change*. (Scotland, 1975.)

BRUNTON: *From School to Further Education*. (Scotland, 1963.)

BRUNTON: *Training of Graduates for Secondary Education.* (Scotland, 1972.)

BULLOCK: *A Language for Life*. (1975.)

CARNEGIE: *Professional Education and Training for Community Education.* (Scotland, 1977.)

CRAIGIE: *Consultation in Educational Matters.* (Scotland, 1982.)

CROWTHER: 15–18. (1959–60.)

DE VILLE: *Review of Vocational Qualifications in England and Wales.* (1986.)

DONNISON: *Public Schools Commission: 2nd report.* 3 vols. Vol.1: Report on independent day schools and direct grant schools. Vol. 2: Appendices. Vol.3: Scotland (see FAULKNER). (1970.)

DUNNING: *Assessment for all: report of the Committee to Preview Assessment in the Third and Fourth Years of Secondary Education in Scotland.* (1977.)

ELTON: *Discipline in Schools.* (1989.)

FAIRLEY: *Pupils' Progress Records.* (Scotland, 1969.)

FAULKNER: *Public Schools Commission: 2nd Report. Vol.3: Scotland.* (1975.)

FLOWERS: *Report of the Joint Working Party on Computers for Research.* (1966.)

GITTINS: *Primary Education in Wales.* (1967.)

GREEN: *Future of In-service Training in Scotland.* (1979.)

HALE: *University Teaching Methods.* (1964.)

HALSEY: *Educational Priority.* 5 vols. (1) EPA: problems and policies; (2) EPA: surveys and statistics; (3) Curriculum innovation in London's EPAs; (4) West Riding Project; (5) EPA: a Scottish study. (1975.)

HASLEGRAVE: *Technician Courses and Examinations.* (1969.)

HENNIKER-HEATON: *Day Release.* (1969.)

HIGGINSON: *Advancing A Levels.* (1988.)

HOLLAND: *Young People and Work.* (1977.)

HOUGHTON: *Pay of Non-university Teachers.* (1975.)

HUDSON: *Central Arrangements for Promoting Educational Technology in the United Kingdom.* (1972.)

JAMES: *Teacher Education and Training.* (1972.)

JONES: *The Brain Drain.* (1967.)

KECHANE: *Proposals for a Certificate of Extended Education CEE.* (1979.)

KILBRANDON: *Children and Young Persons.* (Scotland, 1964.)

LEWIS: *Education of Deaf Children.* (1968.)

LINDOP: *Academic Validation in Public Sector Higher Education.* (1985.)

MCCALLUM: *Future Strategy for Higher Education in Scotland: Report of the Scottish Tertiary Education Advisory Council* (STEAC, 1985.)

MCCANN: *The Secondary Education of Physically Handicapped Children in Scotland.* (1975.)

MCFARLANE: *Education for 16–19 Year Olds.* (1980.)

MCHAFFIE: *Before Five: Pre-school Education in Scotland.* (1971.)

MAIN: *Pay and Conditions of School Teachers in Scotland.* (1986.)

MERRISON: *Report of the Working Party on Postgraduate Education.* (1982.)

MILLAR: *Moral and Religious Education in Scottish Schools.* (1972.)

MUNN: *Structure of the Curriculum.* (Scotland, 1977.)

NEWSOM: *Half our Future (education Between the Ages of 13-16 of Pupils of Average or Less than Average Ability).* (1963.)

NEWSOM: *Public Schools Commission: 1st Report* (integration of public schools within the state system). (1968.)

OAKES: *Report of the Working Group on the Management of Higher Education in the Maintained Sector.* (1978.)

PACK: *Truancy and Indiscipline in Schools in Scotland.* (1977.)

PLOWDEN: *Children and their Primary Schools.* 2 vols.(1) Report; (2) Research and surveys. (1967.)

QUIRK: *Speech Therapy Services.* (1972.)

RAMPTON: See SWANN.

ROBBINS: *Higher Education: Report. Appendices I-V. Evidence VI-XII.* 7 vols. (1963.)

ROBERTS: *Measures to Secure a More Equitable Distribution of Teachers in Scotland.* (1966.)

ROBERTSON: *Future Recruitment and Training of Teachers for Further Education in Scotland.* (1965.)

RODGER: *Ascertainment of Children with Visual Handicap* (Scotland, 1969.)

RODGER: *Conditions of Service of Teachers in Further Education in Scotland.* (1965.)

RUSSELL: *Adult Education: a Plan for Development.* (1973.)

RUSSELL: *Supply and Training of Teachers for Further Education.* (1966.)

RUTHVEN: *Ancillary Staff in Secondary Schools* (Scotland, 1976.)

RUTHVEN: *Organisation of Courses Leading to the Scottish Certificate of Education.* (1967.)

SNEDDON: *Learning to Teach.* (1978.)

STAFFORD: *A 'Special' Professionalism: Report of the Special Needs Teacher Training Working Group.* (1987.)

STEAC REPORT (Scotland). See McCALLUM.

STIMPSON *Non-Teaching Staff in Secondary Schools.* (Scotland, 1976.)

SWANN: *Education for All: Report of the Committee of Enquiry into the Education of Children from Ethnic Minority Groups.* (Swann succeeded Rampton as chairman.) (1985.)

TAYLOR: *A New Partnership for our Schools.* (1977.)

UNDERWOOD: *Report of the Committee on Maladjusted Children.* (Scotland, 1964.)

WADDELL: *Schools Examinations: Report of a Steering Committee Established to Consider Proposals for Replacing the GCE Ordinary-Level and CSE Exams by a Common System of Examining.* Parts 1 and 2. (1978.)

WARNOCK: *Special Educational Needs: Report of the Committee of Enquiry into the Education of Handicapped Children and Young People.* (1978.)

WEAVER: *Report of the Study Group on the Governance of Colleges of Education.* (1966.)

WEAVER: *A Teaching Council for England and Wales.* (1970.)

Do not forget the important reports of the House of Commons Select Committees, set up on an occasional basis to look into specific aspects of education in this country. e.g.:

House Of Commons Select Committee In Education. *Teacher Training.* HMSO.6 vols. 1970.

There is also the ongoing series of reports from one of the standing committees of the House of Commons, e.g.:

HOUSE OF COMMONS. EDUCATION, SCIENCE AND ARTS COMMITTEE. *Session 1986–87. 3rd Report: Special Educational Needs: Interpretation of the Education Act 1981*. HMSO, 1987. 2 vols.
(1) Proceedings of the committee and minutes of evidence. (2) Appendices containing evidence.

Mention should also be made of the interesting series of reports arising from the continuing investigations of the Audit Commission:

Audit Commission. Reports. HMSO. Relevant examples:
Obtaining Better Value in Education: Aspects of Non-teaching Costs in Secondary Education. (1984.)
Obtaining Better Value in Further Education: a Report. (1985.)
Towards Better Management of Secondary Education. (1986.)
Delegation of Management Authority to Schools. (1988)
Assessing Quality in Education. (1989.)

12.2 Finding out about current reports

Important new reports on education will normally receive some attention in the more serious daily newspapers in feature articles, editorials and perhaps the correspondence columns. Fuller treatment of new or recent reports can be expected in the *Times Educational Supplement* (not forgetting the Scottish edition for reports published there) and the *Times Higher Education Supplement*. Their weekly publication makes it possible to give more detailed attention to specific aspects of significant reports, and summaries, extracts and critical reviews may also be provided. Articles will later appear in the more academic educational journals, whose less frequent publication will enable their contributors to put initial reactions into some perspective. However, there is another weekly periodical which should not be overlooked:

Education: the Journal of Educational Administration, Management and Policy.

Weekly. Councils and Education Press.
It regularly reviews developments in education and comments on new reports. Moreover , it frequently incorporates *Education Digests* on particular topics, and some of these have dealt with educational reports, e.g. Warnock, and Scotland's Action Plan. Each digest is designed as a 'short, readable, comprehensive and above all, authoritative guide and update on a particular educational topic'. There are digests on the teaching of particular subjects, and on a variety of issues such as educational broadcasting, independent schools, school libraries, school examinations, and teacher training. A complete list of those available will be found in the latest issue of *Education*. The digests are also available for purchase in sets of ten or more of the same title, or in sets of ten different titles.
Scanning *Education* is a sensible way of keeping up to date on educational matters generally. For example, it has a regular section on 'Parliament: Answers to Questions', which often includes current statistics.

The first appearance of new reports on education is usually noted in the *ACE Digest* which forms an insert in the monthly *ACE Bulletin* (see p.9). The bulletin itself may contain a relevant article. It appears to give particular attention to matters concerned with special education.

Another periodical which could easily be overlooked is the *Survey of Current Affairs*. (HMSO, monthly). It is prepared by the Central Office of Information and covers developments worldwide in many fields of activity. It occasionally includes short summaries of important educational reports or white papers published in this country.

A much better known resource is *Keesings Record of World Events* (see p.159) which could be tried for précis of significant recent reports on education. It has the advantage of appearing weekly, and should be available in most reference libraries.

For recent records of HMI reports on schools and colleges in particular, see 19.3.

12.3 Books about the reports

Brief descriptions of some of the more important educational reports will be found in a few of the dictionaries of education (8.2) and encyclopaedias of education (9.2) already mentioned. There is a select annotated list of reports in the *Education Fact File* (see p.9) and in the *Education Year Book* (see p.57) The latter is probably the most readily available source.

However, several books have been written expressly to discuss and evaluate the more significant reports on education. They will certainly be appreciated by hard-pressed students, and by any others who wish to familiarise themselves quickly with the contents and recommendations of these official documents.

CORBETT. A. *Much to Do About Education: a Critical Survey of the Major Educational Reports.* **4th edn. Macmillan, 1978.**
This has a lively introduction, then deals with the reports in chronological sequence. For each report it gives the names of the chairman and committee members; the terms of reference, with explanatory notes; the main recommendations; and any subsequent action taken on the report. A new edition of this much used work would be very welcome.

ROGERS. R. *Crowther to Warnock: How Fourteen Reports Tried to Change Children's Lives* **2nd edn. Heinemann, 1984.**
This usefully supplements Corbett, A., since it is wider in scope. It discusses reports concerned with key issues in the education, health, and social well-being of children. Each section has four parts: why the committee of enquiry was set up; what it was asked to do; what its recommendations were; and what has happened since the report was published. The reports span twenty years. They include specifically educational reports such as Crowther, Newsom, Plowden, Halsey, Bullock, Taylor, and Warnock. The others are concerned with children and young people in different contexts:

Court. *Child Care Services.* (1976.)
Finer. *One-parent Families.* (1974.)
Houghton. *Adoption of Children.* (1967.)
Houghton. *Children Act.* (1975.)
Latey. *Age of majority.* (1967.)
Platt. *Welfare of Children.* (1959.)
Also included are the reports of the Select Committee on Violence in the Family (1975 and 1977).

KOGAN, M. and PACKWOOD,T. *Advisory Councils and committees in Education.* **Routledge, 1974.**
'The most influential reports in modern educational history ...have been produced by advisory committees and councils in the field. This is an analytical account of the role of these bodies in creating and promulgating educational policies.' The book systematically reviews the contents of 28 reports, starting with the Hadow Report (1926) and ending with the James Report (1971). It also analyses the membership and working of the committees. The final chapter discusses 'the potential role of such committees in relation to the organisational analysis of the whole educational system'. The reports are listed in chronological order at the end of the book and there are references for further reading.

LELLO, J. *The Official View of Education.* **Pergamon, 1964.**
Deals with important reports published before 1964, not in chronological order this time, but in chapters devoted to particular aspects of education, e.g. the youth service, further education, and teacher training. The reports are listed in an appendix, with their terms of reference.

Not many users of the present guide are likely to require information about American educational reports, but there are two convenient compendiums from an influential source:

CARNEGIE COMMISSION ON HIGHER EDUCATION. *A Critical Examination of the Reports and Recommendations.* **Jossey-Bass: USA, 1973.**
The Carnegie Commission subsequently changed its name to describe its functions more fully:

CARNEGIE COUNCIL ON POLICY STUDIES IN HIGHER EDUCATION. *A Critical Examination of Reports and Recommendations.* **Jossey-Bass: USA, 1980.**
The reports in both volumes are carefully presented and summarised. They are worth examining as they illuminate some of the main concerns of American education in comparatively recent times.

12.4 Collections of educational documents

Official reports and documents are very numerous. They can also be very long and indigestible. Students or teachers may not always have the time or the inclination to read them right through, nor may it always be necessary. There are two excellent source books which bring together documents which are important in the history of education in this country. They give extracts from key reports, education acts, etc. and place them in historical perspective, with linking notes and commentaries:

MACLURE, J. S.   *Educational Documents: England and Wales, 1816 to the Present Day.* **5th edn. Methuen 1986.**

The main theme of this volume is 'the creation of an administrative framework - a genuine national education system. This in turn leads to subsidiary themes - the relation between church and state in public education, the training of teachers, the progressive development from elementary to primary and secondary education for all, the growth of technical education from a private to a public activity'. The excerpts are arranged chronologically. In selecting them the editor 'has not always sought the recondite and the recherché and 'has been less interested to chase ghosts and embryos than to arrange the famous and the obvious passages in a useful form... It may be that this collection will persuade more to go back to these secondary but fascinating sources and dig for themselves'. Successive editions have kept this invaluable work up to date. There is an index of members of committees, assessors, etc.

SYLVESTER, D. W. *Educational Documents: 800 – 1816.* **Methuen, 1970.**

This complementary volume covers the earlier period, including the centuries before the real flood of educational reports started. The documentary material has been selected 'to illustrate the main themes of educational history from the Middle Ages to the beginning of the present century... An attempt has been made to provide, as far as space would allow, a balanced selection of material on the curriculum and discipline of various educational institutions, and on the legal and constitutional framework on which they are founded'. The editor accepts that this volume will be much less used than the later one 'since this earlier history has not often figured in courses of education' though 'its importance in adding perspectives to studies of educational development is now being more widely acknowledged'.

These are splendid compilations and are indispensable for those who wish to obtain a more realistic insight into the development of education in this country than can be obtained from the general histories of education. Equally valuable in its way is:

VAN DER EYKEN, W. *Education, the Child and Society: a Documentary History 1900–1973.* **Penguin, 1973.**

It aims to complement, not compete, with the volume by J. S. Maclure above, and it does not confine itself to extracts from official documents. It aims to collect 'the most influential and perceptive thinking on education from that of civil servants to the most radical social critic of the day... The material centres not only on the crucial Education Acts of 1902, 1918, 1936 and 1944, the reports of Geddes, Hadow, Spens, Norwood, Crowther, Robbins, Newsom and Plowden and the political speeches and government circulars of the period...but also on the individual views of novelists, social historians and economists on the development of child psychology, and on some of the experiments which profoundly affected contemporary notions of education'.

On a more specific topic there is:

FOWLER, W. S. *Towards the National Curriculum: Discussion and Control in the English Educational System 1965–1988.* **Kogan Page, 1988.**

This brings together key extracts from the most important political speeches, White papers and HMI reports to trace the development of the concept of a National Curriculum in Britain. It focuses on issues raised and the implications for teachers.

There is an interesting book which collects educational documents of various kinds to illustrate developments in education and teaching since the beginning of the nineteenth century:

GOSDEN, P. H. J. H. *How They Were Taught: an Anthology of Contemporary Accounts of Learning and Teaching in England 1800 - 1950.* **Batsford, 1969.**

It is almost a social history of England over a period of 150 years. Its expressed aim is 'to illustrate some of the main lines of development in the whole field of educational activity'. There are chapters on early voluntary and board schools, the later primary and secondary schools, the growth of science education, the education of women, experimental schools, the training of teachers, and the universities.

Other works worth consulting are:

HYNDMAN, M. *Schools and Schooling in England and Wales: a Documentary History.* **Harper & Row, 1978.**

This is not so much a collection of documents as a continuous text interwoven with short illustrative extracts. Each chapter takes a particular theme, e.g. the training of teachers in the 19th and 20th centuries, so that the overall treatment is not simply chronological. However, the final chapter provides a 'chronological framework' or list of relevant dates, which could be useful to students generally.

BALL, N. *Educating the People: a Documentary History of Elementary Schooling in England 1840–1870.* **M. T. Smith, 1983.**

'The elementary schools of mid-Victorian Britain are portrayed in this book through the evidence of those who established and ran them.' It draws on school records, etc. in order to 'add another perspective to the picture which emerges from official reports and papers'. Each chapter consists of several pages of text followed by notes and a selection of relevant documents.

CRESSY, D. *Education in Tudor and Stuart England.* **Arnold, 1975. (Documents of modern history.)**

'The documents in this volume have been chosen to outline the school system of Tudor and Stuart England, and to illustrate some of the social and political pressures bearing on education in the 16th and 17th centuries.' There is a general introduction and brief notes on each document, which is usually a short extract. The sections are: (1) Perspectives on education; (2) Control of education; (3) The organisation of schools; (4) Schoolmasters; (5) The curriculum; (6) Educational opportunity; (7) Education of Women; and (8) The universities. This is a readable introduction to education during the period.

None of the above-mentioned works includes any documents relating to Scotland. A notable gap was therefore filled by a volume which appeared 'in the wake of the centenary celebrations of the 1872 Education Act' north of the border:

Scottish Public Educational Documents 1560–1960; **ed. H. Hutchison. Scottish Council for Research in Education, 1973.**

'In the study of any branch of history it is tempting to be satisfied with information supplied from secondary sources but there is no substitute for personal acquaintance with the original documents which are the stuff of history.' To prove his point the editor provides extracts from over 220 documents covering a period of 400 years from the Reformation to modern times. There are three parts, each with its own introduction: (1) 1560–1700; (2) 1700–1872; and (3) 1872–1960. The internal arrangement of each part is 'approximately chronological' and the extracts are prefaced by explanatory notes. The development of particular themes can be traced by using the comprehensive index. The volume succeeds in presenting a balanced picture of Scottish educational development. It deserved a better format.

Only one example from America will be given here:

Hofstadter, R. and Smith, W. *American Higher Education: a Documentary History.* **Chicago University Press: USA, 1961.**

'This is designed for the reader who wants to get from original materials an overall view of the development of higher education in America.' The editors hoped that the collection would be 'representative, informative, interesting and serviceable' and they have been largely successful. 'The documents touch not merely on teaching and research, but also on some central aspects of American life and character.' The arrangement is broadly chronological.

If you are interested in documentary material, do not overlook the collections of historical documents which are primarily intended for students of history (see Cressy, D. above). A notable example is:

English Historical Documents; **ed. D. C. Douglas. Eyre & Spottiswoode. 1953 - 1977. 12 vols, for example: Vol.12(1): 1833 - 1874. (1956.) Vol.12(2): 1874 - 1914. (1977.)**

These two volumes are typical of this splendid series. There is a valuable section on education in each of them, with informative introductions.

For the curious, there is a unique source which could provide something of interest:

CRAIG, F. W. S. *British General Election Manifestos 1900–1974.* **Revised edn., Macmillan, 1975.**

A collection of the election manifestos of the three principal political parties. In Appendix 2 there is a list of the occasional manifestos issued by the parties for Wales and Scotland since 1950. As the preface states: 'The manifestos rarely cover any subject in great depth' and this applies to the sections on education. However it is a handy source for anyone who wants to survey the parties' views on education in the twentieth century. There is a European collection: *Political Manifestos of the Postwar Era 1945–1988*. (K. G. Saur: W. Germany, 1989, on microfiche) on 150 fiches which few libraries will be able to afford. It has an index of subjects treated.

To end this section on a less serious note there is a collection not of documents but of cartoons, which have been retrieved from the best known British educational journal:

TIMES EDUCATIONAL SUPPLEMENT. *A Hundred of the Best: TES Cartoons* ed. N. Tucker. Penguin, 1968.
'All the traditional Aunt Sallies are here, and many newer ones. From the timetables of the great comprehensives to the awesome complexities of the latest visual aids the collection adds up to a shrewd and witty commentary on our current educational attitudes.' So states the publisher's blurb, which has a slightly dated air. It also asks the question: 'Are teachers funny? and concludes that they are very funny indeed.

There is a brief work which may or may not persuade you of the truth of this observation:

Best Classroom Jokes; ed. E. Phillips. Wolfe, 1974.
'Most of the jokes in this collection refer to that age-old war in the classroom between teacher and pupil - and in most of them, the pupil comes out best (sorry sir, better).'

12.5 Parliamentary reports and papers

The books described in the previous section would be useful to anyone with a general interest in the history of education. Those with a more serious or research interest should also know about the collections, summaries, and lists of parliamentary reports and papers which are now available in a convenient form. Reference to some of

the works described below will save you considerable searching in other sources:

FORD, P. and FORD, G. *A Breviate of Parliamentary Papers, 1900–1916*. **Revised edn. Irish University Press, 1960.**

FORD, P. and FORD, G. *A Breviate of Parliamentary Papers, 1917–1939*. **Irish University Press, 1969.**

FORD, P. and FORD, G. *A Breviate of Parliamentary Papers. 1940–1954*. **Irish University Press, 1961.**
These cover the whole range of British parliamentary reports and papers issued during the period 1900 - 1954, but in each one there is a special section devoted to education. Here will be found excellent brief summaries of most of the official documents required for the study of British educational history in the first half of the twentieth century. The lists are continued in:

FORD, P, FORD, G. and MARSHALLSAY, D. *Select List of British Parliamentary Papers, 1955–1964*. **Irish University Press, 1970.**

MARSHALLSAY, D. and SMITH, J. H. *Ford List of British Parliamentary Papers, 1965–1974*. **Irish University Press, 1979.**
In these works the papers are simply listed, not summarised, but they are still valuable for identification purposes. Presumably a breviate of the papers will be issued at a later date.

For the larger part of the century there is a similar publication:

FORD, P. and FORD, G. *Select List of British Parliamentary Papers, 1833–1899*. **Irish University Press, 1969.**

Fortunately for those who wish to study nineteenth century British parliamentary papers in detail there is a magnificent set of volumes issued by the Irish University Press. In them are collected and reprinted on a selective basis the complete texts of British parliamentary reports and papers on education:

British Parliamentary Papers. **Irish University Press, 1967–72:**
Education: General. 45 vols.
Education: Scientific and technical. 8 vols.
Education: Poorer classes. 9 vols.

No attempt will be made to describe in detail this rich storehouse of information on nineteenth century education. To take just one example, you will find in these pages the full report of the Argyll Commission on Schools in Scotland, originally issued in 1865–67. All the volumes are beautifully printed and bound. For quick reference to the whole series, which is not limited to education, there is a *Checklist of British Parliamentary Papers in the Irish University Press 1000 -Volume series 1801 - 1899, (1972)*. This provides short abstracts of every paper included in the series.

The identification of many lesser known reports in all fields including education will be made easier by reference to:

RICHARD, S. *British Government Publications: an Index to Chairmen of Committees and Commissions of Enquiry.* **Library Association, 1974–84.**
Vol.1:   1800–1899
Vol.2:   1900–1940
Vol.3:   1941–1978
Vol.4:   1979–1982

These volumes list alphabetically by surnames of chairmen and/or authors every British government report, with minor exceptions, since 1800. It was not until the 1940s that the Stationery Office began to include chairmen's names on the reports so these volumes are indispensable for the whole period covered. The indexes are based largely on the collections in Edinburgh University Library and the National Library of Scotland, and also on those in the British Library Official Publications Library and the Bodleian Library. Volumes 2 and 3 incorporate the earlier indexes covering the period 1911–1971 compiled by A. M. Morgan and L. K. Stephen which are now superseded.

There is another publication which is relevant for reports published in the early 1970s:

Kite, J. *Government Reports 1971–75: Indexes of Chairmen and Subjects.* **Avon County Library, 1977.**

Useful lists of this kind are contained in two brief works described later in this guide:

ARGLES, M. and VAUGHAN, J. E. *British Government Publications Concerning Education during the 20th Century.* **History of Education Society, 1982. (see p.131)**

ARGLES, M. *British Government Publications in Education During the 19th Century.* **History of Education Society, 1971. (See p.131)**

There is a list of reports for the further education sector in:

PETERS, A. J. *A Guide to the Study of British Further Education: Published Sources on the Contemporary System.* **NFER, 1967.**
(Appendix 2: List of reports mentioned which are commonly known by chairman's name.)

Another publication should help you to identify recent official reports:

Committee reports Published by HMSO Indexed by Chairman. **4 per annum. HMSO.**
This lists alphabetically the chairmen of all committee reports, including the chairmen of parliamentary and departmental committees and review bodies. It does not include annuals. The final quarterly issue is also an annual cumulation. Note also: *Reports of the European Communities: an Index to Authors and Chairmen*; compiled by J. Neilson. Mansell, 1981.

General guidance on the use of parliamentary papers will be found in Ford, P. *A Guide to Parliamentary Papers and How to Use Them.* (Irish University Press, 1972). Further information about official publications (both general and educational) will be found in chapter 19 of the present guide.

13 The law of education

The law of education, like the law affecting many other areas of human activity, is full of complexities and ambiguities. Anyone embarking on a study of it is faced with an unenviable task. However, there are one or two excellent general guides (see 13.1) and a number more particularly geared to the needs of teachers and others who are interested in the law of education as it affects them (13.2).

It is not possible here to cover all aspects of the subject but there is one area of special concern to educationists, administrators and teachers: the law of copyright, and a short section (13.3) is devoted to it. Following the publication of the Taylor Report in 1977 and the Education Acts of 1986 and 1988 the role of school governors has become much more significant, and a list of relevant books and pamphlets forms a separate section (13.5) at the end of the chapter.

Readers who make good use of some of the works mentioned in the following pages will find that much of the groundwork has already been done for them. At least they may be spared the labour of poring over Acts of Parliament and the minutiae of statutory instruments.

13.1 Guides to the law of education

The *Education Year Book* (see p.57) includes a short 'Guide to Legislation' which covers the Education Acts and other statutes, with references to Wales and Scotland. The *Education Fact File* (see p.9) has short summaries of the more important Education Acts in recent years. However, the standard guide to the existing law of education is:

LIELL, P. and SAUNDERS, J.B. *The Law of Education.* 9th edn.Butterworths, 1984. (In loose-leaf binder with updating service.)

'It deals mainly with the law of education as it affects that part of the system maintained by local education authorities.'The material is clearly presented but a fuller introduction would have been helpful. Sections are: (A) Introduction; (B) Education Acts; (C) Other relevant enactments; (D) Statutory instruments (Government regulations and orders); (E) Government circulars, circular letters and administrative memoranda; and (F) Cases on the law of education. There are tables of statutes and cases at the end. The index, which refers to paragraphs not page numbers, could be more detailed. There have been twelve updates since 1984. *A Special Bulletin: Education Reform Act 1988* (ed. P. Liell) appeared in 1989 but the relevant material has since been incorporated in Supplement 11.

A shorter summary of the law of education will be found in the:

Citizens' Advice Notes Service (CANS). **National Council for Voluntary Organisations. (In loose-leaf binder with updating service.)**
A digest of current legislation in all fields including education, and a model of its kind. It should be available in most libraries.

There are several books on the Education Reform Act which may of interest:

COULBY, D. and BASH, L. *Education Reform Act: Competition and Control.* **Cassell, 1989.**

Education Reform Act 1988: its Origins and Implications, **eds. M.Flude and M. Hammer. Falmer Press, 1989.**

Guide to the Education Reform Act 1988. **Longman, for the Association of Headteachers, 1989.**

LAWTON, D. *Education Reform Act: Choice and Control.* **Hodder, 1989.**

LEONARD, M. *The 1988 Education Act: a Tactical Guide for Schools.* **Blackwell, 1988.**

MACLURE, S. *Education Reformed: Guide to the Education Reform Act.* **2nd edn., 1990.**

The full text of the Act will be found in *Education Reform Act 1988. Chapter 40.* (HMSO). It has far-reaching implications. For example, it makes provision for a National Curriculum and for schools to opt out of the maintained sector. Numerous books have already appeared on aspects of the National Curriculum and many more can be expected but there is not space to include them here.

The Advisory Centre for Education (see p.9) has published useful short summaries of the 1988, 1986 and 1981 Education Acts, and also:

SALLIS, J.A. *ACE Guide to Education Law.* Latest edn. Advisory Centre for Education.
There are three sections, on England and Wales, Scotland, and Northern Ireland, with brief appendices: (A) Landmarks in the history of public sector education; (B) Government reports on education; (C) Model articles of government for LEA schools. There is a detailed index. A new edition which will take account of the 1988 Act is expected in 1990.

A fuller, more general account will be found in:

NICE, E. *Education and the Law.* Councils and Education Press, 1986.
Intended for professionals in the field of education and interested parents, school governors and others who require a better knowledge and understanding of the legal framework and background to the education service. A separate chapter indicates the differences in the Scottish system. Note the date.

The law relating to special education is dealt with in:

COX, B. *The Law of Special Educational Needs: a Guide to the Education Act, 1981.* Croom Helm, 1984.
A handy guide for local authority advisers, teachers and parents among others. More up to date is:

NEWELL, P. ACE *Special Education Handbook.* Latest edn. Advisory Centre for Education.
Originally published to explain the Education Act 1981 which provided important new rights for parents. It covers the changes introduced by the 1988 Act.

Special education law in Scotland is described in:

SCOTTISH CONSUMER COUNCIL. *In Special Need: a Handbook for Parents of Children and Young People in Scotland with Special Educational Needs,* by G. Atherton, HMSO,1989.
A clear explanation of a complex law. It includes an annotated list of publications and organisations which offer information, advice or practical help.

There are two important handbooks which must be mentioned here. They are primarily concerned with educational administration and both come from authoritative sources:

***Educational Administration,* 3rd edn. written by members of the Society of Education Officers and the Association of Directors of Education in Scotland, eds. K. Brooksbank and K. Anderson. Longman, 1989.**
'This edition has been completely revised and updated in the light of the major innovations of the Education Reform Act: local management of schools, the National Curriculum, the abolition of the Inner London Education Authority, grant-maintained schools, city technology, and other implications for the LEA.' The previous edition was published by Councils and Education Press in 1984.

***College Administration: a Handbook,* 2nd edn. Eds. M. Locke *et al,* Longman, in association with the National Association of Teachers in Further and Higher Education, 1988.**
A thorough and practical guide for college administrators and academic staff. This edition has an almost entirely new text but a smaller and less permanent format. It describes in detail the administration of public sector post school education in England and Wales. It also provides information on the many changes in administration, finance, education law, salaries and conditions of service, staff development and training, and the curriculum which have occurred since the first edition appeared in 1980. The latter will still have to be consulted for fuller treatment of earlier concerns, e.g. the Crombie Regulations on voluntary redundancy in the colleges of education.

A warm welcome must be given to a new quarterly periodical on *Education and the Law,* published by Longman from 1989. Its aim is 'to provide a fully independent and up-to-date source of material on all aspects of the law relating to primary, secondary, tertiary, and higher education'. It has the field virtually to itself.

13.2   Teachers and the law

There has been a steadily increasing interest over the last decade in the legal position of teachers in a variety of contexts. It is reflected in the number of useful guides published in recent years:

BARRELL, G.R. and PARTINGTON, J.A. *Teachers and the Law.* **Methuen, 1985**
'The law' (a quote from Lord Denning in the Introduction)'never stands still. You have to run fast to keep up with it.' This new edition of the standard handbook by Geoffrey Barrell, who died during its production, was therefore very welcome. It had revised chapters covering health and safety at work, and employment protection and discrimination, but now needs updating again. It is clearly presented and readable.

BARRELL, G.R. *Legal Cases for Teachers.* **Methuen, 1970.**
A different kind of book which 'contains a wide variety of cases concerned with education in general and schools in particular'. It was prepared primarily to help practising teachers. There are sections on the administration of education; conditions of service; parents; administration of schools; punishment; negligence; and defamation of teachers. Despite its date, it is still a valuable supplement to *Teachers and the Law* (above).

The Head's Legal Guide, ed. S.B. Howarth. **Oyez Publishing Ltd. (In loose-leaf binder with updating supplements issued quarterly.)**
This ambitious guide is dedicated to Barrell's memory. The basic volume, which appeared in 1985, is large and unwieldy but its usefulness is enhanced by its arrangements for keeping itself up to date. There are six sections: Structure and administration of education; Employment of staff;

Day-to-day running of the school; External dealings; Special education; and Further information (e.g. lists of statutes, statutory instruments, cases, circulars, abbreviations, and useful addresses). An index has been provided but it could have been more detailed. The high cost of the book and its amendments may mean that it is less widely available than it should be. It is a comprehensive manual, well set out and clearly written, and a reliable source of information for headmasters and their staffs. It will be less useful to those in Scotland.

ADAMS, N. *Law and Teachers Today.* **Hutchinson, 1983.**
'Almost everything a teacher does has a legal context.' This book tries to present relevant information in a readable and interesting way. It poses realistic problems related to the everyday life of the schools with practical advice.

BLOY, D. and HARRISON, G. *Essential Law for Teachers.* **Oyez, 1980.**
This 'does not aim at comprehensiveness, rather to provide a service to the working teacher' in England and Wales, and to explain his/her legal rights and obligations.

IRELAND, K. *Teachers' Rights and Duties.* **Macmillan, 1985.**
Aims to provide a straightforward account of how laws and regulations affect the ordinary teacher. There is a 'selective index'.

PARTINGTON, J. *Law and the New Teacher.* **Holt, Rinehart, 1984.**
Intended for the newcomer to the teaching profession, this book presents the law's view of the young teacher's daily work and the problems that often arise. There is a subject index of topics.

A short pamphlet produced specially for Scottish teachers deserves mention:

FRASER, A. *The Teacher and the Law.* **Revised edn. Moray House College of Education, 1982.**
Within its limited format this provides an adequate commentary with some useful appendices. It was issued by the Scottish Centre for Studies in School Administration at Moray House College in Edinburgh.

There is a more recent Scottish work, fuller and wider in scope:

SCOTTISH CONSUMER COUNCIL. *Law of the school: a Parent's Guide to Education Law in Scotland;* by G. Atherton *et al.* HMSO, 1987.
Prepared by the Scottish Consumer Council primarily for parents of schoolchildren at all stages. It is clearly written and fairly recent. Arrangement is by topics alphabetically, e.g. discipline and punishment, education authorities, employment of schoolchildren. There is a note on 'where to find out more' at the end of each section. It will be useful to teachers, administrators, governors and others.

13.3 Copyright and education

Nowadays copyright is a matter of considerable importance to all those who are involved in teaching and the preparation of teaching and learning materials, more especially because of the increasing emphasis on resource based learning.

The Copyright Act of 1956 was proving so unsatisfactory, particularly in relation to the newer media, that anyone who wished to copy parts of books or periodicals, transfer a sound recording from disc to tape cassette, record a television broadcast, or make use of computer programmes, was becoming very uncertain about the legal implications.

Some of the general guides to the law of education already described include information and guidance on copyright. There have been numerous other publications, substantial or slight, which were designed to help teachers and librarians in particular to tread a safe path through the minefield. However most of these have now become dated by the passing of the new Copyright, Designs and Patents Act of 1988.

The most accessible brief account of copyright in this country (and the USA) will be found in two chapters of the *Writers' and Artists' Yearbook* (A.& C. Black), which is updated annually. On the general guides to the law of education, those in looseleaf format (e.g. Liell and Saunders, (see p.46) have stood up best because they have been able to update their contents readily.

Although some publications on the new copyright law have already appeared these are aimed at lawyers rather than teachers or educationists. There is one however which has an excellent chapter on copyright as applied to education:

DORKIN, G. and TAYLOR, G. *Blackstone's Guide to the Copyright, Designs and Patents Act 1988.* Blackstone Press, 1989.
The chapter deals with reprography, education and libraries; audio and visual recordings; computer technology; and cable and satellite broadcasting, and gives a clear outline of the current position. The full text of the Act is included in the book. Also to be welcomed is a new edition of a well-established book whose publication is imminent:

FLINT, M. *A User's Guide to Copyright.* 3rd edn. Butterworths, 1990.
The previous edition explored the copyright problems of particular professions, and chapter 18 was concerned with schools, universities and other educational establishments. It is a well organised and lucid book which gives particular attention to the newer media.

Other accounts of copyright which have proved useful over the years but which now require new editions are:

TAYLOR, A.J. *Copyright for Librarians.* Tamarisk, 1980.

WHALE, R.F. and PHILLIPS, J. *Whale on Copyright.* 3rd edn. ESC Publishing Ltd, 1983.

PLOMAN, E.W. and HAMILTON, L.C. *Copyright: Intellectual Property in the Information Age.* Routledge, 1984.

LAHORE, J. *et al. Information Technology: the Challenge to Copyright.* Sweet and Maxwell, 1988.

They could still be useful to those who wish to follow the discussion in the 1980s on possible changes to the copyright law in the UK in consequence of the Whitford Report (1977). The international aspects of copyright are fully treated in Ploman, E.W. and Hamilton,L.C. (above).

The National Council for Educational Technology (formerly the CET) has produced a range of publications in recent years dealing with copyright problems in relation to education, which have proved very useful to all concerned. Most of these have been the work of Geoffrey Crabb, the Rights Development Officer who has established himself as an authority in this field. The most recent (1990) is *Copyright Clearance: a Practical Guide,* which will be indispensable to teachers and others who are endeavouring to keep within the law in their use of copyright material. A new edition of *Copyright Agreements Between Employers and Staff in Education* is also being prepared.

Other interested bodies have published helpful short guides over the years including The British Copyright Council, The Library Association, The Museums Association, The Society of Authors and the Publishers' Association. The Library Association has now produced a more detailed series of guidelines which interpret the 1988 Act for librarians in all types of libraries. It is also worth looking at current issues of the periodical *Education and the Law* (see p.48).

There is space for only a brief account of recent developments here. After some years of negotiation and experiment, traditional photocopying in universities, polytechnics and colleges is being licensed following agreement between the Copyright Licensing Agency (CLA) and the appropriate governing bodies. Three-year licences will allow for the copying of extracts under fair dealing regulations from most books and periodicals published in Britain, Western Europe and the USA. The income from copying fees will be transmitted to authors and publishers. These arrangements seem both sensible and workable.

Again, following the new Copyright Act off-air recording by institutions for educational purposes has been legalised. This means that it is currently permissible to record programmes of general interest like *Horizon* as well as specifically educational broadcasts (but not Open University programmes for which separate arrangements exist: see below). Moreover the recordings may now be kept indefinitely without having to be 'wiped' after a prescribed period as in the past. This has made it possible for school and college resource centres to start building up substantial collections of video recordings for instructional purposes.

However, from June 1990 'recognised educational establishments' (the definition is already causing serious concern to those likely to be excluded) will have to obtain new licences under the Act if they wish to continue to record programmes. The Educational Recording Agency (ERA) on which the TV companies are represented will be responsible for issuing the licences. Local Education Authorities will be able to take out one licence on behalf of all the schools and colleges in their areas. The licence permits the recording of whole radio and TV broadcasts (including cable output) There is no limit on the number of copies which may be made and no payment is required apart from the original licence fee, but the recordings may not be adapted or modified, nor may they be sold or hired out. They may be used for inter-library loan providing lenders and borrowers are all licensed educational establishments.

Arrangements for recording Open University programmes are different. Guild Sound and Vision, who have operated a scheme for the past ten years, have negotiated a new Licensing Scheme which will also run from June 1990. It will allow legal recording of OU and Open College TV broadcasts under the new Copyright Act. It will no longer include Channel 4, which has decided to leave the scheme. Further details will be found in the current *Guild Catalogue* (see p.141).

A full account of these new licensing schemes is given in *Viewfinder* (no.9, May 1990), the magazine of the British Universities Film and Video Council.

13.4 Guides for governors

Following the publication of the Taylor Report: a New Partnership For Our Schools (1977) a number of books appeared which were designed to help existing or new governors to acquire a fuller understanding of the context in which they operate. However, the Education (No.2) Act 1986 made extensive changes to the constitutions of school governing bodies, their powers and their functions, and these powers were further extended by the 1988 Education Reform Act. This should be remembered when consulting some of the books listed below:

BAKER, L. *The School Governor's and Parent's Handbook.* Foulsham, 1990.

BROOKSBANK, K. and ANDERSON, K. *School Governors: a Handbook of Guidance for Governors of County and Voluntary Schools.* 2nd edn. Longman, 1987.

BULLIVANT, B. *You are the Governor: How to be Effective in your Local School.* Bedford Square Press, 1988.

BULLIVANT, B. and WALLIS, E. *What Does it Mean?: a Glossary of Educational Terms for Newly Elected Governors.* Home and School Council. 1988. (Includes acronyms)

BURGESS, T. and SOFER, A. *The School Governor's Handbook and Training Guide.* 2nd edn.Kogan Page, 1986.

DAVIES, B. and BRAUND, C. *Local Management of Schools: an Introduction for Teachers, Governors and Parents.* Northcote House, 1989.

EVERARD, K.B. and MORRIS,G. *Effective School Management.* 2nd edn. Chapman, 1990.

FIDLER, B. and BOWLES, G. *Effective Local Management of Schools.* Longman, 1990.

FOWLER, W.S. *Teachers, Parents and Governors: their Duties and Rights in Schools.* Kogan Page, 1989.

Governors' Guide. Times Educational Supplement, 1990. (Eight part series reprinted in plastic wallet.)

Governors' Handbook. Latest edn. Advisory Centre for Education. (A collection of ACE information sheets, with a glossary of terms.)

HARDING, B. *A Guide to Governing Schools.* Harper & Row, 1987.

LEONARD, M. *School Governor's Handbook.* Blackwell, 1989.

Local Management of Schools: some Practical Issues, eds C. Wilkinson and E. Cave. Routledge, 1989.

LOWE, C. *The School Governor's Guide.* Croner Publications, 1989.

MACBETH, G. *School Boards.* Scottish Academic Press, 1990.

MAHONEY, T. *Governing Schools: Powers, Issues and Practice.* Macmillan Education, 1988.

MARTIN, L. *The School Governor's Handbook.* Blackwell Education, 1989.

ROGERS, R. *Considering the Options.* Advisory Centre for Education, 1989. (ACE handbook on opting out, giving detailed guidance.)

SALLIS, J. *The Effective School Governor: a Guide to the Practice of School Government.* Latest edn. Advisory Centre for Education. (Pamphlet.)

SALLIS, J. *Schools, Parents and Governors: a New Approach to Accountability.* Routledge, 1988.

School Governing Bodies, ed. M. Kogan et al. Heinemann Education, 1984.

WRAGG, E.C. and PARTINGTOn, J.A. *A Handbook for School Governors*. 2nd edn. Routledge, 1989.

There is a useful digest of the 1986 Act in SALLIS J. *Education (No.2) Act 1986: ACE Summary* (Advisory Centre for Education, 1987). The author writes a regular column 'Governors' forum' for the *ACE Bulletin* and another, 'Agenda', for the TES in which she answers questions on matters relevant to governors.

The Department of Education and Science has issued a pamphlet: *School Governors* (1988)

More recent publications are listed in the *ACE Digest* which forms part of the *ACE Bulletin* (see p.9)

There is a periodical: *The School Governor* (4 per annum, published by the School Governor, 73 All Saints Road, King's Heath, Birmingham, B14 7LN). It aims to provide practical, readable and authoritative information on curriculum, finance and new legislation.

14 Directories

Directories are among the most useful reference sources. Educational directories provide details of institutions, schools, organisations, associations, personnel, services, courses, careers, qualifications, etc. and you will find them indispensable for locating this kind of information quickly. Not all directories are published in book form, and the final section in this chapter (14.17) gives some idea of the range of educational information available on online services such as Campus 2000, NERIS and MARIS On-Line(formerly MARIS-NeT).

As we have seen, directories are sometimes called year books since they are usually, though not always, published annually with updated information. An attempt has been made here to divide them into categories but this is not easy since there is frequently an overlap between one category and another. For example, directories of courses may also provide descriptions of the institutions which offer them.

The first section (14.1) is devoted to some well-known general directories which are often the quickest source for basic educational information and statistics. However, not all the works described in this chapter are directories. Some more general books and guides have been included where these would be useful, e.g. in sections 14.5 (Going to university or college), 14.11 (Adult and continuing education; open learning), and 14.15 (Guides to careers).

Although this chapter is the longest in the guide, there may be other directories devoted to particular areas or aspects of education which have not been included here. Useful lists will be found in *Bibliographical Aids and Reference Tools for the Literature of Education* (see p.127) and *British Educational Reference Books* (see p.13) although the latter is now rather dated.

New directories are appearing all the time and even well-established ones may change their titles or their format in an effort to acquire more readers or to provide a more useful service. The fullest descriptive list of British directories in all fields is:

Current British Directories: a Guide to Directories Published in the British Isles. Latest edn. **CBD Research Ltd.**
> There is also a *Current European Directories* from the same publisher which includes some international directories. It is revised less frequently than the British list.

14.1 General directories

Some of the general directories mentioned in this section should be available in every reference collection. They all contain some educational information and/or statistics:

Whitaker's Almanack. **Whitaker, annual.**
> Librarians have always regarded this as one of the handiest reference tools available. It is not specifically concerned with education but contains a surprising amount of information related to it, e.g. lists of HMIs, universities, polytechnics, societies and organisations, and so on. There is also a succinct account of the UK educational system. Use of the detailed index is essential.

Britain: an Official Handbook. **HMSO, annual.**
> This is issued by the Central Office of Information. It is much more than a directory. It is an authoritative, reliable and illustrated survey of British life and institutions which is revised and updated every year. It is a first source for basic information about the administration of this country, including the educational system and the social services. It is factual, concise and up to date with many useful statistics. A valuable bibliography which included many official publications used to appear at the end of the book, but has unfortunately been discontinued.

Municipal Year Book and Public Services Directory. **Municipal Journal Ltd, 2 vols, annual.**
> Gives full details of local authorities, including directors of education, number of schools, etc. and lists organisations concerned with education. There is a useful review of educational developments during the year. For Scotland we have:

***The Scottish Companion*. Carrick, 2-yearly.**
This is described as 'an all-embracing source of
reference to the public life of Scotland'. It gives
essential brief information on organisations,
institutions and other bodies, with their aims and
objectives and names of principal officers, etc. A
new feature of the 1989-90 edition is a complete
listing of Scottish secondary schools. Carrick has
also issued a *Scottish Education Directory* (see p.57), a
Schools' and Colleges' Who's Who (see p.100), and a
Universities' Who's Who (see p.100).

There is a *Scottish Government Yearbook*
(Edinburgh University Press, annual) which
usually contains one or two interesting
articles on aspects of Scottish education,
e.g. the anglicising of Scottish universities
(1989–90).

***Statesman's Year Book*. Macmillan, annual.**
First published in 1864 this is the standard
handbook to the countries of the world, updated
every year. Part 1 deals with international
organisations, Part 2 with individual countries from
A-Z. The educational systems of each country are
described factually under the heading 'Justice,
Religion, Education and Welfare'. Basic statistics
are incorporated in the text. It is a convenient
source of detailed information in compact form.

***Europa World Year Book*. Europa Publica-
tions, 2 vols, annual.**
A reliable source of political, economic, statistical
and commercial information on the countries of the
world. Again, brief information is given on the
educational system of each country and basic
statistics are included. Other Europa year books
can be consulted for more detailed information
about particular countries or regions, e.g. *Africa
South of the Sahara; Far East and Australasia; Middle
East and North Africa; USA and Canada; Western Europe.*

***Commonwealth Yearbook*. HMSO, annual.**
Prepared for the Foreign and Commonwealth
Office this includes brief information on national
educational systems under country headings.

A selection of national year books of
individual countries should be found in
most reference collections. These will often
provide fuller information than the general
directories. There are also more specialised
directories:

***Civil Service Yearbook*. HMSO, annual.**
This is prepared by the Cabinet Office. It indicates
who does what, and where, in the Civil Service
including the DES and the SED.

***Guide to the Social Services*. Family Welfare
Association, annual.**
There is a chapter concerned with education: pre-
school; primary and secondary; further education;
the youth and community service; and adult and
continuing education.

***Social Services Year Book*. Longman, annual.**
A standard compendium. It includes lists of special
schools in each local authority under the heading
'Education Department'.

***Voluntary Agencies Directory*. Bedford Square
Press, annual.**
Lists about 2,000 organisations which 'are active in
every area of Britain and in all aspects of its social
and economic life' with details of aims, activities,
publications, etc. A classified index includes
agencies concerned with education and training.

14.2 Educational systems

Some of the encyclopaedias of education
described in 9.2 have detailed descriptions
of national educational systems. The most
recent are the *World Education Encyclopedia*
(see p.24) and the *Encyclopedia of Comparative
Education and National Systems of Education*
(see p.25).

There are several directories whose purpose is to describe the educational systems
of different countries:

***Systems of Higher Education: United Kingdom*,
ed. T. Becher et al. International Council for
Education Development, 1978.**
One of a series of twelve books planned by the
ICED to provide a comparative analysis of how
different countries were adjusting their systems to
meet changing demands. Arrangement: (1) The
purpose and structure of higher education in
Britain; (2) The government and management of
the higher education system; (3) Effectiveness in
higher education. Note the date.

***Educational Systems in the European
Community*, ed. L. Elvin. NFER-Nelson, 1981.**
This excellent guide describes the educational
systems of member countries, covering the whole

field from pre-primary to university education and teacher training. Brief bibliographies which include many official publications are appended to the articles. There is a good account of the educational system of the UK with separate sections on Scotland, Wales and Northern Ireland, and illustrative charts which enable the reader to compare the systems of different countries. A new edition would be welcome.

Higher Education in the European Community: Student Handbook. Latest edn. Kogan Page.
Intended primarily for those who are considering a period of higher education in one of the member countries. However, it is also a good source for relevant information on the educational systems of the countries concerned. It is published for the Commission of the European Communities.

Handbook of Primary Education in Europe, eds M. Galton and A. Blyth. David Fulton Publishers in association with the Council of Europe, 1989.
Much of the material here is based on reports and case studies collected by the Council as part of its five-year project 'Innovation in Primary Education in Europe.' It covers aims and content; policy and practice; role, status and professionalism in teachers, etc. There is a bibliography.

Vocational Training Systems in the Member States of the European Community: Comparative Study. CEDEFOP: HMSO, 1984.
CEDEFOP is the European Centre for the Development of Vocational Training. The text is based on information supplied by nine countries including the UK. The numerous charts and diagrams, which are a main feature, include valuable statistical information. There is a more recent work from the same source: *Vocational Training and Job Creation Schemes in the Countries of the European Community.* CEDEFOP: HMSO, 1987.

International Handbook of Educational Systems, ed. J. Cameron et al. Wiley, 1983–4, 3 vols.
Vol. 1: Europe and Canada. 1983.
Vol. 2: Africa and the Middle East. 1983.
Vol. 3: Asia, Australasia and Latin America. 1984.
This book was inspired 'by the success and usefulness of the profiles of educational systems compiled over the previous ten years by the British Council'. The systems of each country are described under standard subheadings. Statistics drawn from the *Unesco Statistical Yearbook* (see p.92) have also been included. There are diagrams showing the structure of each system and references for further reading.

International Guide to Education Systems, ed. B. Holmes. Unesco, 1979.
Published by Unesco for the International Bureau of Education this gives short profiles in English, French and Spanish which describe the educational systems of the member states of Unesco. The arrangement is alphabetical within each region. There is a statistical appendix which provides basic data for each country.

World Guide to Higher Education: a Comparative Survey of Systems, Degrees and Qualifications. 2nd edn. Bowker: Unesco, 1982.
Provides 'a comparative world-wide country by country survey of the most characteristic elements of both the systems and the main stages of higher education... a glossary of degrees and qualifications awarded in each system, and a table showing the period of study required for degrees and qualifications in particular subject areas'. The glossaries are helpful, e.g. under Austria we find explanations of terms such as Berufsreifeprüfung, Magister, Reifezeugnis and Vorprüfung. In general, 'the approach is practical rather than scholarly'.

A similar work written from a British standpoint is the *International Guide to Qualifications in Education* (see p.78) which contains descriptions of the educational systems in 140 countries. There is an older standard work which may be found in well established libraries:

World Survey of Eduction. Unesco, 1955–71. 5 vols.
Vol. 1: Handbook of educational organization and statistics. 1955.
Vol. 2: Primary education. 1958.
Vol. 3: Secondary education. 1961.
Vol. 4: Higher education. 1966.
Vol. 5: Educational policy, legislation and administration. 1971.
These handbooks are rather dated now, but they still provide a wealth of basic information about the educational systems of the world. Although the fullness of treatment varies from country to country there is no comparable work on this scale.

Although it is not a function of this guide to survey the textbooks available on different aspects of education, much useful information on national systems of education can be obtained from standard works of this kind. Those who would like a recent overview of the higher education system in Britain would find the following books of interest:

British Higher Education, ed. T. Becher. Allen & Unwin, 1987.

STEWART. W.A.G. *Higher Education in Postwar Britain*. Macmillan, 1989.

14.3 Associations and organisations

The first few works mentioned here are general directories which include educational information:

Directory of British Associations and Associations in Ireland. Latest edn. CBD Research Ltd.
> One of a series of directories from this publisher. It covers 'the interests, activities and publications of... professional institutes, learned societies, research organisations... cultural, sports and welfare organisations'. The subject index has about fifty entries under the heading Education.

Trade Associations and Professional Bodies of the United Kingdom, ed. P. Millard. Latest edn. Pergamon.
> A basic directory. Addresses and telephone numbers are given but no additional information. Educational examples range from the Association for Independent Education to the Welsh Schools Association.

Councils, Committees and Boards: a Handbook of Advisory, Consultative, Executive and Similar Bodies in British Public Life. Latest edn. CBD Research Ltd.
> Gives essential details about each body including its terms of reference, responsibilities, duties and activities, and publications. There are indexes of chairmen, abbreviated names, and fields of activity and interest. Useful as the only work on its subject

Directory of European Professional and Learned Societies. Latest edn. CBD Research Ltd. 2 vols.
Vol. 1: National, industrial, trade and professional associations.
Vol. 2: National, learned, scientific and technical societies.
> Covers continental Europe, Iceland, Malta and Cyprus. The UK is excluded. Only brief information in tabular form is given. Arrangement is by subject interest subdivided by countries. There are indexes of names and acronyms, and subject indexes in English, French, and German. Formerly the *Directory of European Associations*.

Encyclopaedia of Associations. Latest edn. Gale Research Co.: USA. 4 vols.
Vol. 1: National organizations of the US.
Vol. 2: Geographical and executive index.
Vol. 3: New associations and projects.
Vol. 4: International organizations
> A massive work. Vol. 1 has a large section on educational organisations, followed by one on cultural organisations. The great majority you will not have heard of before and are unlikely to meet again. There is a keyword index. The encyclopaedia is available online from Dialog.

These are all general directories. The others are confined to educational organisations, etc.:

PAYNE, P. and WILLETT, I. *Information Services in Education: an Inventory of Organizations and Associations in the United Kingdom Providing Information Services related to Education*. Lancaster University Centre for Educational Research and Development, 1978.
> Claims, probably justifiably, that organisations and associations are often neglected as sources of information. The book gives details of about 250 which may be in a position to answer short enquiries within their field of interest. They range from the School Library Association to the Scottish Council for Research in Education. Note the date.

Directory of Educational Documentation and Information Services. Latest edn. IBE: Unesco.
> One of the IBETA series of publications from the International Bureau of Education. It is revised

every few years. Arrangement: National services; regional services; international services; other member institutions. Basic information only is given and there is no index. There are very few British entries. There is a *Directory of Adult Education Documentation and Information Services* from the same source.

Some of the dictionaries of abbreviations described in 8.2 may help to identify organisations and associations connected with education, since addresses may be given. Telephone directories are indispensable in checking for the latest information.

14.4 Educational institutions

This section is concerned with general educational directories; directories of schools (including independent schools), colleges, universities, etc. in this country; and directories of higher educational institutions elsewhere. The first is an international handbook.

World of Learning. **Europa Publications, 2 vols, annual.**
This directory is a standard reference source in its field. Although it is primarily concerned with educational institutions, its scope is much wider, and it could also have been included in the previous section. It provides essential minimum details of universities and colleges, learned societies and associations, research institutions, libraries, museums and art galleries throughout the world, with reference also to the people active in them. There is a comprehensive index of institutions.

Education Year Book. **Longman, annual.**
The most frequently consulted of all educational directories in this country. It was known for many years as the *Education Committees Year Book,* but it changed its name with the 1979 edition. It is the best organised and most comprehensive of the British directories, and is useful for information about LEAs, educational institutions, organisations and schools. There is a wealth of other information, e.g. about educational publishing, including lists of educational publishers and journals, educational broadcasting, computers in education, and educational equipment. There is even a section of educational statistics. Another useful feature is a

Guide to Reports which briefly summarises the remits and recommendations of the principal educational reports applying to England and Wales since 1926, with a few from Scotland and one from Northern Ireland. This is an indispensable handbook for teachers, administrators, and the general reader.

Education Authorities Directory and Annual. **School Government Publishing Co., annual.**
This well-established directory covers much the same ground as the *Education Year Book* (above), sometimes in more detail, sometimes not. The two publications therefore usefully complement each other. The *Education Year Book* has a greater range of general information. This has fuller information on universities and colleges, for example. The index is at the front of the book.

Scottish Education Directory. **Latest edn. Carrick.**
Aims to be a comprehensive source of reference to education in Scotland, from primary school to university. It has sections on: Government Offices (the SED and regional authorities); educational bodies; the Scottish universities, with entries for each department listing the names of academic staff; the central institutions; the teacher training colleges; and the colleges of further education. Names of heads of department in the colleges are given. All secondary schools, independent schools, and primary schools are listed alphabetically under regions. This directory is to be discontinued and merged with *The Scottish Companion* (see p.54). Carrick also publishes the *Schools' and Colleges' Who's Who* and the *Universities' Who's Who* (see p.100).

Primary Education Directory. **School Government Publishing Co., annual.**
Brings together information not easily acquired in any other source. It gives the name, address, and headteacher of every state primary school in the UK. The number and age range of pupils are added if known. Middle Schools are included. The main arrangement is geographical.

There are numerous guides to independent schools in this country. No attempt will be made to give detailed descriptions here, but a list of the most familiar and readily available guides is provided for reference:

Choosing Your Independent School: a Guide to More than 1,350 Boarding and Day Schools for Boys and Girls Aged 3–19 in the United

Kingdom and Eire. **Ruskin Book Services, annual.**
Published for the Independent Schools Information Service (ISIS) which also issues free annual lists of member schools on a regional basis, including one for Scotland.

Equitable Schools Book: the Discriminating Parents' Guide to Independent Secondary Schools. **Latest edn. Papermac. (Previously** *The Schools Book*; **by the editors of** *The Student Book* **(see p.61).**

Gabbitas Truman and Thring Guide to Boarding Schools and Colleges. **Northcote House, annual. (There is also a** *Gabbitas Truman and Thring Guide to Independent Further Education* **(see p.68).**

Guide to British Independent Schools. **Fontana, annual.**

Independent Schools Yearbook: Boys' Schools, Co-educational Schools and Preparatory Schools. **A & C Black, annual. (Formerly the** *Public and Preparatory Schools Year Book.***)**

Independent Schools Year Book: Girls' Schools. **A & C Black, annual. (Formerly the** *Girls' School Year Book.***)**
The titles of these two yearbooks were changed in 1986 because the term 'independent school' was considered to be more appropriate than 'public school'. Both have excellent careers sections.

Parents' Guide to Independent Schools. **SFIA Educational Trust: Hobsons, two volumes in one, 2-yearly.**
The most handsomely produced of all these schools directories. It gives profiles of over 2,000 schools, with advice on what to look for, comparative statistics, and maps. Formerly in two separate volumes, the first annual, the second 2-yearly.

Schools of England, Wales, Scotland and Ireland: a Book of Reference for Parents, Principals and Students, with Scholarships, Careers and Continental Sections and a Directory of Schools and Colleges. **E.J. Burrow, annual.**

Which School: a Parent's Guide to Education. **Truman & Knightley, annual. (Formerly**

Schools: a Geographical Directory of Independent Schools, etc.) **The same publisher issues a** *Directory of Catholic Schools and Colleges.*

Details of independent schools in Europe will be found in the:

International Schools Directory. **European Council of International Schools, annual.**
Provides descriptions of member schools of the ECIS, which are independent of the state system, in Europe and throughout the world.

Parents who would like some advice on selecting a school (not necessarily an independent school) for their children could usefully consult the books by ITZIN, C. *How to Choose a School* (Methuen. 1985) and MARKS, J. *et al. Choosing a State School* (Hutchinson, 1989.) Note also:

STILMAN, A. and MITCHELL, K. *Choosing Schools: Parents, LEAs and the 1980 Education Act.* **NFER: Nelson, 1986.**
'The 1980 Education Act and the 1981 regulations aim to provide parents with a greater choice of schools and more information to help them decide. This is the first large-scale study of parental choice since the legislation came into force.' Drawing on research in four LEAs, the authors try to identify the major factors influencing parents when faced with having to choose a school for their children. The book is based on research sponsored by the NFER.

It is difficult for parents to make informed choices at different stages in their children's educational careers without a fuller understanding of the educational system as a whole. The following books may be helpful to them and to those who wish to take a more active role as governors. (See also 13.4: Guides for governors).

BARNES, P. and WOODHEAD, M. *Parental Participation in Schooling.* **Open University Press, 1990.**

DOCKING, J. *Primary Schools and Parents: Rights, Responsibilities and Relationships.* **Hodder, 1990.**

MARTIN, C. *Schools Now: a Parents' Guide.* **Lion Publishing, 1988.**

O'CONNOR, M. *How to Help Your Child Through School.* **Columbus, 1989.**

Parent's Handbook, eds. A. McIntosh and R. Barnes. **Newpoint, 1989.**

WRAGG, E.C. and PARTINGTON, J.A. *Schools and Parents.* **Cassell, 1989.**

Note also:

Scottish Consumer Council. *Keeping Parents Posted: Information About Children's Schooling and Other Educational Matters,* **by F. Allen** *et al.* **SCC in association with the National Consumer Council and the Welsh Consumer Council.**
'Covers, in handy guide form, the various official and semi-official sources of information that are open to parents, such as inspectors' reports, school handbooks, council papers and government publications.'

Directories of institutions beyond school but excluding universities for the most part include:

Compendium of Sixth Form and Tertiary Colleges. **Greenhead College, Huddersfield, annual.**
This is compiled by the Standing Committee of Sixth Form and Tertiary Colleges. It is a list of member colleges with information about the number of students, courses provided, administration and organisation, etc.

Directory of Technical and Further Education. **Longman, annual.**
This now comes from 'the same editorial stable' as the *Education Year Book* (see p.57) but gives fuller information within its special field. At the beginning there is a helpful guide to terminology: e.g. sixth form college, tertiary college; and another to abbreviations. There are details of government and public offices; the regional framework of FE; technical and FE colleges throughout the UK, arranged by local authorities; polytechnics in England and Wales, and central institutions in Scotland; universities; correspondence colleges; examining bodies; employment and careers; allied organisations and societies; etc. The emphasis in

the sections on polytechnics and universities is on the sciences and the social sciences. The names of heads of departments, schools, and faculties are usually given. This work should be compared with the *Directory of Further Education* (see p.67).

Full accounts of the institutions which provide teacher training and related courses in England and Wales will be found in the *NATFHE Handbook* (see p.69) which is published annually.

Institutions and organisations concerned with adult and continuing Education are described in the *Year Book of Adult Continuing Education* (see p.31) and the *Scottish Handbook of Adult Continuing Education* (see p.71).

Universities in Britain and the Commonwealth are covered by the well-known:

Commonwealth Universities Yearbook: a Directory to the Universities of the Commonwealth and the handbook of the Association. **Association of Commonwealth Universities. 4 vols., annual.**
This is the standard guide. It provides detailed information on all the universities included, with complete lists of their academic staff, but its most frequent use is for information about universities in the UK. Recent editions have an interesting article on universities in Britain by Dr. A.E.. Sloman, which gives an account of their historical development and current trends. It is followed by a directory to subjects of study and an index to postgraduate courses of instruction. More extensive information will of course be found in the calendars and handbooks of individual universities. The ACU also issues for quick reference a straightforward *List of University Institutions in the Commonwealth.*

Note also the:

Guide to Education and Training Resources in the Developing Countries of the Commonwealth: a Selection of Post-Secondary Courses and Institutions. **Commonwealth Secretariat, irregular.**
This excludes universities which are covered by the *Commonwealth Universities Yearbook* (above). It includes institutions offering post-secondary courses requiring less than full university entrance standards, and institutions offering courses at first degree, postgraduate or advanced level. The main

arrangement is by geographical location. There is an alphabetical index of institutions and courses, and a select bibliography.

Correspondence Institutions in the Commonwealth. Latest edn. International Extension College.

Provides brief details of university, official, and other non-profit making organisations, arranged by country, then alphabetically.

Universities and colleges in Europe are covered by:

Higher Education in the European Community: Directory of Higher Education Institutions. Latest edn. Office for Official Publications of the European Communities.

A sister publication to the *Student Handbook* (see p.55). Aimed at academic staff who wish to make contact with corresponding institutions in other countries. Only basic details are given.

Information on American universities and colleges will be found in:

American Universities and Colleges. American Council on Education: USA, 4-yearly

A substantial volume which is the standard guide to institutions of higher education in the US. Much of it is devoted to detailed descriptions of individual institutions in each state from Alabama to Wyoming. However, there are introductory chapters on aspects of higher education in the US, and numerous appendices on accreditation, degree abbreviations, etc. plus institutional and general indexes.

American Junior Colleges. American Council on Education: USA, 4-yearly.

Published as a companion volume to *American Universities and Colleges* (above). It is arranged by states, then by colleges, with information on enrolment, curricula, admission and graduate requirements, history, fees, student aid, teaching staff, student life, and special facilities. There is an index of institutions.

Accredited Institutions of Postsecondary Education and Programs. American Council on Education: USA, annual.

Reports on the accredited and pre-accreditation status of American universities and colleges. Part 1 contains brief basic information about the institutions, part 2 gives fuller information about those

which have been accredited since publication of *American Universities and Colleges and American Junior Colleges* (both 4-yearly, see above). It therefore acts as a supplement to them.

Comparative Guide to American Colleges: for Students, Parents and Counselors. Latest edn, Harper & Row.

Unlike the other American directories mentioned here this is designed primarily as a guide for consumers of higher education: intending students, their parents and counsellors. It attempts 'to provide insight into the essential nature of each institution' and to explain the differences amongst the many hundreds of colleges and universities from which a choice has to be made. Arrangement is by institutions, alphabetically.

For universities outside the Commonwealth, and excluding America, there is the:

International Handbook of Universities and Other Institutions of Higher Education. Macmillan, 2-yearly.

Planned as a companion volume to the *Commonwealth Universities Yearbook* and *American Universities and Colleges*, already described. Entries are arranged alphabetically by country, subdivided by institution. Lists of faculties and departments are followed by brief accounts of the history and academic structure of the institutions. There are also notes on admission requirements, degrees and diplomas awarded, and so on. The handbook is compiled by the International Association of Universities, which is also responsible for the:

World List of Universities, Other Institutions of Higher Education and University Organizations. Macmillan, 3-yearly.

This has a rather different purpose. 'It has been designed as a concise directory likely to be helpful in facilitating exchanges throughout the world of higher education.' Part 1 is arranged alphabetically by country. Basic information is given for each institution, followed by brief descriptions of national academic and student bodies. Part 2 is a guide to the principal international and regional organisations concerned primarily with higher education. Entries throughout are in French and/or English where this would be helpful. The book is published in two editions: British and American.

There are several directories compiled by the International Bureau of Education in Geneva. One is the *Directory of Special Educa-*

ion (IBE: Unesco, 1986), the others list esearch organisations (see p.177).

14.5 Going to university or college

Applications for admission to full-time undergraduate courses in all universities, with he exception of the Open University and he University of Buckingham, must be made through the Universities Central Council on Admissions (UCCA). The UCCA scheme does not include postgraduate study; external degree courses; part-time or evening courses; and diploma or certificate courses of one year's duration, for which separate application must be made.

Most students and their advisers will already be familiar with the *UCCA Handbook: How to Apply for Admission to a University*, which is issued annually and is indispensable. It should be used in conjunction with the relevant university prospectuses, which are obtainable free from the universities themselves. The detailed advice in the *UCCA Handbook* should be strictly followed by all students. UCCA also publishes a useful booklet *Mature Students and Universities* which is available free. There is a brief guide *How to Complete your UCCA Form* by A.S. Lumley (Trotman, annual).

A new centralised admissions system for advanced courses in polytechnics was introduced from the 1986 entry. The Polytechnic Centralised Admissions System (PCAS) is applicable to intending students for all courses except initial teacher training, and art and design. The *PCAS Guide for Applicants* has already become as familiar as the *UCCA Handbook* to students and their advisers. In Scotland students apply directly to the central institutions.

Applications for teacher training courses in England and Wales are made to the Central Register and Clearing House (CRCH) in London. The CRCH issues a free booklet *Teacher Training Courses and How to Apply* which should be used by all intending students. Again, applicants in Scotland should apply direct to the college of their choice. Fuller information about courses of teacher training is given in 14.9.

There are two substantial paperback guides which provide a relatively informal approach to educational institutions in this country, largely from the student point of view. In this respect they differ from the formal directories of colleges, courses, etc. which have always held the field:

The Student Book: the Applicant's Guide to UK Universities, Polytechnics and Colleges, eds. K. Boehm and J. Lees-Spalding. Macmillan, annual.
'Every year because of bad or inadequate information thousands of students end up studying for the wrong degree in the wrong institution. The result is a wasted opportunity and three wasted years. The aim of this publication is to help students to avoid a similar fate'. 'What you need to know' is covered in six sections: (1) How to go about it (Before you apply; How to apply; How to get the money; How to survive your first year A - Z; What's what in higher education); (2) Where to study (notes on each institution from official sources, followed by student views of what it's like, and 'Pauper Notes'); (3) Maps; (4) Subject and places index; (5) What to study (teachers in higher education define their own particular study areas and indicate their approach to teaching them; and (6) Index. Designed for students and sixth formers, their parents and teachers.

Student Eye: the CRAC Guide to Universities and Polytechnics as Seen by Students. CRAC/Hobsons.
One of the best of the numerous guides published by the Careers Research and Advisory Centre in Cambridge (see p.79). It gives a view of student life at universities and polytechnics from the inside. 'It is based on alternative prospectuses, handbooks, student newspapers and other publications' and also on official prospectuses and printed materials. Additional information is acquired from visits, interviews, personal accounts and conversations, and there is a good mixture of fact and opinion. This guide emphasises the social aspects of student life which tend to be neglected in the more formal type of publication.

It may be helpful to mention a number of short books (not directories) which provide general guidance on going to college or university for students, parents, mature students, adult learners and others. Reference should also be made to 14.15 (Guides to careers) and 14.16 (Guides to employment) since the choice of courses at college or university is closely related to decisions about future careers and job prospects.

ACRES, D. *How to Get to College*. **Macdonald & Evans, 1986.**

ACRES, D. *How to Prepare for Going to College: the Student Survival Handbook*. **Macdonald & Evans, 1985.**

ACRES, D. *How to Survive at College*. **Northcote House, 1987.**
These three books are written by an experienced student counsellor and provide for all age groups.

BELL, J. *et al. Mature Students: Entry to Higher Education: a Guide for Students and Advisers.* **Longman, 1986.**
An attractively produced and clearly presented guide. Particularly good on sources of further information for mature students. Other useful books are described in 14.11 (Adult and continuing education; open learning.)

BELL, J. and RODERICK, G.W. *So You Want to Get a Degree?* **Longman, 1984.**
Gives practical help and advice to school leavers and mature students, with relevant addresses and pointers to additional information.

COX, E.H. *New Signposts for Sixth Formers: a Guide to Entering Higher Education.* **Trotman, 1989.**
Explains how admission procedures work, the range of courses on offer, the qualifications needed for entry, how to prepare for interviews, etc. with references to sources of further information.

COX, E.H. and HEDGE, P. *Student Survival Guide.* **Trotman, 1989.**
Has sections on preparing for college, methods of teaching and assessment, revision and examination techniques, finance, vacation jobs, careers advice, postgraduate study, preparing a c.v., and finding a job.

DIXON, D. *Higher Education: Finding your Way: a Brief Guide for School and College Students.* **Latest edn. HMSO.**
This is sponsored by the UK Government Education Departments and contains very practical advice with lists of relevant publications. It has been revised and re-issued periodically.

FLETCHER, J. *The Woman Student's Handbook: Handbook for School Leavers and College Entrants.* **Northcote House, 1987.**
'Deals with all aspects of college life from subject and career choice to applying for places and grants, being at college, social and married life, being a mature or overseas student, and much more.'

Getting into University. **Latest edn. Trotman & Co.**
Provides brief guidance on choosing the right institutions, subjects and courses, application strategies, etc. Other titles are:

Getting into Oxford and Cambridge
Getting into Polytechnic
Getting into Colleges and Institutes of Higher Education.

GILBERT, J.K. *Staying the Course: How to Survive Higher Education.* **2nd edn. Kogan Page, 1984.**
Outlines the decisions facing sixth formers preparing to enter college or university and gives advice on how to cope when they get there: facing the problems of transition; making the best use of academic and social opportunities; and how to survive first year exams.

Graduates and Jobs: Some Guidelines for Young People Considering a Degree. **Latest edn. HMSO.**
An attractive pamphlet prepared jointly by the DES and the Department of Employment. Its aim is 'to help young people in schools and colleges by providing them with some indicators to the job prospects for graduates in different subjects'. There are tables of statistics with advice on how to use them. The DES also publish a series of booklets entitled *Choose your Course* (see p.80).

HEAP, B. *How to Choose your Degree Course.* **Trotman, annual.**
This guide has become firmly established over the years as a valuable aid to sixth form and college leavers. Designed as a companion to *Complete Degree Course Offers* (see p.65).

Making the Most of Higher Education, ed. E. Rudinger. Consumers' Association, 1987.

Advises on subjects and courses to follow; getting a place at university or college; how to study efficiently; taking advantage of opportunities offered; and making new qualifications the stepping-stone to a career.

Raynor, B. The Abbey National Student Guide to Living, Studying and Jobhunting. Latest edn. Longman.

Aims 'to ease you through all the stages of being a student (one of life's experiences which is rarely repeated)'. A lively summary with brief but sound advice on most of the relevant topics.

Sunday Times Good University Guide incorporating 'The Good Polytechnic Guide' and 'The Good CHE Guide'. Latest edn. Grafton Books.

The original version of this book appeared in the *Sunday Times Magazine*. It is interesting and clearly presented, and students and their parents will find it helpful. The aim is 'to apply to institutions of higher education the kind of critical scrutiny that the *Good Food Guide* or the *Michelin Guide* applies to hotels and restaurants'. However the information on colleges, especially those in Scotland, is rather meagre. The book should not be used without reference to more official works. There is also a *Sunday Times Good Career Guide* (see p.80).

Your Choice of Degree and Diploma: a Guide to Where to Study and How to Apply. Latest edn. CRAC/Hobsons.

A guide to university, polytechnic and college courses, with advice on interviews, visits, grants, and sponsorships.

Also likely to be useful is *The Sixth Former's Guide to Visiting Universities, Polytechnics and Other Colleges*. CRAC, annual, which gives details of all planned open days in UK institutions, with advice and information on contacts, etc.

Taking a Year Off, by V. Butcher and S. Swanson (Trotman, 1989), which has a 'magazine-style' format, looks at the option of taking a year off before, during or after higher education or during employment. There is a well-known CRAC publication: A *Year Off – a Year On* (see p.84) on the same subject).

For students coming to this country from abroad there are two well-established publications:

Higher Education in the United Kingdom: a Handbook for Overseas Students and their Advisers. Longman, 2-yearly.

Produced by the British Council in conjunction with the Association of Commonwealth Universities. Details are given of institutions admitting overseas students, courses available, entry to Britain, knowledge of English required, money matters, etc. There is a directory of facilities for study and a list of relevant addresses. There is also an account of student life in Britain.

Studying and Living in Britain: a Guide for Overseas Students and Visitors. Northcote House for the British Council, annual.

Intended for anyone from abroad who is visiting Britain for the first time. There is guidance on deciding whether to come; arriving in Britain; costs, customs and services; the British way of life; and making the most of Britain. Lists of British Council offices, embassies, and societies and institutions, are also provided. It is a useful complement to Higher Education in the United Kingdom (above).

Note also WOOLFENDEN, J. *How to Study and Live in Britain* (Northcote House, 1990), which offers information and advice to both the long and short term student visitor.

There is a more specialised handbook for students coming to this country from overseas:

Where to Study in the UK: a Guide to British Professional Qualifications, Colleges and Courses. Latest edn. Kogan Page.

Gives the history and aims of 30-40 key professional associations, with entry requirements, exemptions, awards, qualifications, etc. and details of colleges and schools in the public and independent sectors which prepare students for examinations in particular areas, e.g. accounting, computing, management, business administration.

14.6 Guides to degree courses

The fullest information about degree courses is usually to be found in the calendars (official handbooks) and student prospectuses of individual universities and colleges. University calendars can be rather formidable and quite expensive and most students will consult them in libraries. Student prospectuses are free to intending students and are much more digestible and readable. They contain the general information that students need to know, and they are written in a practical and helpful way.

'Alternative prospectuses' are issued by student associations in some universities and colleges. They are written by students for students and give an inside view of the institution, its resources, facilities, courses, teaching methods, and so on. The best ones can give a more realistic picture of an institution not obtainable in any other way. They are often written with a touch of humour not evident in more official publications. Allowance must be made for the subjective and personal opinions expressed but usually they represent a consensus of student views which can be helpful in deciding which institution, faculty or course to apply for. Reference could also be made to the consumer guides *The Student Book* and *Student Eye* (see p.100).

Calendars and student prospectuses of individual institutions are not particularly helpful if you wish to compare the courses which many different places have to offer. Fortunately there are well-established directories specially designed for this purpose and they are described in the next few sections. An effort has been made to divide them into groups according to types of institutions, but the problem of overlap still arises, e.g. degree courses are available in universities, polytechnics, and colleges of higher education, and you will have to look in more than one section to acquire all the relevant information about them.

The most essential guide to degree courses in universities is:

University Entrance: the Official Guide.
Association of Commonwealth Universities, annual.

This appeared for the first time in 1987. It is produced by the Committee of Vice-Chancellors and Principals, and is the only official guide to university entrance requirements. 'It replaces the once familiar *Compendium of University Entrance Requirements* which was produced by the Committee for some 25 years and which came to be regarded as the essential guide for teachers and careers advisers. It was therefore a book for specialists. *University Entrance* is designed for a much wider readership, especially sixth-formers, college students, and their parents. It is compiled in full consultation with universities using data supplied by UCCA, and contains a great deal of authoritative information of the kind applicants themselves feel is important.'

The main sections are: Getting started; Map; Universities in outline (with illustrations of each one); Grade tables; Index to all subjects; Flow charts: Choosing your degree course, and How to apply for university entrance (inside the front and back covers). There are useful subject overviews. Also listed are O and A level requirements for single, dual and multiple subject degrees, plus entry statistics and estimated grades of offers. All this information is clearly presented in a large and attractive format. Scottish universities are included but there is a separate publication:

Scottish Universities Entrance Guide. Scottish Universities Council on Entrance (SUCE), annual, with supplements.

This short guide is published by SUCE on behalf of the eight Scottish universities: Aberdeen, Dundee, Edinburgh, Glasgow, Heriot Watt, St. Andrews, Stirling, and Strathclyde. It contains basic information about entry requirements, application procedures, etc. An appendix gives brief descriptions of first degree courses and explains how they differ from corresponding courses at English universities.

Other well-established, although non-official, guides are:

Which Degree: a Comprehensive Guide to all Full-time and Sandwich Courses. Newpoint, 5 vols, annual.
Vol. 1: Arts, humanities, languages.
Vol. 2: Engineering, technology, environment.
Vol. 3: Mathematics, medicine, sciences.
Vol. 4: Business, education, social sciences.
Vol. 5: Universities, polytechnics, colleges.

This is probably the best known of the remaining directories. In vols 1–4 courses are broken down into key subject areas to make choices easier. The presentation and layout are extremely helpful. Vol.5 has useful accounts of each institution under the headings: Introducing the university; What facilities are there?; What's going on?; Where can I live?; Where can I get help?; How do I apply?; and How can I find out more?

Complete Degree Course Offers: Current Information on Entry to British Universities, Polytechnics and Colleges; B. Heap. Trotman, annual.

A familiar handbook which 'aims to provide guidelines for the applicant who is going through the processes of choosing courses and institutions... It also describes how applications should be prepared and how applicants are selected. Finally, in the tables, details are given of the levels of offers made by universities, polytechnics and colleges for their degree and diploma courses, together with some indication of how applications are received and considered by the various departments'. There is a separate chapter on the Scottish universities and an index of subjects.

Vocational Degree Course Offers; B. Heap. Latest edn. Trotman.

Formerly *Professional and Vocational Degree Course Offers*. This has the same editor and publisher as the previous work. It focuses on universities and polytechnics offering degree courses in areas such as accountancy, banking, engineering, and law. It indicates facilities, numbers admitted to courses, etc. There are tables of qualifications required for entrance, and for membership of relevant societies and institutions. Sandwich courses are included.

Degree Course Guides: Guides to First-Degree Courses in the UK. Latest edn. CRAC: Hobsons.

A series of over thirty subject guides which give detailed comparisons of first-degree courses in universities, polytechnics and colleges in this country. They are available separately or in two bound volumes. Together they cover all the major subject areas, half of the titles being updated each year. In 1987 the guides became available on floppy discs. In many respects these are the most useful of all the non-official works described here. 'Each guide gives details of the nature of degree-level study in a particular area, covering both general factors and variations in specific courses' and 'offers comparative information that enables prospective students to narrow down their choice of institutions'. For example there are notes about teaching methods and forms of assessment, and tables showing the numbers of students and staff involved in particular courses at different universities. Sources of further information are given.

Degree Course Index: a Comprehensive Listing of All Full-time and Sandwich Courses at all Universities, Polytechnics and Colleges in the United Kingdom. Segal Information Services, 3 vols.
Vol. 1: Arts and humanities.
Vol. 2: Business and social studies
Vol. 3: Science, engineering and technology

In each volume courses in related groups are listed together, e.g. creative and performing arts. This is essentially a quick reference guide, in paperback format, with minimum information, and has not been appearing regularly.

Much information about courses available and entry qualifications required at universities and colleges in this country is available through Campus 2000 (see 14.17).

Special mention must be made here of the degree courses offered by the Open University (OU), and those validated by the Council for National Academic Awards (CNAA).

According to the *Education Year Book* (see p.57) over 70,000 students are engaged in studying for OU degrees. The various guides produced by the OU therefore assume some importance. Apart from the formal *Student Handbook*, published regularly with two supplements each year, there is:

OPEN UNIVERSITY. Guide to the BA Degree Programme. Annual.

An attractive, informal and illustrated guide. Sections: Introduction to the OU; How you study; How to become a student. There is a list of Regional Centres and Study Centres.

Other essential guides to OU programmes are described in the appropriate section of this chapter, e.g.:

Open Opportunities (see p.73).
Professional Development in Education (see p.70).
Research Degree Prospectus and Student Handbook (see p.66)
Taught Master's Degree Prospectus (see p.67).

Open University Enterprises Ltd (OUEE), the marketing division of the OU, produces a valuable catalogue:

OPEN UNIVERSITY. *Undergraduate Course Material: Complete Listing.* **Annual**
It gives details of the OU course units which are currently available to outside users, a checklist of OU courses, and details of OU purchasing and distribution arrangements, etc. It lists the relevant study units, videotapes, films, and audiotapes (but not the set books) for each course.
A separate *Set Books List* (annual) in newspaper format, is available from the OU. *Undergraduate Courses* (annual), also in newspaper format, is designed to help students to make appropriate choices from the whole range of courses available.

Degrees in the non-university sector in this country are awarded by the Council for National Academic Awards (CNAA) to students who have successfully completed courses validated by the CNAA at approved polytechnics and colleges. The essential guides are:

COUNCIL FOR NATIONAL ACADEMIC AWARDS. *Directory of First Degree and Diploma of Higher Education Courses.* **Annual.**
It gives a conspectus of all courses validated by the CNAA at institutions of higher education. About 2,000 full-time and part-time courses are included from over 130 different institutions. The CNAA is now the largest degree awarding body in the UK. More than a third of all students who are taking degrees in this country are on CNAA approved courses.

COUNCIL OF NATIONAL ACADEMIC AWARDS. *Handbook of CNAA's Policy and Regulations.* **Annual.**
Contents: (A) Charter and statutes; (B) First degree, DipHE and Certificate courses; (C) Postgraduate and post-experience courses; (D) Research degrees; (E) Notes for examiners; (F) Admissions; (G) Validation policy and procedures; (H) Policy statements; (J) Appendices and (K) Indexes.

14.7 Postgraduate study

The standard guides are described below. Some of the resources in the following sections are also relevant: 14.5 (Guides to careers), 14.16 (Guides to employment), and 14.12 (Study abroad; educational exchanges); 14.13 (Grants for study at home and abroad).

British Universities Guide to Graduate Study (BUGGS). **Association of Commonwealth Universities, annual.**
Concerned with taught graduate courses, not with research of a kind that leads to a doctorate. Courses are listed in over 50 subject groups, e.g. engineering and technology; arts-education; languages and literatures. There are sections on fees, grants and awards, and an index of course titles. There is also a series of university profiles. Attractively presented in A4 format.

DOG Guide to Postgraduate Study: the Complete Guide to Postgraduate Courses and Institutions. **Newpoint, annual.**
Provides a comprehensive listing of all full-time taught courses and research opportunities in universities, polytechnics and institutes/colleges of higher education in the UK; application details on all postgraduate institutions; and specialist advice on choosing a subject, selecting a course and obtaining a grant. More information on postgraduate opportunities can be found in *Graduate Opportunities* (GO) (see p.83) from the same source.

Graduate Studies: the Guide to Postgraduate Study in the UK. **CRAC: Hobsons, annual.**
'Provides summaries of research facilities and courses, and basic information about the institutions in which postgraduate study is available'. Education is included in the Humanities and Social Sciences. General advice is given about career prospects and financial support. The amount of detail makes it more suitable for careers advisers than for students, for whom a shortened version is available:

Students' Guide to Graduate Studies in the UK: a Concise Personal Guide to Postgraduate Courses and Research. **CRAC: Hobsons, annual.**

Compiled from the data bank collected for the parent work (above). Lists postgraduate courses and research facilities in the UK plus information about the institutions. It enables the user to pinpoint where to pursue further study. There is a section on the Postgraduate Certificate of Education (PGCE).

As in the previous section the guides produced by the OU and the CNAA require special mention:

OPEN UNIVERSITY. *Research degree prospectus and Student Handbook.* **Annual.**

Contents: (1) Introduction; (2) Research opportunities; (3) Application and registration procedures; (4) Areas of study available (including the School of Education);. (5) Some regulations; and (6) Other programmes of study.

OPEN UNIVERSITY. *Taught Master's Degree Prospectus.* **Annual.**

Gives details of all the taught master's degrees, including the MSc in Advanced Educational and Social Research Methods which may not be offered after 1991.

COUNCIL FOR NATIONAL ACADEMIC AWARDS. *Directory of Postgraduate and Post-experience Courses.* **Annual.**

This has special relevance for practising teachers. Approved CNAA courses are arranged by subject headings alphabetically including Education. There is a college index and a subject index.

14.8 Courses at polytechnics and FE colleges

Much information on courses at polytechnics and FE colleges in this country is included in directories described in the previous two sections (14.6 and 14.7). Further details of all the courses offered, including non-advanced courses, can be found by consulting more specialised directories:

Compendium of Advanced Courses in Colleges of Further and Higher Education: Full-Time and Sandwich Courses in Polytechnics and Other Colleges Outside the University Sector. **London and South-Eastern Regional Advisory Council for Further Education, annual.**

Gives details of courses and entrance requirements for non-university institutions in England and Wales with a brief section on Scotland. The arrangement is by subject areas, e.g. education, and social sciences. Each Regional Council also publishes an annual directory with information about all courses, full-time and part-time, available at colleges in its region.

Polytechnic Courses Handbook: Full-Time and Sandwich Advanced Courses, England and Wales. **Committee of Directors of Polytechnics, annual.**

An official handbook which gives descriptions of each polytechnic, its academic activities and student amenities. It also describes the courses available in different subject areas throughout the country.

ASSOCIATION OF COLLEGES FOR FURTHER AND HIGHER EDUCATION: *Handbook.* **ACFHE, Sheffield City Polytechnic, annual.**

Another official handbook with more limited coverage.

Survey of Polytechnic Degree Courses, **E. Whittington. Latest edn. Trotman.**

Gives information on all full-time and sandwich courses offered on full-time or sandwich basis by the polytechnics and 'those Scottish institutions which most resemble polytechnics', i.e. the central institutions. It is now arranged by subject areas, e.g. social studies which includes education. A new *Survey of HND Courses* from the same author and publisher appeared in 1990.

Directory of Further Education: the Directory of Further and Many Higher Education Courses in the United Kingdom. **CRAC: Hobsons, annual.**

A substantial handbook giving details of full-time, part-time block and day-release courses: degree, professional, BTEC, SCOTVEC, City and Guilds, college, GCE A level, SCE H grade, plus entrance requirements, college information, etc. There is a key to abbreviations. It should be compared with the *Directory of Technical and Further Education* (see p.59).

Sandwich Courses: a Guide to All Courses in Universities, Polytechnics and Colleges Which Combine Full-Time Study with Training and Experience in Industry and Commerce. CRAC: Hobsons, annual.
Contains a full list of sandwich courses under subject headings. It explains what sandwich courses are and gives information on sponsorship, pay, allowances and future prospects.

Association for Sandwich Education and Training (ASET) Journal. ASET, annual.
A detailed directory of all advanced level sandwich courses offered in polytechnics, universities, institutions of further and higher education, and colleges in Scotland. It also contains statistics on the number of degree and diploma sandwich students by subject. Designed for employers, providers, students, and careers officers.

Signposts: a Review of 16–19 Education. Further Education Unit, annual.
A guide to the jungle of post-16 courses of general, vocationally specific, and pre-vocational education.

COPE: Compendium of Post-16 Education and Training in Residential Establishments for Handicapped Young People. Latest edn. Wiltshire Careers Service.
Lists courses and indicates sources of help and finance. Users are referred to the publications of the National Bureau for Handicapped Students (now the National Bureau for Students with Disabilities) and the Institute of Careers Officers for further information.

City and Guilds Handbook: Subjects, Awards and Services. City and Guilds of London Institute.
The CGLI does not itself provide courses. It awards certificates for achievement on courses taken at educational institutions throughout the country. They range from yacht and boatbuilding to aeronautical engineering. The handbook provides information on City and Guilds awards, assessment and credit accumulation, special services, contacts, and so on.

For details about courses in Scotland we have the:

Scottish Central Institutions Handbook. Paisley College of Technology, annual.
The Scottish Central Institutions are in some respects comparable with the polytechnics in England and Wales, although they vary widely in size and in the range of courses they provide. The handbook gives full information about the courses, most of which are vocationally orientated. CNAA degrees are offered in a variety of subjects.

SCOTTISH VOCATIONAL EDUCATION COUNCIL. The National Certificate Catalogue of Module Descriptors. Latest edn.
SCOTVEC was set up in 1985 following the implementation of the SED's Action Plan for 16+ in Scotland. It was formed by the merger of the Scottish Business Education Council (SCOTBEC) and the Scottish Technical Education Council (SCOTEC). SCOTVEC is responsible for the new National Certificate which is designed for students in non-advanced further education in Scotland who are following modular programmes in central institutions, further education colleges and schools. The programmes are made up of modules or units of study (mostly of 40 hours) and may include any number and combination of modules taken on a full-time or part-time basis.
   The National Certificate catalogue lists all the module 'descriptors' currently available or under development (over 2,000 in total). They are divided into categories, e.g.: Interdisciplinary studies; Business and administration; Pure and applied sciences; and an appendix gives examples. Equivalences have been agreed between certain City and Guilds (CGLI) certificates and specific National Certificate programmes. A separate *Guide to Equivalences* is available. News about developments is published in the *SCOTVEC Journal* (irregular), and for more recent information, in *SCOTVEC Information Sheets*.
   SCOTVEC is also responsible for continuing and refining the system of advanced courses at HNC, HND, and postgraduate level formerly offered by SCOTBEC and SCOTEC. Further information is available from SCOTVEC, or from individual colleges (central institutions and FE colleges).

The *Directory of Day Courses in FE* (annual), which was issued by the SED, ceased publication with the 1985–86 edition. It gave information about advanced and non-advanced courses in Scotland, but excluded those provided by the universities and colleges of education.
Independent further education in this country is covered by:

Your Choice: with the Conference for Independent Further Education. CIFE: Hobsons, annual.
'Designed for young people and their parents who find a conventional school environment cannot fully

meet their needs.' It has information on the CIFE's member colleges with details of what they offer, and indicates those which conform to the Code of Conduct and have received official approval. The CIFE also issues a separate *List of Members and Guide to Courses*.

Gabbitas Truman and Thring Guide to Independent Further Education. **John Catt Ltd, annual. (Cover title is *Education After 16*)**
   Gabbitas Truman and Thring claim to be the oldest and largest educational consultancy in the UK. Sections are: 1. Colleges of independent further education, GCE and tutorial colleges. 2. Professional schools and colleges. 3. English language schools. 4. Colleges of arts. 5. Institutes of health and beauty. 6. American colleges in the UK. 7. European and international schools. There are introductory essays, a glossary of abbreviations, and a general index. There is also a *Gabbitas Truman and Thring Guide to Boarding Schools and Colleges* (annual).

Directory of Independent Training and Tutorial Organisations (DITTO): a Guide to Alternative Education. **2nd edn. Careers Consultants Ltd, 1985.**
   DITTO was written largely to fill a gap and it was a pioneering work in a difficult area. Its arrangement is by courses, with a number of appendices and a brief bibliography. There is an index of organisations and another of subjects. It may have been of some help in treading a path through the maze of private colleges and other tutorial organisations - good, bad, and indifferent, but it appears to have ceased publication.

Other, more general directories include details of independent colleges. For example the well-known *British Qualifications* (see p.78) has a list of private colleges which have been approved by the appropriate bodies.

It should be remembered that much detailed information about courses in polytechnics, FE colleges, etc. is available on Campus 2000 (see 14.17). One of its advantages is that it can provide up-to-date details of current vacancies for places at educational institutions throughout the country. Attention is also drawn to the:

Higher Education Information Service. **Middlesex Polytechnic.**
   This provides computer held information to anyone wishing to study for a degree, diploma or certificate course either full-time or sandwich at UK polytechnics and institutions of higher education. The information is continually updated, and the service is provided free to any part of the world.

14.9 Teacher training courses

Applications for teacher training courses in England and Wales are channelled through the Central Register and Clearing House (CRCH) or the Graduate Teacher Training Registry (GTTR). These bodies amalgamated in 1962. The CRCH deals with entry to undergraduate (B.Ed) initial teacher training courses and some one-year specialist and certificate courses, e.g. those for art and technical teachers. The GTTR deals with applications for one-year postgraduate courses of initial teacher training.

As already indicated (see p.61) the CRCH issues a free booklet: *Teacher Training Courses and how to Apply* and there is another brief guide: *Graduate Teacher Training Registry: Information for Graduates*. CRCH also issues an annual report which surveys the entry pattern for both undergraduate and graduate students in the previous year, with useful statistics.

The training of teachers in England and Wales takes place in a variety of institutions which are listed in the title of the standard guide:

NATFHE Handbook: the Handbook of Initial Teacher Training and Other Degree and Advanced Courses in Institutes/Colleges of Higher Education, Polytechnics, University Departments of Education in England and Wales, **compiled by the Central Register and Clearing House. NATFHE: Linneys ESL, annual.**
   It is published for the National Association of Teachers in Further and Higher Education. Before 1977 it was issued by the Association of Teachers in Colleges and Departments of Education (ACTDE). The title has been altered several times and this is a reflection of the changing pattern of teacher training in recent years. Sections 1-6 provide general information about NATFHE, CRCH and GTTR (see above), the types of courses available,

how to make applications, etc. Sections 7-10, the main body of the guide, are arranged by types of courses. Within each section there is an alphabetical list of institutions providing the courses with detailed information about them. Finally there are charts summarising the inform- ation presented, a section on grants, an index of subjects and courses, and an index of institutions. The handbook is carefully compiled and edited. If it is not too easy to use this it is because the teacher training and other courses described do not follow an easily recognisable pattern.

There is a separate guide to courses in the colleges and institutes of higher educa- tion, which are primarily concerned with teacher training:

Colleges and Institutes of Higher Education Guide. **Standing Conference of Principals and Directors of Colleges and Institutes of Higher Education (Edge Hill College of Higher Education), annual.**
It covers courses in the arts, social sciences, technical subjects, and teacher training. The arrangement is alphabetical by institutions. Each entry has four sections: undergraduate courses; postgraduate courses; professional courses; and general information. A poster-size leaflet summarising the information is included.

Unfortunately there is no complete guide to courses at the Scottish colleges of educa- tion and it is necessary to consult the pros- pectuses for individual colleges. In 1990 there were five remaining: Craigie (Ayr), Jordanhill (Glasgow), Moray House (Edin- burgh), Northern (Aberdeen and Dundee) and St. Andrew's (Glasgow) which is a Catholic college. The *STEAC Report* on future strategy for higher education in Scotland (1985) recommended that the number of colleges should be reduced from seven to four, and that existing teacher training courses at Stirling University should be discontinued. However, a favour- able review of the Stirling courses by the SED ensured their survival.

Entry requirements for the Scottish col- leges of education are set out in:

SCOTTISH EDUCATION DEPARTMENT. *Memorandum on Entry Requirements to Courses of Teacher Training in Scotland.* **Annual.**

Note that there is also a:

Directory of Teacher Training Facilities in Commonwealth Countries. **Commonwealth Secretariat, irregular.**

14.10 In-service courses

Undoubtedly, in-service training (INSET) will continue to play an important part in equipping teachers to cope with the rapid changes in education and teaching methods in the years ahead. Information about forth- coming courses in England and Wales is given in:

Long Courses for Teachers, **organised by universities, polytechnics and colleges. DES Publications Despatch Centre, annual.**
This is prepared by the Teacher Branch of the DES. Formerly issued as the *Programme of Long Courses for Qualified Teachers.*

Short Courses for Teachers, **organised by Her Majesty's Inspectorate in England and Wales for teachers and others engaged in the educational service in England and Wales. DES Publications Despatch Centre, annual.**
From the same source. Formerly issued as the *Programme of Short Courses for Qualified Teachers*. It is arranged in broad subject categories, from 'Able Children' to 'Special Educational Needs'.

Both of these directories are available on Campus 2000 (see 14.17). There used to be a *British Council List of British Short Courses*, but it ceased publication in 1982.

Many teachers will be familiar with the periodical *Teacher's Time*. Eye-to-Eye Publi- cations, 5 per annum. It has a regular sec- tion: 'Course and Conference Diary' which gives details of forthcoming conferences, etc.

The educational press generally, es- pecially the *Times Educational Supplement* (and its Scottish edition) carry advertise- ments for in-service courses emanating from universities, colleges and LEAs. So do national and local newspapers. Prospecuses and lists of courses are readily available from individual institutions and may be found in academic and public libraries.

Scottish teachers will use similar sources. In addition there is an annual publication:

NATIONAL COMMITTEE FOR THE IN-SERVICE TRAINING OF TEACHERS. *National Courses and Other Courses of Interest Organised for the Benefit of Teachers and Others Engaged in the Educational Service in Scotland.* **Annual.**

Many of the Open University's courses are of potential interest to teachers:

OPEN UNIVERSITY. *Professional Development in Education.* **Annual.**
An attractive illustrated brochure for teachers and others on courses, study packs, diplomas and higher qualifications including the MA in education. There is a separate brochure on the Advanced Diploma in Educational management. Another brochure *Open Opportunities* (see p.73) gives details of further opportunities for personal and professional development.

For college lecturers, there is a publication issued free by the DES:

PICKUP Directory: Update your Skills!: the Red Book Guide to Courses: over 250 opportunities for College and Polytechnic Teachers. **DES, annual.**
It is available from the DES Publications Despatch Centre. The main sections are: (1) PICKUP inset courses; (2) Other inset opportunities, including the Open University. (For further information about PICKUP see p.85). Note also:

FURTHER EDUCATION STAFF COLLEGE. *Annual Directory.* **Coombe Lodge, Blagdon, Bristol, BS18 LRG.**
The FE Staff College at Coombe Lodge is well known for its continuing series of short courses which are of particular interest to promoted staff. The college also undertakes outreach work on a negotiated basis. Details are included in the directory.

The Scottish School of Further Education, which is a constituent part of Jordanhill College in Glasgow, offers programmes of in-service training for FE lecturers throughout Scotland. The Curriculum Ad-

vice and Support Team (CAST) in the School has produced a wide range of curricular materials to support delivery of SCOTVEC National Certificate modules (see p.68). There is also an excellent series of Action Plan Staff Development (APSD) modules.

A guide to courses for teachers and others in one specific area should be mentioned here:

Courses Leading to Qualifications in Educational Technology. **National Council for Educational Technology, annual.**
A directory of institutions in the UK offering major courses lasting a year or more, and others lasting at least one term. For shorter courses see *Short Courses for Teachers* (above) issued by the DES.

14.11 Adult and continuing education; open learning

This section is concerned with sources of information on learning opportunities for adults. Attention is also given to open learning opportunities. A wide variety of handbooks and guides is described, although there is an excellent manual by Dale, S. and Carty, J. (see p.128) which may be consulted for fuller information. Chapter 6 (Organisations and Associations, pp. 73–97) is especially valuable.

Many of the directories mentioned in previous sections include information about continuing education opportunities for adults and mature students. For example, the guides to degree courses aimed primarily at school leavers are equally useful to adult returners. However, the directories and guides in this section will be particularly helpful to more mature students.

There are two year books, one for England and Wales and one for Scotland, which should be known to those who require up-to-date information in this field:

Year Book of Adult Continuing Education: a Directory of Opportunities. **National Institute of Adult Continuing Education, annual.**
> Provides details of LEAs in England and Wales; adult education centres and staff; university extramural departments; art centres; residential colleges; societies and institutions; industrial training boards; broadcasting authorities and other relevant organisations. A list of journals is included.

Scottish Handbook of Adult and Continuing Education. **Scottish Institute of Adult and Continuing Education. Network Scotland, annual.**
> Formerly the *Handbook of Adult Education in Scotland*. Designed 'as a guide to public sector education and training opportunities for those with an interest in this area, and particularly individuals and agencies who are called upon to provide advice to enquiring members of the public'. There is an overview of current developments; an alphabetical directory of major types of providers in Scotland; information about grants and further sources of information and advice; and details of relevant organisations.

Network Scotland, which co-operates in the production of the above handbook, is an organisation set up to provide advice, by telephone and correspondence, to adults who want to find out about education and training at any level. It provides free printed information on a wide variety of learning opportunities, including open learning and the Open Tech (see below). It is also an agency for the TAP (Training Access Points) initiative, funded by the Training Agency.

Most people will be familiar with the prospectuses for adult education classes issued by the LEAs and by the university departments of extra-mural education throughout the country. They are readily available in academic and public libraries, or obtainable on request from the authorities and institutions concerned.

The National Institute of Adult Continuing Education issues a twice-yearly guide, *Time to Learn*, which lists available courses in date order, including study tours abroad, summer schools and courses for families, and a range of academic and lei-sure subjects for study.

A useful guide for adults who wish to know more about opportunities at college and university is the one by BELL, J. *Mature Students: Entry to Higher Education* (see p.62). Another book, by BELL, J. and RODERICK, G.W. *So You Want to Get a Degree* (see p.62) also contains advice for mature students. The same authors have written:

BELL, J. and RODERICK, W. *It's Never too Late to Learn: the Complete Guide to Adult Education.* **Longman, 1982.**
> This is intended for adults who hope to obtain a qualification, learn a new subject or train for a new career, and indicates the most likely routes and sources of help available. There is a work on similar lines which is designed for mature women students:

PERKIN, J. *It's Never Too Late: a Practical Guide to Continuing Education for Women of All Ages.* **Impact Books, 1984.**
> It is worth quoting from the book's cover: 'Returning to education takes courage and determination. This book cannot give you that, but it will provide plenty of advice and information about all aspects of becoming a mature student... gaining confidence, choosing a course, getting a grant, fitting in at college, getting down to study, getting the family on your side, caring for children, applying for jobs'. Most readers will be grateful for this readable and practical handbook.

Perhaps the most thorough and clearly written guide is:

Second Chances: a National Guide to Adult Education and Training Opportunities; **by A. Pates and M. Good. Latest edn. Cambridge Training and Development Ltd (CTAD) for COIC and NIACE.**
> It includes information on providers, courses, and contacts and is designed for 'anyone wanting to further their education or training in any way... or feels that it is time for a change, a new direction, a fresh start, a second chance'. There are many useful addresses and telephone numbers.

Other recent books are *Learning Opportunities for Adults*; ed. T. Corner (Routledge, 1990); the *Mature Students' Handbook;* by I. Rosier and L. Earnshaw (Trotman, 1989);

and the *Kogan Page Mature Student's Handbook: Making a Fresh Start with Full-Time, Part-Time and Distance Courses*, by M. Korving (Kogan Page, 1990).

Two short official guides should be known to mature students who are planning to enter higher education:

COMMITTEE OF VICE-CHANCELLORS AND PRINCIPALS. *Mature Students: a Brief Guide to University Entrance*. Latest edn.

COUNCIL FOR NATIONAL ACADEMIC AWARDS. *Opportunities in Higher Education for Mature Students*. Annual.

Part-time courses are covered in:

Part-Time Degrees, Diplomas and Certificates: a Guide to Part-Time Higher Education Courses at Universities, Polytechnics and Colleges. Latest edn. CRAC: Hobsons.

ECCTIS (the Educational Counselling and Credit Transfer Information Service) has produced two valuable directories:

ECCTIS Handbook: a Guide to Credit Transfer Opportunities Offered by Advanced Further and Higher Education Institutions in the UK. ECCTIS, annual.
'Credit transfer' is defined as 'either admission at the beginning of a course with alternatives to the normal entry requirements, or exemptions from studying parts of a course'. The information given here could be very helpful to mature students.

Access to Higher Education Courses Directory: a Guide to Courses throughout the United Kingdom Especially Designed for Adults Who Want to Enter Higher Education and Do Not Have the Normally Required Entry Qualifications. ECCTIS in co-operation with the CNAA and the Forum for Access Studies, annual.
First issued in 1989. It lists courses and providing institutions, open college networks, other routes to higher education, counselling service, relevant publications and other information sources.

The *ECCTIS Database*, which was developed by the DES in association with the Open University, is available on Campus 2000 (see p.85). The DES recently awarded

a contract for the management and operation of ECCTIS to a consortium: ECCTIS 2000, comprising CRAC (see p.79), Hobsons, PCAS (see p.61), TTNS (see p.85) and British Telecom.

Educational guidance services are listed in:

Directory of Educational Guidance Services for Adults, by J. Alloway and L. Opie. Latest edn. Unit for the Development of Continuing and Adult Education (UDACE).

The Open University, the Open Tech, and the Open College are all closely concerned with adult and continuing education. It is not a coincidence that they have also been involved in developing new approaches to teaching and learning, particularly distance and open learning. In addition to the guides mentioned in previous sections (14.6, 14.7, 14.10), the OU produces:

OPEN UNIVERSITY. *Open Opportunities: Continuing your Personal and Professional Education with the Open University*, annual.
This gives some idea of the wide range of programmes, courses and study packs now available in the OU's Associate Student Programme. They include courses to help further a career; courses to develop personal interests; and family and community courses. There are detailed descriptions of all courses offered, as well as guidance on applying for courses and other opportunities for study. There is a list of regions, regional centres and study centres. Mention should also be made of *Community Education Packs and Courses (1990)* issued by OU Department of Community Education.

An extensive range of learning and training opportunities, and many learning materials, are described in the:

Open Learning Directory. Latest edn. Training Agency.
A comprehensive source of information on open learning opportunities with details of courses available throughout the UK, presented in eye-catching panels. There are also very useful accounts of open learning and the benefits it offers. It is designed for employers, trainers, advisers and individuals, and is one of the most attractive, best organised and easy to use directories currently available. First published as the *Open Tech Directory* (National Extension College) in 1985, it changed its

title with the 1988–89 issue. The Open Tech Programme formed an integral part of the Adult Training Strategy administered by the Manpower Services Commission (now the Training Agency). Its aim was to make it as easy as possible for adults to acquire and update their skills.

MARIS On-Line (see 14.17) holds information about materials suitable for use in open learning schemes. Note also the *Open Learning Directory* (see p.139) published by the Great Ouse Press, which is a substantial catalogue of distance learning and independent study materials.

Reference was made above to ECCTIS which is available on Campus 2000. So is the *National PICKUP Directory* (see p.85) which contains details of thousands of short work-related courses, mainly at public sector institutions. There is a quarterly printed version.

Open learning systems aim to provide learning opportunities at a time, place and pace suitable for the individual student. In other words, the courses are designed to meet personal circumstances and needs. They may involve learning at home, in college, or a combination of both. Some courses may include residential periods. Most are administered by FE colleges and the tutor input varies. In their simplest form, the student may have access to a learning booth, appropriate equipment, and learning aids, with minimum guidance.

Since the establishment of the Open College, opportunities have been considerably extended. A key role is being played by the open access centres (mainly in FE colleges) which provide the necessary support for students who are taking the Open College route. There is a *BBC Television Programme Information Pack* financed with the support of the Open College. It includes a description of the new approaches to skills training offered by the Open College through TV and radio, workbooks, audio and video casettes, and practical kits.

The *Access to Higher Education Course Directory* (see above) has sections on open learning opportunities for adults. There is an established directory in Scotland which is more directly concerned with these areas

Open Learning in Scotland. Scottish Council for Educational Technology, annual.

Formerly the *Directory of Open Learning Opportunities in Scotland,* this useful guide lists courses suitable for those who wish to study at their own pace and in their own time. It also offers information on where to go for help and advice. Courses are grouped by subject, but there is also an alphabetical course index, and a list of providing organisations and institutions with their addresses. (See also *Network Scotland* on p.72).

SCET, the publisher of the directory, has a continuing interest in open learning which it shares with its parent organisation the National Council for Educational Technology (NCET) south of the border. One of the major sub-committees of SCET, the Scottish Committee on Opening Learning 'advises on and offers co-ordinating assistance in' the whole field of open learning in Scotland. The SCET Learning Systems Unit has probably the largest collection of open learning packages in Scotland. Both SCET and NCET have produced a series of open learning guides.

There is another organisation concerned with open learning:

Open Learning Federation, c/o Barnet College, Wood Street, Barnet, Herts, ENS 4AZ.

It brings together individuals active in the field of open learning; endeavours to generate policy and good practice; assists in the production, appraisal, and exchange of open learning materials; and promotes the exchange of information. There are regional groups including one for Scotland.

The National Extension College has issued two guides written by R. Lewis for tutors and advisers who have limited experience of open learning approaches: the *NEC Guide to Open Learning* (NEC,

)86), and the *Schools Guide to Open Learning* NEC: SCET, 1986). The guides are themselves in open learning form, and could elp tutors to produce an action plan for their own open learning scheme. The Open University publication *Open Learning*, ublished in 1988, is excellent on general rinciples and teaching methodology.

Two books which adult students would find elpful in the context of open learning are:

pen Learning for Adults, eds M. Thorpe and . Grugeon. Longman, 1987.

.ACE, P. *How to Win as an Open Learner*. CET, 986. (The same author has written an *Open earning Handbook*. Kogan Page, 1989.)

Fuller perspectives are provided in:

pen and Distance Learning: Selected Readings; ed. D. McConnell. Kogan Page, 1988.
The readings are taken from the *Aspects of Educational Technology* year books (see p.30) and the journal *Programmed Learning and Educational Technology*.

An overview of recent developments in olleges is provided in *Flexible Learning in erspective* (Further Education Unit, 1989). There is also a short bibliography which ould be useful to students and tutors alike:

Open Learning: a Select Bibliography of Recent Works, compiled by P. Starbuck. Jordanhill College Library, 1988.
It lists books and periodical articles published since 1980. Sections are: Open learning; Distance learning; Correspondence courses; Flexistudy; The Open Tech; and The Open College.

Finally, there is an information pack (one of a series) on *Open and Flexible Learning* NCET, 1990), which is well worth acquiring. It provides definitions; describes organisations involved, e.g. the National Open Learning Association (NOLA), and the Open Polytechnic (due to be launched in 1990), which have not been mentioned here; gives sources of information on materials and current developments; and concludes with a selected reading list.

14.12 Study abroad; educational exchanges

This brief section, which is concerned with opportunities for students at all levels to study in foreign countries or to participate in educational exchanges, should be read in conjunction with 14.13 (Grants for study at home and abroad). The book *How to Study Abroad* by T. Tinsley (Northcote House, 1990) is also worth reading.

Study Abroad: International Scholarships; International Courses. Unesco, 2-yearly.
This closely printed paperback is the fullest compendium available in its field. It provides details of international programmes at post-secondary level offered at institutions located in over 100 countries. It also includes information about scholarships, grants, etc. Opportunities for mature students are mentioned.

Higher Education in the European Community: Student Handbook. Latest edn. Kogan Page.
Published for the Commission of the European Communities. It provides reliable and recent information on institutions, qualifications, applications, grants, fees, and accommodation. It also describes the educational systems of the countries concerned.

Research Opportunities in Commonwealth Developing Countries: Universities; Non-University Institutions: a Register. Latest edn. Association of Commonwealth Universities.
Published by the ACU in association with the Commonwealth Secretariat for academic staff and graduate students. It lists areas of strength at over 120 universities and describes the kind of research undertaken by each of 300 non-university institutions.

The main source of information about educational visits and exchanges is:

Central Bureau for Educational Visits and Exchanges. Publications. Latest eds.
The Central Bureau is a government agency which is responsible to the government education departments in the UK for developing contacts, co-operation, visits and exchanges with other countries. It issues a variety of useful publications which should be available in public as well as

academic libraries, e.g.: *School Travel and Exchange; Study Holidays; International Youth Travel and Exchange; Adventure and Discovery; Volunteer Work Abroad; Working Holidays; Young Visitors to Britain.* Most of these contain detailed information arranged by countries, with addresses of relevant organisations and lists of useful publications. Their practical approach is very refreshing, and they are frequently updated.

Some of the directories mentioned in 14.16 (Guides to employment) are also relevant in this context, especially the series issued by Vacation-Work Publications. Note also:

SCOTTISH EDUCATION DEPARTMENT. *Exchange and Interchange Opportunities Abroad for Teachers and Assistants.* Annual.
> The appendix to this circular describes the opportunities that exist for teachers from Scotland to exchange posts with teachers from the Commonwealth, the USA and Europe. It also provides information about the employment of English language assistants abroad and foreign language assistants in this country. The procedures relating to the operation of the various schemes are outlined.

14.13 Grants for study at home and abroad

This section describes some of the publications which provide information about student grants, sponsorships, scholarships, awards, etc. for study and/or research at home and overseas. A few of the directories mentioned elsewhere, e.g. *Study Abroad* (see p.75) include information of this kind, but the undernoted publications are more directly concerned with these matters. If you are particularly interested in research, you could also refer to 14.7 (Postgraduate study) and 25.6 (Organisations concerned with research).

DEPARTMENT OF EDUCATION AND SCIENCE. *Grants to Students: a Brief Guide.* Annual.
> Gives details of grants available from LEAs to students who are taking up first degree and comparable courses at universities and polytechnics; DipHE courses; initial teacher training courses; and HND courses. It includes information about students' and parents' contributions. The DES also issues a *Guide to Grants Courses Designated as Comparable to First Degree Courses for the Purpose of Awards.*

SCOTTISH EDUCATION DEPARTMENT. *Guide to Students' Allowances.* Annual.
> This is a similar guide for Scottish students.

Sponsorships Offered to Students by Employers and Professional Bodies for First Degrees, BTEC/SCOTVEC Higher Award or Comparable Courses Beginning in 19—. Careers and Occupational Information Centre, Annual.
> COIC was part of the Manpower Services Commission (MSC) (now the Training Agency). The booklet lists employers, industrial and professional organisations, and government departments which give financial help to young people of academic promise who are taking higher education courses, mainly in scientific and technical subjects. The awards may be given in addition to an LEA grant. There is an index of course subjects.

Students and Sponsorship. CRAC: Hobsons annual.
> Intended for all students seeking sponsorships for degree courses. It looks at the expanding range of options available for students about to enter further and higher education.

The National Union of Students issues a number of booklets and leaflets on student grants. The *Student Welfare Manual* (annual) contains a good section on grants and finances. *The Student Money Guide* by A. Moore and G. Roberts (Curtis, 1989), has a section on student loans. There is also a *Guide to Postgraduate Funding* (latest edn, Newpoint). Much fuller information will be found in the:

Grants Register. Macmillan, twice-yearly.
> A standard guide for those considering postgraduate study or advanced professional training. It aims 'to provide full current information on awards for nationals of the United States and Canada, the United Kingdom and Ireland, Australia and New Zealand, South Africa and the developing countries'. It includes details of scholarships, fellowships, exchange opportunities, vacation study awards, travel grants and so on.

There is a subject index to help users. This substantial volume can be supplemented by a number of smaller guides:

Scholarships Abroad: Scholarships Offered to British Students by Overseas Governments and Universities. **British Council. Annual.**
The scholarships listed here are intended primarily for students of British nationality normally resident in this country graduating from British universities and other institutions of higher education. However, some countries will consider applications from Commonwealth students temporarily resident in Britain. The scholarships are tenable for a full academic year but some bursaries are available for shorter periods.

The following guides are all issued by the Association of Commonwealth Universities:

Financial Aid for First Degree Study at Commonwealth Universities: a Guide to Scholarships, Bursaries, Grants, Loans, etc. for Commonwealth Students Who Wish to Study for a First Degree at a Commonwealth University outside Their Own Country. **ACU, twice-yearly.**

Scholarships Guide for Commonwealth Postgraduate Students. **ACU Awards Information Service, 2-yearly.**
Gives details of scholarships, etc. open to graduates of Commonwealth countries who wish to undertake postgraduate study or research at a Commonwealth university outside their own country. Appendices cover awards at non-university institutions, and awards tenable in the UK by UK graduates. (See also *Research Opportunities in Commonwealth Developing Countries: a Register (p.75).*)

Awards for Commonwealth Universities Academic Staff: Fellowships, Visiting Professorships, Grants, etc. **ACU, 2-yearly.**
Details of awards for those who wish to carry out research, make study visits, or teach for a period at universities in another Commonwealth country.

Grants for Study Visits by University Administrators and Librarians. **Latest edn. ACU.**
Information about financial aid available for training and research purposes. An appendix lists courses and conference held in Commonwealth countries from time to time.

There is a comparatively new directory which is designed to help deprived persons in the community:

Educational Grants Directory: Voluntary and Charitable Help for Children and Students in Need, **eds. L. Fitzherbert and M. Eastwood. Directory for Social Change, 1988.**
It 'describes non-statutory sources of financial help for the education of needy children and students'. Coverage is of England and Wales only although many of the trusts operate nationally. It gives background information on areas of educational need, and also sources of further information and advice. The directory does not include awards or scholarships for academic excellence or research.

There are several other directories which may be included here as possible sources of funding, although they are not primarily concerned with education. The first could be particularly useful:

Charities Digest. **Family Welfare Association, annual.**
This has a chapter on education and includes details of exhibitions and scholarships. It concentrates on national charities and those in the London area but there are some Scottish ones. There is a subject index.

The others are concerned with community and welfare:

Directory of Grant-Making Trusts. **Latest edn. Charities Aid Foundation.**
Claims to be 'an indispensable tool for all those who are engaged in the search for funds'. It gives details of the locations, objects, policies and resources of about 2,500 grant-making bodies. Part 2 lists trusts in a classified arrangement. Educational trusts are included.

Space will allow only a few examples of American directories which give details of scholarships and grants in the US:

Scholarships for International Students: a Complete Guide to Colleges and Universities in the United States. **Latest edn. Octameron Press: USA. (Distributed in Britain by CRAC: Hobsons.)**
'For students who are interested in study in the USA and are looking for financial aid.' Sections are: (1) Choosing a college; (2) Paying for college; (3) Visa and immigration; (4) Customs and lifestyle; (5) College ad university data; (6) Scholarships and general information.

Graduate Scholarship Book: the Complete Guide to Scholarships, Fellowships, Grants and Loans for Graduate and Professional Study. **Latest edn. Prentice-Hall: USA.**
'A comprehensive listing of financial aid available specifically for graduate study in the US.'

Annual Register of Grant Support: a Directory of Funding Sources. **Marquis Who's Who Inc.: USA, annual.**
A large volume which is a standard reference source on non-repayable financial support for academic scholars and researchers in the US. It is impressive in the range of detailed information it provides.

14.14 Educational qualifications

There is one indispensable directory concerned with educational qualifications in this country:

PRIESTLEY, B. *British Qualifications: a Comprehensive Guide to Educational, Technical, Professional and Academic Qualifications in Britain.* **Kogan Page, annual.**
A well-established work which covers the subject in considerable detail. Contents: (1) Teaching establishments; (2) Secondary school examinations; (3) Further education examinations; (4) Awards made by universities, polytechnics and other institutions; (5) Membership of professional associations; (6) Qualifications listed by trades and professions; (7) Accrediting bodies. There is an index of abbreviations (at the front) and a general index. Material extracted from Priestley has appeared in a convenient format:

LAYTE, O. *A Dictionary of British Qualifications: Abbreviations and Qualifying Bodies.* **Kogan Page, 1985.**

An alphabetical listing of professional, academic, educational and technical qualifications available in Britain today. The abbreviation, its full name, and where appropriate the address and telephone number, are given for each entry.

A–Z of First Degrees, Diplomas and Certificates: a Guide to Qualifications Awarded by Universities and Polytechnics in the UK. **Kogan Page, annual.**
A quick reference source for school leavers and their advisers to pinpoint where courses can be studied and the relevant institution contacted for further details.

AUSTIN, M. and ASHCROFT, F. *A Simple Guide to British Qualifications.* **Great Ouse Press, 1983.**
Designed primarily for employers but also for students and their parents. It covers general vocational and commercial qualifications. There is an index of qualifications arranged by their initials

Locate: List of Common Abbreviations i Education and Training (see p.18) has brie notes on qualifications in four areas general; pre-vocational; vocational; an professional.
Where to Study in the UK (see p.63) in cludes information on British Qualifica tions for overseas students. Reference coul also be made to the DES's *Guide to Grants Courses Designed as comparable to First Degre Courses for the Purpose of Awards* (see p.76).

Educational qualifications throughou the world are covered in:

International Guide to Qualifications i Education. **2nd edn. Mansell for the Britis Council: National Academic Recognitio Information Centre, 1987.**
A detailed survey of education at all levels in 140 countries, arranged alphabetically by country. Each national system of education is described and the qualifications offered are compared with those in Britain. This is a valuable work for comparative purposes. NARIC was formerly known as the National Equivalence Information Centre. It also publishes a shorter *Guide to Overseas Qualifications.*

World Guide to Higher Education: a Comparative Survey of Systems, Degrees and Qualifications. **2nd edn. Bowker: Unesco, 1982.**
(Already described on p.55). Again the main arrangement is by countries. The patterns of education for each one are given in some detail, with glossaries of degrees and qualifications awarded.

14.15 Guides to careers

It is not possible to list here all the publications which contain careers information.

However, many of the best known and most useful guides to careers have been included and described.

Some of the sources mentioned in other sections, e.g. 14.5 (Going to university or college) and 14.16 (Guides to employment) contain information and advice on choosing careers. So do some of the school year books, e.g. the *Independent Schools Yearbook* (see 14.4.)

Most of the books on careers have at least some references for further reading. A more extended bibliography will be found in DIBDIN, K. and TOMLINSON, J. (see p.127) although this needs updating. It should be remembered that there is a fair amount of careers, information on Campus 2000 (see under *Occupations* below).

Quite a few of the guides to careers and employment come from publishers or organisations which specialise in this field, e.g. CRAC: Hobsons, Kogan Page, Newpoint, and Vacation-Work. Their catalogues are always worth scanning for new titles. A brief description of CRAC in particular may be useful here:

CAREERS RESEARCH AND ADVISORY CENTRE (CRAC), Bateman Street, Cambridge, CB2 1Z.

> CRAC works entirely in the field of careers education. It aims to create links between the worlds of education and employment, and more especially to help graduates, school leavers and the qualified with their career decisions. It is joint sponsor with Hatfield Polytechnic of the National Institute for Careers Education and Counselling (NICEC), which aims to advance the progress of careers education in Britain through the education and training of guidance staff. CRAC issues a wide range of items which are published on its behalf by Hobsons Press.

The most substantial guides to careers are:

Occupations: the Essential Reference Source for Careers and Jobs. Careers and Occupation Information Centre (COIC). Annual.

> COIC was part of the Manpower Services Commission (MSC), now the Training Agency. *Occupations* (formerly the *Annual Careers Guide*) is a large-format paperback which includes a mass of clearly presented information from the COIC Database. There are introductory sections on topics such as occupational change and open learning. These are followed by lists of careers and career opportunities under broad subject headings, e.g. teaching and cultural activities; social and related services; and business management services. This arrangement follows the Careers Library Classification Index (CLCI) which groups jobs and careers with similar backgrounds. However, there is a general alphabetical index of careers and occupations.
>
> COIC is responsible for gathering vocational and careers information of concern to young people and adults, and distributes materials to schools. It issues a bulletin *Newscheck*. (9 per annum) which reviews new literature on careers. COIC also provides information on more than 300 careers through Campus 2000 (see p.85).

Careers Encyclopaedia, ed. E. Segal. Latest edn. Cassell.

> Revised and updated every three years or so, this well-established careers guide provides 'independent and impartial information for school and college leavers, graduates, their parents, teachers, and careers advisers'. It is not an encyclopaedia in the usual sense. Introductory chapters are followed by detailed surveys of careers grouped into broad areas, e.g. information technology; professional, scientific and social services. More frequent revision would enable it to take account of rapid changes in the employment market for school leavers. It is an impressive publication nevertheless.

Other less ambitious directories and guides to careers are:

BURSTON, D. *An A–Z of Careers and Jobs.* Latest edn. Kogan Page.

> Short accounts of more than 300 careers and occupations, from accountancy to occupational psychology, for young people still at school. Those requiring detailed information will be disappointed. Less than a page on average is given to each career.

Careers Book, eds. K. Boehm and J.L. Spalding. Papermac, annual.

> Provides 250 jobs profiles and key information to aid career choice. There was an *Alternative Careers Book*, 2nd ed, 1989, from the same source.

Daily Telegraph Careers A–Z. Latest edn. Collins.

'The information in this book is based on more than 100,000 enquiries to the Daily Telegraph Careers Information Service, run by Careers Intelligence.' There are brief articles on over 300 different occupations, interspersed with articles on related topics, e.g. Industrial Training Boards; City of Guilds and London Institute; preparation of a curriculum vitae. Articles covering a range of careers appear in the *Daily Telegraph* on Mondays.

DONALD, V. *How to Choose a Career.* **Latest edn. Kogan Page.**
Focuses on essential points to be considered. Describes qualifications and training required, and grants available, for careers in various sectors of employment.

FENNELL, E. *The Parents' Guide to Careers and Courses.* **Latest edn. Newpoint.**
'Practical information and guidance on the maze of issues and opportunities faced by young people in planning careers and further education, YTS or other training.'

GABRIEL, J. *Unqualified Success: a Comprehensive Guide to Jobs for School Leavers.* **Latest edn. Penguin.**
A guide to hundreds of jobs open to those with no formal qualifications. It includes checklists of the personal qualities needed, the pros and cons of the job, likely employers, jobs in related fields, and sources of further information.

MILLER, R. and ALSTON, A. *Equal Opportunities: a Careers Guide.* **Latest edn. Penguin.**
This Penguin handbook 'gives information on job opportunities for young people of both sexes as well as for those who want to start a career later in life... A unique feature is the section under each job category which assess the current position of, and opportunities for, women'. Unusually the female pronoun is used throughout.

SEGAL, A. *Career Choice.* **Pan, 1981.**
'Choosing and finding a career, and getting started, is a complex and difficult business nowadays. Future uncertainties make it more so.' This paperback of over 400 pages is one of the most readable guides, full of useful information and good advice. It deserves a new edition. Meantime the author has edited a *Parents' Guide to Careers* (Rosters, 1990).

Sunday Times Good Career Guide, ed. P. Wilby. **Granada, 1985.**

A companion volume to the *Sunday Times Good University Guide* (see p.63). It is a substantial well-produced paperback which offers positive help and advice in a contemporary context. If it is revised and updated regularly it could become a standard work.

TAYLOR, F. *After School: a Guide to Post-School Opportunities.* **2nd edn. Kogan Page, 1987.**
Practical and clearly written. There are chapters on careers education in school; vocational guidance; job-finding agencies; information sources and aids; sources of further education and training; options at 16+, 17+, 18+; alternatives (e.g. travel, self-employment and voluntary work); and applications costs and grants.

Which Subject? Which Career?: a Guide to Subjects and Courses at 14, 16, and 18 and the Careers to Which They Lead. **Latest edn. Consumers' Association and Hodder/Hobsons.**
A well organised handbook which examines what each option involves and how it is linked to possible career paths, with reference to many additional sources of information. Covers YTS, TVEI, etc. and describes 200 careers by subject, indicating the qualifications needed and assessing prospects. A publication with a similar purpose is:

Focus at 18: Education, Employment and Training Opportunities for 18 Year Olds. **Newpoint, annual.**
This is admirably clear and a mine of useful information. Sections are: (1) Making your choice; (2) The education route; (3) Options in education and training; (4) The employment and training combinations; (5) Reference indexes.
Focus at 18 is designed by Newpoint to be used in conjunction with *Focus at 16*: a magazine in regional editions, covering education; education and training; and employment and training; and also with the:

Adviser's Handbook. **Newpoint, annual.**
This was developed from the *Careers Adviser's Handbook* which is superseded. It is intended primarily for professional advisers of 18-year-olds. It follows the same pattern as *Focus at 18* but includes an overview of the basic theories underlying all advisory work, and other features. Recent editions have chapters on employment and training in Scotland and Northern Ireland.

CRAC (see above) has published a series of short paperbacks to help pupils to make decisions at various stages. They include:

ecisions at 13/14+; Decisions at 15/16+; ecisions at 17/18+; Your Choice of A Levels; eyond A Levels; Jobs and Careers After A Levels; our Choice of Degree and Diploma (see p.63); *tarting Points: Suggestions for Study Covering 00 Courses and Cross-Referenced Against O and Levels and A Grades*; and *A Year Off: a Year n* (see p.84). They have been revised and pdated as required and can all be recomnended.

There is a series of brief leaflets issued y the DES called *Choose Your Course*. They re designed for school leavers and the itles include *Choosing at 16* and *On From O evels*. They are available from the DES ʼublications Despatch Centre. Other useul leaflets from the DES are: *A Career in eaching; Back to School; Teaching as a Career;* nd *Why Teaching?*

For handicapped pupils and students here is:

fter 16 – What Next? Latest edn. National ʼureau for Handicapped Students (now the ʼational Bureau for Students with ʼisabilities).
A general guide to the opportunities available for young people with disabilities. It gives information on grants, benefits, etc. and indicates other sources of advice. Other relevant leaflets are issued by the Bureau. Note also:

ʼHOMPSON, M. *Employment for Disabled People.* ʼogan Page, 1986.
It ʼdescribes the current employment situation for the disabled, and discusses policy legislation, attitudes, and schemes'.

The above is one of a series of careers ʼooks published by Kogan Page, and there ιre similar series from other publishers, ʼ.g. Batsford and Newpoint. They are usully well represented in public and school ibraries. Two titles on teaching as a career nay be given as examples:

ʼHILVER, P. *A Career in Teaching.* Batsford, ʼ987.

ʼAYLOR, F. *Careers in Teaching.* 3rd edn. ʼogan Page, 1988.

For young people in Scotland there is:

Career Through School: the Radio Scotland Guide to Educational Choices Open to 14-17 Year Olds in Scotland. BBC Education Scotland, 1986. (Available from SCOTVEC)
This attractive brochure was produced to accompany a Radio Scotland Career Through School Week. Its main aim 'is to offer help in making decisions at important stages in a young person's career through school and beyond'. It is very clearly presented and indicates where to turn for further information.

There are two annual guides, both fairly short, which are produced by teachers' associations for careers teachers and advisers rather than students or pupils:

NATIONAL ASSOCIATION OF CAREERS AND GUIDANCE TEACHERS. *Annual Guide.*
A series of papers on careers topics, not strictly a guide to careers.

NATIONAL UNION OF TEACHERS. *NUT Guide to Careers Work.* Annual.
Articles of general interest followed by an ABC of careers, with very brief information about the type of work involved, entry requirements and potential employment.

There are other guides, primarily designed for teachers, which could be more generally useful because of the information they provide about resources in this field:

AVENT, C. *Practical Approaches to Careers Education.* Latest edn. CRAC/Hobsons.
Planned as 'a comprehensive but concise handbook for newly appointed or trainee careers teachers as well as a reference source for the more experienced'. It sets out the principles of careers education, surveys the resources available, and offers practical ideas and suggestions. Contents: (1) Mainly for heads; (2) Mainly for heads of departments; (3) For the careers team.

SUMMERSON, E.J. *Careers Information and Careers Libraries: a Practical Guide.* Revised edn. Careers Consultants Ltd, 1984.
Aims to help careers teachers, careers officers and librarians to set up libraries and to collect careers information. There are substantial appendices giving addresses of suppliers of careers literature, publishers of careers books, and sources of further

information. The same publisher has issued a *Handbook of Free Careers Information* 'to help careers officers make full use of the vast fund of careers material available to them'.

More recent than either of these is:

CLEATON, D. and FOSTER, R. *Practical Aspects of Careers Guidance*. Omnibus edn. Trotman, 1989. (Spiral binding.)
It 'sets the careers education scene and deals with the organisation of school guidance work, liaison with internal and external agencies, individual guidance and techniques of assessment, and careers information and resources'.

Some careers services in local education authorities have produced careers handbooks which could be very useful to careers guidance staff and teachers, and often to pupils too. An excellent and substantial example is *Choices at 16+: Education and Training Handbook,* from Strathclyde Regional Council Careers Service.

For those who wish to keep up to date with new developments there is an abstracting periodical:

Careers Abstracts. 6 per annum. Kogan Page.
This provides abstracts from specialised careers publications, i.e. journals, magazines and newspapers. Each issue contains about 100 abstracts, copies of which can be ordered through the associated 'copy article service.' First published in 1986.

The National Institute for Careers Education and Counselling (NICEC) publishes an annual *Register of Research and Development in Careers Guidance (*see p.187) which provides summaries of ongoing research and development projects.

The rapid expansion of careers literature and the need for constant updating of directory-type information mean that printed sources are not always adequate for careers advisers in particular. The development of computerised databases is providing at least part of the answer. Mention has already been made of the careers information which is available on Campus 2000. The Newpoint Publishing Co. has produced a useful series of:

Job Knowledge Indexes (*JKI*). Newpoint.
These provide information on a wide variety of jobs and careers in the form of questions and answers. They are available as resource packs or on computer disc for BBC B, RML 480Z, and Commodore 64 machines. Each of the discs contains one group of careers, e.g teaching, with a true-or-false questionnaire.

Another venture in computer assisted careers education is:

JIIG-CAL (*Jobs Ideas and Information Generator – Computer Assisted Learning*). NFER.
It was instigated jointly by the DES and the SED in 1980, and is carried out by the NFER. It is still being developed, but has already proved a worthwhile resource for careers education. 'The desk-top interactive version can provide valuable help to counsellors who have equipment powerful enough to receive it.' (TES, 13.11.87.)

A computerised careers guidance system *PROSPECT* is being piloted for the DES by Newpoint during 1990. It is designed for stand-alone use on a microcomputer. Mention should also be made of *CASCAID* (the Careers Advisory Services Computerised Aid Careers Guide) operated by the Leicestershire County Council Cascaid Unit. A handbook is published annually.

Some ideas of the range of careers software now available can be obtained from the *Microelectronics Education Programme* (MEP) *Catalogue of Reviews.* The Somerset Careers Service also issues a list of *Careers Software Available on Microcomputer.*

14.16 Guides to employment

Most of the well-known guides to employment described here are for graduates or for students in their final years at university or college. However, a few which are suitable for school leavers are included. There are also some directories of vacation job opportunities and guides to working overseas. Students who have been using tandard careers guides (see 14.15) should lso consult some of the directories mentioned below. They often present a more ealistic picture of the employment scene, nd give helpful information about employers and their training systems.

Register of Graduate Employment and Training (ROGET): the Official AGCAS Compendium. Central Services Unit, annual (with supplement).

AGCAS is the Association of Graduate Careers Advisory Services in Universities and Polytechnics. The CSU provides support for these services. ROGET is an alphabetical list of employers with details of their recruitment policies, training practices and activities. The indexes are an important feature. They enable job-seekers to identify employers offering a specific kind of work or recruiting graduates of a particular discipline. There are useful introductory sections. *ROGET in Scotland* is published separately. The CSU also issues over 70 careers booklets on behalf of AGCAS, as well as a fortnightly *National Vacancy List for Graduates*.

Graduate Employment and Training (GET). CRAC: Hobsons, annual.

The GET system involves reading the editorial section; selecting employers through the indexes; comparing employers; and studying employers' advertisements. There is an alphabetical list of employers recruiting graduates, with details about their main activities, products, subject areas, etc. There are indexes of degree subjects and occupational categories, and a geographical index. A *Graduate Studies Supplement* caters for those going on to postgraduate work.

Graduate Opportunities (GO): a Guide to Opportunities for Students at Universities and Other Institutions of Higher Education. Newpoint, annual.

Aimed at 'those who are investigating all their career opportunities'. It provides detailed profiles of UK and overseas employers with graduate vacancies, as well as key facts on over 1,700 employers; advice on where and how to seek employment; and details on professional associations. There is a comprehensive index. It was designed as a companion volume to *Postgraduate Opportunities (POGO)* which is no longer published.

Directory of Opportunities for Graduates (DOG). Newpoint, 3 vols, annual.

Although it is more selective than the works already mentioned, this is one of the more practical and realistic guides to career possibilities. It has clear accounts of the qualifications and qualities required in different professions and occupations, and helpful case studies to make the briefing more effective. The volumes cover: (1) Accountancy, finance, legal work, insurance, commerce/statistics; (2) Engineering, science, patent work, computing, architecture, building, surveying; and (3) Management, administration, marketing, sales, retailing. Each volume has a section listing major employers of graduates in the field concerned, with other relevant information.

The directory should be used in conjunction with the *DOG Guide to Postgraduate Study* (see p.66) which was planned as the fourth volume of the series. The same publisher issues a *Guide to Graduate Careers Services* (annual), and a fortnightly *Graduate Post*, which covers career and recruitment topics, postgraduate study, current vacancies, etc.

More general guides to employment include:

Opportunities: the Annual Guide to Opportunities and Trends in Employment. Newpoint, annual.

This is available in four regional editions: South; Midlands and Wales; North; and Scotland. It is an annual guide to employment, training, and further education. Each edition includes a directory of local and national employers offering career and training opportunities to young people in the region covered.

The Job Book: the Handbook of Employment and Training for School Leavers. CRAC: Hobsons, annual.

Intended for graduates as well as school leavers. An alphabetical list of 1,000 or so companies with details of opportunities they provide, information about training schemes and so on. There are subject and geographical indexes. It also describes national certificates and diplomas; professional and graduate qualifications; and the entrance and training requirements of professional bodies. An excellent publication.

Job Finder's Book, R. Sandys and A. Stace. Latest edn, Kogan Page.

'A simple and practical guide to the mechanics of getting a job. It provides job-seekers with all the information and advice they need to put them ahead in the job hunt.'

Jobfile: a Compendium of Job Information. Hodder, annual.

Compiled from information contained in the Jobfile of the JIIG-CAAL computerised careers guidance and information system (see p.82) used in LEAs, schools and colleges. It provides concise information on over 600 jobs.

The Good Job Guide: the Daily Telegraph Guide to Employment Opportunities and Key Employers. Latest edn. Newpoint.

Aims to provide 'everything in the job-changer must know'. Sections are: (1) Aspects of employment; (2) UK and overseas employers; (3) Charities and voluntary organisations; (4) Recruitment consultants; (5) Professional and training associations; (6) Post-experience courses; (7) Appendices on employers and institutions; (8) Index of careers and locations.

Two short books published by Newpoint: *Coping with Jobhunting* and *Coping with Interviews* give useful advice in this area.

There are numerous directories which give practical help to students who would like to work during their vacations, or find temporary or even permanent jobs overseas:

A Year Off: a Year On: a Guide to Jobs, Voluntary Service and Working Holidays During your Education. CRAC: Hobsons. Latest edn.

Possibilities for voluntary service and paid work in Britain and abroad for those who would like 'a break from study, a year's relief from the grind of academic work before going up to college or university, or a year (or less) between graduating and taking up a permanent job'.

Vacation-Work Publications issue a range of relevant publications which will already be familiar to many students. They are regularly updated:

Directory of Jobs and Careers Abroad. Directory of Summer Jobs in Britain

Directory of Summer Jobs Abroad (excludes USA
Directory of Work and Study in Developing Countries
International Directory of Voluntary Work
Vacation Traineeships for Students
Work your Way Round the World

Vacation-Work also distributes:

Internships USA (on-the job training opportunities). (USA)
Summer Employment Directory of the United States. (USA)

The undernoted guides are intended primarily for those seeking more permanent posts abroad:

Working in the European Communities: a Guide to Graduate Recruiters and Job Seekers. CRAC Hobsons, 1985. Supplement and Continuation, 1986.

The basic volume describes 'the recruitment policies of four major European countries and their education systems'. A general introduction on Europe is followed by sections on Belgium, Germany, France and the Netherlands. The supplement covers Denmark, Ireland, Italy and the UK. There are useful references to further sources of information.

Working Abroad: the Daily Telegraph Guide to Living and Working Overseas. Kogan Page, annual.

A more substantial and detailed guide which contains general advice on most points, although health matters are excluded. Part 1: General aspects; Part 2: Country surveys. There are lists of sources and relevant addresses.

Two recent books: *How to Get a Job Abroad* and *How to Teach Abroad* by R. Jones, both published by Northcote House in 1989 could be helpful. The latter contains practical advice on job-hunting, applications, contract negotiation, culture shock, tax and personal finance, and an A–Z guide to teaching English as a foreign language.

14.17 Online services: Campus 2000; NERIS; MARIS On-Line

Those who are looking for information of the kind described in this chapter are not nowadays restricted to printed sources. A rapidly increasing amount of information is becoming available through information networks which are already serving educational institutions of all types in this country and abroad. The most important ones are described in this section.

Campus 2000

Prestel, the British Telecom Viewdata System, provided the first large database on education in this country. Prestel Education was a very large store of mainly directory-type information on educational institutions, courses, careers, resources, etc. Another well-known database: TTNS (The Times Network Systems Ltd, formerly The Times Network for Schools) provided a range of information, particularly on curricular aspects of education, and an electronic mailing facility, for use by teachers and pupils.

The services offered by Prestel Education and TTNS were amalgamated early in 1989 to form a new service – Campus 2000 – which is already subscribed to by a large number of educational institutions at home and overseas. Access to the service can be achieved via the Dialcom network at the cost of a local call throughout the UK.

The aim of Campus 2000 is to provide educational information of common interest and to help institutions and individuals to share and exchange it in the easiest possible way. 'There are two main elements: databases which hold vast libraries of diverse but useful information, and electronic mail to ensure speedy and efficient contact with the central resources and amongst users'. It claims already to link the majority of secondary schools, most of the further and higher education sector and a rapidly growing number of secondary schools.

'In order to cater for obviously different needs, Campus 2000 is offered in two forms, each of which may be enhanced.' CAMPUS offers electronic mail (inland and international), a directory of users, campus conferencing, LEA databases, SEND (the Special Educational Needs Database) and the Primary Database. Campus Plus adds specialist databases (including careers and modern languages) and Prestel Education. Subscribers to either of these forms may opt for Campus Premium on payment of an additional charge. This will give them access to ECCTIS (information on courses and entry requirements) (see below), NERIS (a national database of mainly curricular materials) (see below), and Profile (access to text published in newspapers and magazines). All subscribers receive a yearbook and a publication *Campus forum* once a term.

The brochure advertising Campus 2000 (there is also a video) gives fuller descriptions of its main services and how they are used under the headings Campus Mail, Campus Conferencing, Campus Careers, Campus Modern Languages (which has an international dimension), Campus Business Studies, Campus Sport, Campus for Primary Schools (seen as a major growth area), Campus Special Needs (a database maintained by the Scottish Council for Education Technology in collaboration with special needs professionals throughout the UK), and Campus Manager which is being developed to help LEAs with their local management of schools (LMS) following the Education Reform Act 1988. It will include an LMS database.

Most of the original Prestel Education databases are retained on Campus 2000. *ECCTIS* (the Educational Counselling and Credit Transfer Information Service) available on Campus Premium offers information about courses from non-advanced to postgraduate levels in UK universities, polytechnics and colleges, and also about their entry requirements. *ECCTIS* is also available on CD–ROM.

The *UCCA Course Vacancy Database* indicates which universities still have places vacant during the clearing period from mid-August to the end of September. Polytel provides current vacancy information on all first degree, DipHE and HND courses at polytechnics, including art and design and teacher education courses. Both databases are updated daily.

The *National PICKUP Directory* provides basic details of thousands of short work-related courses mainly at public sector institutions. It is arranged in subject divisions with regional subdivisions. The directory is also available on microfiche and on floppy discs. A printed version: the *PICKUP Short Courses Directory* is published by Guildford Educational Services.

New Signposts has information on more than 300 careers which is supplied by COIC (The Careers and Occupational Information Centre) (see p.79). It includes advice on finding a job and a free mailbox to contact COIC and request a search. The database is updated three times a year.

Educational Telesoftware gives details of computer software on a variety of subjects which could be of interest to educational institutions and the domestic market. The details are supplied by schools, colleges, LEAs and commercial publishers.

Obviously the information available on Campus 2000 can be more up to date than that appearing in printed directories published once a year always assuming that the information providers, who range from the DES to the independent University of Buckingham, keep the data they are presenting under constant review. Nevertheless it can be frustrating to use Campus 2000 a times. For example if you are trying to fin out about courses at a particular college after some searching you may simply b referred to the College's prospectus, and i you ask about grants you may be advise only to apply to your LEA. It is not unusua to be led up blind alleys and the problem i partly the indexing system though effort are always being made to improve it Generally, however, Campus 2000 is a ver useful additional resource for directory type information on education.

NERIS

NERIS (the National Educational Resour ces Information Service) which is a pre mium service on Campus 2000, is also avail able on subscription via direct access o through the JANET network. It aims t provide teachers, lecturers and suppor agencies with information about curricu lum materials and developments through out the UK. Initially funded by the Depart ment of Trade and Industry, it is now a educational trust with charitable status anc is moving towards being self-financing. I was mainly concerned in its early stages with the secondary age phase, but now has curriculum coverage from pre-school tc post–16.

NERIS makes it possible to identify a very wide range of teaching and learning resources (currently over 30,000) which have been produced by educational institutions and other organisations. Full descriptions of each resource are given, with details of any projects, case studies and examples, and often the full text of worksheets, teacher notes, or evaluative reviews. These may be printed out or adapted for classroom use by means of a word processor.

National Curriculum documents held on NERIS, and also on separate discs, include information about statutory and non-statutory guidelines for English, mathematics and science. Other topics, e.g. technology will be added on an ongoing basis. With the support of the SED, a comprehensive datafile about national support materials for the Scottish Standard Grade has also been entered.

Undoubtedly the Welsh, Scottish and Northern Ireland dimensions are helping to ensure that the service will meet the needs of potential users throughout the UK. Moreover the CD-ROM version of NERIS (the annual subscription includes termly updates) offers access which eliminates local call charges and makes possible the use of alternative search facilities, including free text searching, for those institutions which have the appropriate hardware.

NERIS claims to have the most comprehensive catalogue of computer software currently available in the UK. It also provides advance information on new publications from most UK educational publishers, and details of educational broadcasts. The database as a whole is not difficult to access. The *User Guide* handbook provides guidance on search terms and strategies. The Basic System is designed to help beginners to become used to online searching and includes a Word List. The Extended System, which is recommended for serious researches, has a *Thesaurus* and truncation options. There are plans to provide a printed thesaurus.

The database is now expanding rapidly and its use is increasing as schools and colleges become aware of its benefits. There is an international dimension to NERIS. Many countries are showing an interest, particularly in the CD-ROM version and there is a growing willingness on the part of agencies abroad to become information providers. The future of NERIS seems assured.

MARIS On-Line

The other important educational database is MARIS On-Line, formerly MARIS-Net (the Materials and Resources Information Service Network). It started life as a Government funded project in 1983 but was acquired by William Dawson Holdings in 1989 and incorporated into the Training Information Network along with the Directory of Training.

MARIS On-Line provides a national and international information service for vocational education and training from a growing series of databases. They include Open Learning Materials; Management Training Opportunities; Training Resource Materials; Computer Based Training and Interactive Video (CBT and IAV); Training Films and Videos; Short Courses (merged with the *PICKUP Training Directory of Short Courses* in 1990); Training Services; Open Learning Bibliography; and the National Open Learning Library.

The Training Development Information Service (TDIS), at present being piloted by the Training Agency, should be available soon. The Training Agency is also negotiating for the National Council for Vocational Qualifications (NCVQ) Database to be hosted on the MARIS computer. It will be made available via TDIS to all subscribers.

MARIS On-Line is now available on CD–ROM, and in addition offers a personal telephone search service and an electronic messaging system (ENVOY). Access to MARIS is also possible through PSS/Prestel. In order to make its services more widely available it is in the process of installing over 2,000 Training Access Point (TAP) terminals in public places throughout Britain. To help subscribers MARIS conducts one-day workshops at the Ely Headquarters of the company, which provide hands-on experience of all the databases and services. The printed version of the *MARIS Thesaurus,* originally produced in 1984, is now an integral part of the materials database.

MARIS claims to provide immediate, detailed and up-to-date information on virtually every learning package or course over a wide range of subjects. It seems appropriate therefore that it has taken over production of the *Open Learning Directory*

(see p.73) which has proved its usefulnes in recent years.

It will be obvious from the brief account given here that these educational data bases, unlike the bibliographic database (online and CD–ROM) described in 26. and 26.8 are not intended primarily for the serious researcher. They could be useful t anyone who is involved or interested i education and training.

The *ACE Bulletin* for 20 February 198 contained an Education Digest on *Database for Education.* This was a useful review o those available at the time and man readers would be surprised by their numbe and variety.

15 Statistical sources [   ]

Some of the works already mentioned, e.g. encyclopaedias, year books and directories, include statistics.

A wealth of statistics will be found scattered through any major encyclopaedia. Many of them could be useful for historical or comparative purposes, but no one should rely on encyclopaedias for up-to-date statistics. The year books published by the major encyclopaedias, on the other hand are good sources for fairly recent statistics, notably the *Britannica Book of the Year,* which incorporates a World Data Survey (see p.27). The *Annual Register* (see p.28) has a six-year statistical survey.

The general directories mentioned in 4.1, e.g. *Whitaker's Almanack* (see p.53) and the *Statesman's Year Book* (see p.54) are good providers of basic statistics, both general and educational. Some of these year books and directories have long histories. Whitaker was first published in 1868 and the Annual Register over a century before that. Libraries usually keep a file of at least some back issues so that you can locate relevant statistics for earlier years.

However, there are numerous works that consist almost entirely of statistics and these are the main concern of this chapter. Some are general, and some are devoted entirely to educational statistics. Most of them are compiled from official sources. The ones described here are mainly British and American, but sources of further information are indicated.

15.1 General statistical sources: UK

There are four handbooks of official statistics which should be available in any medium-sized reference collection. The first three are prepared by the Central Statistical Office.

Annual Abstract of Statistics. **HMSO, annual.**
This is the best known general source for British statistics. It covers the whole range and provides comparative tables for the last ten years or so. Note that the references in the index are to table numbers not page numbers. An index of sources is also included. Complete volumes of the *Annual Abstract of Statistics* from 1860 to date are available on microfilm and those from 1970 to date are on microfiche. (See a recent issue for details.) The *Monthly Digest of Statistics* which provides more recent figures does not include education.

Regional Trends. **HMSO, annual.**
Brings together detailed information to highlight regional variations in the UK. It includes tables on different aspects of education. The title was formerly *Regional Statistics* and before that the *Abstract of Regional Statistics.*

Social Trends. **HMSO, annual.**
Designed to give a broad description of British society, updated every year. 'The focus in each section is on current policy concerns. 'It has more tables on education than *Regional Trends,* and there are also numerous charts with useful introductory comments. This is an invaluable survey which could be used for a variety of purposes. It shows educational statistics in a broader context. The 1990 edition has a section on projected social trends over the next 20 years.

Scottish Abstract of Statistics. **Scottish Office, annual.**
Compiled by the Scottish Office Statistical Unit. It covers the whole field of Scottish statistics with a separate section on education. It includes an outline of the Scottish educational system, a description of the sources for the statistics, and explanatory notes on the tables which include comparative figures for preceding years.

There is a concise and convenient summary of British statistics for the general reader:

Key Data. **HMSO, annual.**
First published in 1986 this provides key statistics from other CSO handbooks, e.g. *Social Trends* (above). It includes many tables, maps and charts. An earlier publication of a similar kind was *Facts in Focus.* 5th edn. Penguin, 1980, also prepared by the CSO.

An example of a more specialised source is:

Women and Men in Britain: a Research Profile.
**Equal Opportunities Commission: HMSO,
1987.**
> 'A digest of statistics depicting the position of
> women and men in the various facets of life in the
> mid-eighties.' Part 2: Education and training, gives
> figures for Great Britain. There is a more general
> and more recent review in *Women and Men in Britain*
> 1989, also from the EOC. Another EOC
> publication: *Facts that Figure* (1988), provides 'some
> introductory statistics for teachers on the education
> of boys and girls, with particular reference to the
> issue of equal opportunity'.

15.2 Educational statistics: UK

The main producers of educational statistics south and north of the border in this
country are the Department of Education
and Science and the Scottish Education
Department. Both of them in recent years
have been trying to find alternative and
more effective ways of making statistical
data available. This has meant that several
well established series of statistical publications are no longer available. However,
they will be included here as they are still
useful for retrospective coverage.

The most convenient general source for
specifically educational statistics in Britain
at present is:

DEPARTMENT OF EDUCATION AND SCIENCE.
Education Statistics for the United Kingdom.
HMSO, annual.
> Prepared by the DES in collaboration with the
> Welsh Office Education Department, the Scottish
> Education Department, the Northern Ireland
> Department of Education and the Universities
> Funding Council. It 'brings together the main
> statistics of the different national education
> systems to give a general picture of education in
> the UK as a whole. It contains a summary guide to
> sources of more detailed educational statistics.
> Included are statistics of schools, pupils, teachers,
> students at further education institutions and
> universities, awards and finance, together with
> explanatory notes to the tables'. There is an
> inserted leaflet *Education Facts and Figures, England.*

A convenient summary of educational
statistics in England and Wales will be
found in:

DEPARTMENT OF EDUCATION AND SCIENCE. *Digest
of Statistics.* **HMSO, annual.**
> It is a handy size for easy reference and the figures
> are as recent as possible. There are thirty simple
> tables showing the statistics most often needed on
> educational finance, school pupils and teachers,
> school leavers, 16–19 year olds, further and higher
> education, overseas students, etc. Note also:

DEPARTMENT OF EDUCATION AND SCIENCE.
Statistics of Education: Data Sets. **DES,
annual.**
> The DES started to produce these data sets when
> *Statistics of Education* (see below) ceased publication
> in 1981. The data sets include:

> **Digest of statistics (England) (see above)**
> **Finance and awards (England and Wales)**
> **Further education (England)**
> **Further education student: staff ratios
> (England)**
> **Schools (England)**
> **School leavers (CSE and GCE) (England)**
> **Teachers in service (England and Wales)**

> They are available direct from the DES (not
> HMSO) in the form of complete or individual sets,
> tables, or loose sheets. The address is: DES, Room
> 337, Mowden Hall, Staindrop Road, Darlington
> DL3 9BG.

The statistics in the above publication
are updated in specific areas by the *Statistical Bulletins* which have been issued by the
DES at irregular intervals since 1978. A
complete list of them is available from the
DES Library. More recent issues are listed
in the *ACE Digest* (see p.9) and the whole
year's issues in *DES Publications* (see p.134).

The previous standard source for educational statistics in England and Wales was:

DEPARTMENT OF EDUCATION AND SCIENCE.
Statistics of Education. **6 vols, annual.
(Ceased publication)**
Vol.1: Schools.
Vol.2: School leavers, CSE and GCE.
Vol.3: Further education.
Vol.4: Teachers.
Vol.5: Finance and awards.
Vol.6: Universities.
> There was always a considerable time lag in the
> publication of these volumes. More recent figures
> were to be found in the *Statistical Bulletins* already
> mentioned. However, the main series of volumes
> ceased publication as already indicated in 1981.
> Some of the statistics which appeared in vol.6 are
> being published in *University Statistics* (see below).

Fuller current educational statistics for Wales are available in:

WELSH OFFICE. *Statistics of Education in Wales*. HMSO, annual.

In Scotland the SED has issued its own series of *Statistical Bulletins* since May 1977 and these are now the main source for published statistics on Scottish education. They appear at irregular intervals throughout the year and like the *DES Statistical Bulletins* (above) each one deals with a different topic. A virtue of the bulletins is that the statistics are set firmly in context. The SED also issues annually *Basic Educational Statistics (Scotland)* in the form of a small folded card. The previous standard source for Scottish educational statistics was:

SCOTTISH EDUCATION DEPARTMENT. *Scottish Educational Statistics*. HMSO, annual. (Ceased publication.)
This covered the whole range of Scottish educational statistics: schools, further education colleges and higher education, but the final edition which appeared in 1977 covered schools, pupils and teachers only.

Detailed university statistics will be found in:

***University Statistics: Statistics of United Kingdom Universities*. Universities' Statistical Record for the Universities Funding Council, 3 vols. annual.**
Vol.1: Students and staff
Vol.2: First destinations of university graduates.
Vol.3: Finance.
The Universities' Statistical Record, a computer-based information system, was set up in 1968 to meet the need for more comprehensive statistics on the different areas of university activity. Comparative statistics for earlier years are given. There is a helpful introduction and commentary in each volume. *Universities Management Statistics and Performance Indicators in the UK* is available from the same source.
The Universities Funding Council replaced the University Grants Committee in 1989. Some university statistics will be found in the *UGC's Annual Survey*, and the *Qinquennial Reviews* are also

worth checking for earlier years. Other relevant annual reports containing statistics are those of UCCA (see p.61), the PCAS (see p.61), the CRCH (see p.69), and the CNAA (see p.66). Statistics for the OU are not included in *University Statistics* above. They will be found in *Open University Statistics: Students, Staff and Finance*, published by the OU itself from 1987.

Some statistics for polytechnics are included in the *PCAS Annual Report* (see p.33). Follow-up surveys of students can be found in: *First Destinations of Polytechnic Students* (Committee of Directors of Polytechnics, annual). The Association of Careers Advisers in Colleges of Higher Education publishes *First Destination Statistics* (ACACHE, annual).

The clearest short guide to sources of information in this field, how they compare, and how they may be obtained, is:

COUNCIL FOR NATIONAL ACADEMIC AWARDS. *A Guide to Higher Education Statistics*. Latest edn. CNAA Information Services.

It is worth remembering that major official reports such as the *Robbins Report* on higher education (see p.39) often contain statistical evidence. Many of the statistics in Robbins were specially collected by the Committee for the purpose.

Facts and figures about overseas students will be found in:

***Statistics of Students from Abroad in the United Kingdom*. British Council, annual. (Formerly issued as *Statistics of Overseas Students in the United Kingdom*.)**

For recent educational statistics in local authorities throughout the UK there is a standard source:

CHARTERED INSTITUTE OF PUBLIC FINANCE AND ACCOUNTANCY. *Education Statistics*. CIPFA, 2 vols. annual

Vol.1: Estimates
Vol.2: Actuals
These volumes, which are published separately with an interval between, provide statistics on all parts of the education service administered by local

authorities: nursery, primary, secondary and special schools; polytechnics and colleges; and adult education, etc. Apart from financial information they give details of school and pupil numbers, pupil-teacher ratios, pupils receiving school meals and so on. Since the volumes have been published for many years they are valuable for comparative purposes.

National statistics can often be supplemented by those issued by local authorities on a local or regional basis. There is a good example from Scotland's largest region:

STRATHCLYDE REGIONAL COUNCIL, DEPARTMENT OF EDUCATION. *Annual Data Review.*
First published in 1986 with the title *Education Data Review.* Under various headings from Nursery to FE it provides a useful statistical picture of education in the region.

If you would like to take your study of British educational statistics a little further there is a summary guide to sources in the DES's *Education Statistics for the United Kingdom* (see p.90). A fuller account of official educational statistical sources will be found in:

Guide to Official Statistics. **Latest edn. HMSO.**
This is compiled by the Central Statistical Office (CSO). It attempts to cover all official and some important non-official sources in the UK. The section on education is excellent because it describes under various headings (e.g. number of schools and pupils, teacher training, universities) the main publications which you will need to consult to find all the relevant statistics.

A briefer CSO guide in pamphlet form: *Government Statistics: a Brief Guide to Sources* (annual), lists the statistical publications currently available from HMSO. It is reproduced in *Key Data* (see p.89). There is also a *Statistical News* (4 per annum), which provides an account of current developments in British official statistics. Each issue contains articles dealing with aspects of the subject in depth. For information about other possible sources we have:

Sources of Unofficial UK Statistics. **2nd edn. Compiled by D. Mort, Gower, 1989.**

Refers not only to traditional-type statistical publications but also to journals, year books, annual reports, monographs and conference proceedings. It includes some educational sources.

15.3 Educational statistics: other countries

Some of the general sources for statistics on the countries of the world were mentioned in the introduction to this chapter. Of these the *Statesman's Yearbook* (see p.54) is probably the most useful. Educational statistics for each country are incorporated in the text under the heading 'Justice, Religion, Education and Welfare'.

The *Europa World Year Book* (see p.54) has some educational statistics for the world's countries, and the regional directories from the same publisher could also be used, e.g. *USA and Canada,* and *Western Europe.* However, you can expect to find more detailed information in the year books produced by individual countries, which there is no space to describe here.

The standard handbook for international statistics is the:

Unesco Statistical Yearbook. **Unesco, annual.**
This unwieldy volume is compiled from official sources and contains about 100 pages of comparative statistics on education and culture. The educational statistics cover institutions; teachers and students at different levels; public expenditure on education; and the illiterate population. There is also a *Unesco Statistical Digest: a Statistical Summary of Data on Education...Culture and Communication* (annual).

Educational statistics for most countries of the world will be found in the volumes of the *International Year Book of Education* (see p.28) published by Unesco from 1948-69 and from 1980 onwards. Many less recent educational statistics are included in the five volumes of the *World Survey of Education* (see p.55) also published by Unesco.

The United Nations compiles a handy annual containing basic international statistics:

***World Statistics in Brief: United Nations Statistical Pocket Book.* UN: HMSO, annual.**
It has 'standard data for individual countries...and there is a section on education...An insert contains selected statistics for the major regions and the world as a whole'. The UN also publishes a *Monthly Bulletin of Statistics*.

More specifically for European countries we have:

***Basic Statistics of the Community: Comparison with Some European Countries, Canada, the USA. Japan and the USSR.* Latest edn. Eurostat: Statistical Office of the European Communities.**
This includes statistics on education and training with the numbers of pupils and students in full-time education.

There is a volume which covers almost two decades of educational statistics in member countries of the Community:

***Development of Higher Education 1950–1967.* Organisation for European Economic Co-operation (OEEC), 1970.**
This provides, in addition to the statistical tables, short notes on the development of education in each country. The main statistical categories covered are: enrolments, new entrants, and degrees awarded.

Valuable statistical information for vocational education in the Community is contained in the CEDEFOP publication: *Vocational Training Systems in the Member States of the European Community* (see p.55).
The OECD (Organisation for Economic Cooperation and Development) formerly issued an *Educational Statistics Year Book* (2 vols. 1: International tables. 2: Country tables). They were intended for use in the comparative study of educational systems but they have not been published since 1975. There is a retrospective survey from the same source: *Educational Trends in the 1970s: Quantitative Analysis* (OECD, 1984).
Current statistics for member countries

of the OECD will be found in:

***Educational Statistics in OECD Countries.* Latest edn. OECD.**
The *Reviews of National Policies for Education* series, also published by the OECD, contain relevant statistics for individual countries.

A convenient summary of American educational statistics will be found in the standard handbook:

***Statistical Abstract of the United States.* US Bureau of the Census: USA, annual.**
The section on education 'presents data primarily concerning formal education as a whole, at various levels, and for public and private schools. Types of data shown relate to the school-age population and enrolment, educational attainment, education personnel, and financial aspects of education'. The emphasis is on national data but there are tables on regions and individual states. An appendix: Guide to Sources of Statistics, contains detailed references to the primary sources of statistical information in the US under subjects including education.

For specifically educational statistics in the US there is the:

***Digest of Education Statistics.* National Center for Education Statistics: USA, annual.**
It provides summary data on pupils and staff, finances and organisation at elementary, secondary and higher education levels. Projections of enrolment, graduates, teachers, and expenditure appear in the twice-yearly *Projections of Education Statistics* from the same source. A related publication, *The Condition of Education*, provides an annual overview of trends and current issues.

Those requiring a more detailed statistical analysis of American higher education would find the undernoted work of some help though not for recent information:

Harris, S.E. *A Statistical Portrait of Higher Education.* McGraw-Hill: USA, 1972.
A 1,000-page volume prepared for the Carnegie Commission on Higher Education.

No effort can be made here to indicate all the possible sources for national and international educational statistics. Reference should be made to the following publications which may be available in the larger academic and public reference libraries:

Bibliography of Official Statistical Yearbooks and Bulletins, ed. G. Westfall. **Chadwyck-Healey, 1986.**

Directory of International Statistics. **Latest edn. United Nations Statistical Office.**

Subject Guide to Sources of Comparative International Statistics (SISCIS). **Latest edn. CBD Research Ltd.**

Statistics Sources: a Subject Guide to Data on Industrial, Business, Social, Educational, Financial and Other Topics for the United States and Internationally. **Latest edn. Gale Research Co: USA.**
Statistics Europe: Sources for Social, Economic and Market Research. **Latest edn. CBD Research Co.**

There are similar volumes for Africa, America, Asia, and Australia. All are edited by Joan Harvey.

There is a *European Directory of Non-official Statistical Sources*: (ed. D. Mort, Euromonitor Publications, 1988), but its cost will keep it out of all but the largest libraries.

More specifically for education we have:

HAMILTON, M.C. *Directory of Educational Statistics: a Guide to Sources*. **Pierian Press: USA, 1974.**

Note the date. This handbook is concerned with sources for comparatively recent and also historical statistics going back to 1870. Official statistics are included. Entries are by broad categories, e.g. general surveys and summaries; international education; education in Great Britain.

16 Biographical Sources [   ]

The biographical approach to education provides human interest. The quickest way to find out if your library has a full-length book on a particular educationist is to check the subject index or name index at the main library catalogue under the person's name.

If you are looking for a short biography of someone, you could start with the general or subject encyclopaedias (16.1). You could also consult the general biographical dictionaries (which are many) or the biographical dictionaries of educationists (which are few) (16.2). If you require basic information about living persons you will turn to publications of the *Who's Who* type (16.3). Indexes to sources of biographical material generally are described in 16.4. Some idea of the great wealth of biographical resources now available may be obtained from:

Biographical Sources: a Guide to Dictionaries and Reference Works: ed. D.J. Cimbala *et al.* Oryx Press: USA, 1986.

16.1 Biographies in encyclopaedias

The major general encyclopaedias usually have a substantial number of biographical entries. For example the excellent *Colliers Encyclopedia* (USA) (see p.21) has some good articles on people important in the history of education, e.g. Joseph Lancaster. You should check both the main body of the encyclopaedia and the very detailed index (for other references) in each case. Note that most of the biographical articles in the *New Encyclopaedia Britannica* (see p.21) have now been transferred from the Macropaedia to the Micropaedia. Encylopaedia year books (see 10.1) usually have brief biographies of people who have been prominent (or have died) during the year.

More specifically, the *Encyclopedia of Edu-* *cation* (USA) (see p.23) and some of the other educational encyclopaedias described in 9.2 should be examined for biographical material. Do not forget the smaller one-volume encyclopaedias and dictionaries for brief information which may be adequate for your purpose. If not they may provide pointers to fuller information elsewhere. It could also be worth checking encyclopaedias on subjects related to education.

16.2 Biographical dictionaries

Biographical dictionaries may be national or international, and include people from past or present or both. Some of the best known ones are devoted to people no longer living, and this must be remembered when deciding which ones to consult.

This section describes the most familiar and/or readily available biographical dictionaries, starting with British examples, adding some which are international in scope and several which are restricted to Americans, and concluding with dictionaries of educationists. The latter are few in number if we exclude works of the *Who's Who* type (see 16.3). This is why the more general biographical dictionaries feature so prominently in this section.

The most famous of all biographical dictionaries is British and it must be given pride of place here because of its continuing usefulness for the serious researcher, the student and the general reader:

Dictionary of National Biography: from the Earliest Times to 1900; eds L. Stephen and S. Lee. OUP, re-issue, 1908–9. 22 vols. Supplementary vols (various editors) cover the years 1901–11; 1912–21; 1922–30; 1931–40; 1941–50; 1961–70; 1971–80; 1981–85, with an index to biographies 1901–85.

The Dictionary of National Biography (DNB) originally published in 63 volumes from 1885–1901, is almost a national institution. It includes people of British origin no longer living who have distinguished themselves in all fields, including education. The main work finished at 1900 and the supplements cover approximately ten-year periods, except for the latest volume (published in 1990) which starts a five-year sequence. Articles are authoritative, readable, and often lengthy, and many in more recent times are written from personal knowledge of the subject. There are lists of references at the end of each article. Undoubtedly the DNB is the richest source of biographical information that we have.

Note that there is also a *Concise Dictionary of National Biography* (OUP, 2 vols, 1: From the beginnings to 1900, 2nd edn 1906; 2: 1901–1970, 1982), which acts as a useful index to the main work. *A Chronological and Occupational Index to the DNB* is in preparation. This will help anyone who whishes to make a study of educationists during particular periods.

There is another invaluable work which overlaps the later volumes of the DNB:

Obituaries from The Times, compiled by F.C. Roberts. Newspaper Archive Developments, in progress, 1975—.
Vol.1: 1961–1970, (1975)
Vol.2: 1971–1975, (1978)
Vol.3: 1951–1960, (1979)
Note the sequence in which the volumes appeared. This is obviously an excellent source for biographical information about major figures, and some who were not so prominent, in the second half of the twentieth century. Unlike the DNB, it is not confined to people of British origin. However, it is included here because its main use will be in conjunction with the DNB for British subjects. The articles, which are notably readable, have not been rewritten for publication so that they are a good reflection of contemporary opinion. Although the obituaries have been specially selected, there is a full index in each volume to all obituaries published in *The Times* during the period. It is to be hoped that later and possibly earlier coverage will be achieved.

Obituaries from The Times complements the later volumes of the DNB. A remarkable new work is in progress to supplement the earlier volumes:

British Biographical Archive. K.G. Saur: West Germany, in progress. (Microfiche)

This claims to be 'the largest and most wide-ranging biographical dictionary of British historical personages ever to be made available...Over 15,000 biographies in the BBA do not appear in the DNB: either the persons were not illustrious enough or not thought appropriate for inclusion'. It is 'a one-alphabet cumulation of about 300 of the most important English language biographical reference works originally published between 1901 and 1929'. There is an *American Biographical Archive*, also on microfiche, from the same publisher (see p.98). Another massive microfiche enterprise is *British and Irish Biographies 1840–1940* (Chadwyck-Healey, in progress).

There are two smaller scale biographical dictionaries or British subjects aimed at a wider readership. The first is concerned with people no longer living who have been prominent during this century:

OXBURY, H. *Great Britons: Twentieth Century Lives*. OUP, 1985.
This records the lives of over 600 men and women who died between 1915 and 1980. The entries which are of reasonable length are always interesting. Unusually for a work of this kind it contains photographs, cartoons and drawings to evoke the 20th century background. There is an index which makes it easy to track down the key figures in any particular field, but the heading Education yields only a dozen, e.g. Cyril Burt and H.A.L. Fisher – a disappointing haul.

The second is devoted exclusively to women, and is retrospective:

Europa Biographical Dictionary of British Women: Over 1,000 Notable Women from Britain's Past, ed. A. Crawford *et al*. Europa, 1983.
This spans 1,900 years of British life from Boadicea to the present. It includes 'women whose place in history is recognised and who are therefore to some extent established names. For the rest, the bias has been towards women whose work has had some sort of public impact.' The range is wide and there is much interesting information not readily available elsewhere. Unfortunately it lacks a subject index. (See also the *Macmillan Dictionary of Women's Biography* on p.97)

The largest of the general biographical dictionaries, i.e. those which are international in scope, is a multi-volume American work:

*McGraw–Hill Encyclopedia of World
Biography*, ed. D.I. Eggenberger McGraw-
Hill: USA, 1973. 12 vols.
> This provides reliable short biographies of people
> from all periods for students at school and college
> level. It is attractively produced with an index
> listing biographees under subjects, e.g. education.
> Wherever possible portraits have been added to the
> entries. There are references for further reading.

The largest of the one-volume biographical dictionaries is:

Webster's Biographical Dictionary, ed. W.A.
Neilson, Merriam: USA, 1980.
> More than 40,000 concise biographies, both
> historical and contemporary, are included.
> American and British subjects are given fuller
> treatment than others.

The standard one-volume British work is:

Chambers Biographical Dictionary, ed. J.O.
Thorne and T.C. Collocott. Revised edn.
Chambers, 1984.
> The entries in this familiar and well-used work are
> concise, but it is an excellent source for basic
> information, not least about Scots. Details of over
> 15,000 people are included. The editors have
> adopted a policy of 'clothing bare facts with human
> interest and critical observation...We have not been
> as extravagant as Curle, whose biographies were
> said by Arbuthnot to have added a new terror to
> death, nor have we sought to emulate the pious
> eulogies which prompted Carlyle to write: "How
> delicate, how decent is English biography, bless its
> mealy mouth"'.

Chambers is ideal for ready reference, or
for occasional browsing. A similar but less
well-established work is the:

Macmillan Dictionary of Biography, eds B.
Jones and M.V. Dixon. 3rd edn. Macmillan,
1989.
> There is no introduction to explain its principles of
> compilation but it is clearly aimed at the general
> reader. Some entries have the briefest of references
> for further reading. Note also the:

*International Dictionary of 20th Century
Biography*, ed. E. Vernoff and R. Shore.
Sidgwick & Jackson, 1987.
> Concise biographies of notable modern men and
> women who have made their mark in almost every

field of human endeavour, including education (e.g.
John Dewey). The selection is broadly based and
representative of the movements and trends of the
20th century.

*Longman Dictionary of 20th Century
Biography*, eds A.Isaacs and E.Martin.
Longman, 1985.
> This is aimed at a popular audience. Its object is to
> provide, in a compact and readable form, a brief
> outline of the lives of twentieth century men and
> women who have had an impact, either directly or
> indirectly, on our lives.

Macmillan Dictionary of Women's Biography,
compiled and edited by J.S.Uglow. 2nd edn.
Macmillan, 1989.
> Contains essential details of women from all
> periods and cultures with an emphasis on the
> British Isles, North America, the Commonwealth
> and Europe. Most entries contain a reference to an
> autobiography or a serious biographical study.
> There is a helpful introductory section of additional
> reference sources for those who are seeking further
> information about women in particular countries or
> specific subject fields. (Note also the *Dictionary of
> British Women Writers*. Routledge, 1989.)

Worthy of notice here are two splendid
volumes which include a wide range of
'critical biographies' of people who have
made significant contributions to, or been
prominent in society during the last two
centuries. The articles differ from those in
most other biographical dictionaries since
they are more concerned with people's
ideas than with the details of their lives:

Makers of Modern Culture, ed. J.Wintle.
Routledge, 1981.
> This volume concentrates on 'those figures who
> have done most to shape our views and sensibilities
> in the period since 1914 – from Freud to R.D.Laing,
> from Proust to Garcia Marquez, from Picasso to
> Warhol, from Chaplin to Godard, from Debussy to
> Stockhausen, from Shaw to Pinter, from
> Wittgenstein to Popper, from Durkheim to
> McLuhan, from Yeats to Ginsburg, from Wells to
> Castaneda' and one might add, from Walt Disney to
> the Beatles. It is unique in its coverage of con-
> temporary ideas, with many temptations for the
> regular browser. It was the first of a projected series
> designed to extend coverage retrospectively.

*Makers of Nineteenth Century Culture.
1800–1914*, ed. J.Wintle. Routledge, 1982.

Again, this provides 'critical examination of the works of leading novelists, poets, dramatists, artists, philosophers, social thinkers, mathematicians and scientists of the period' as well as statesmen, historians and so on. The entries are just as concisely written and readable.

In both volumes, there are sensible brief references for further reading. Each index contains entries for all the persons who have been, or will be, included in the other volumes in the series. The indexes also have 'thematic references' to help the reader to explore the key ideas and movements during the period covered. If the series is ever completed it will form one of the most rewarding world biographical surveys available. (See also the *Dictionary of Biographical Quotation of British and American Subjects* on p.104, which is the ideal companion volume).

There is a book with a similar purpose, on a more modest scale:

Fontana Dictionary of Modern Thinkers, eds A. Bullock and R.B. Woodings. Fontana, 1989.
This is a new edition of the *Fontana Biographical Companion to Modern Thought* (1983). A bulky paperback which supplies the biographical entries missing from the *Fontana Dictionary of Modern Thought* (see p.17). Coverage is from 1900 to the present day. As the editors say: 'Few people could identify more than a few hundred out of the nearly 2,000 names in this book' but they may come across references to any of them and wish to obtain further information. Readers will be helped by the brief notes on additional sources at the end of each entry. The classified index makes it possible to identify figures prominent in particular fields, e.g. education, psychology, sociology.

For people of American origin, there are two standard works, either or both of which should be found in medium-sized reference collections:

Concise Dictionary of American Biography, ed. J.G.E. Hopkins. Scribner and OUP: USA, 1964.
This is a one-volume abridgement of the parent work, which will be available only in larger libraries. It does not include people who have died since 1940. Every biography in the original DAB is summarised, but some of the entries are very brief. Note the date.

Webster's American Biographies, eds C. Van Doren and R. McHenry. Merriam: USA, 1974.

This is designed for 'anyone looking for background information on significant Americans, living or dead...It presents a concise and authoritative reference collection of prominent men and women from all periods and all walks of American life'. The entries average about 300 words. There is a careers and professions index and a geographical index. Note the date.

Also worth noting, for those who have access to it, is the counterpart of the *British Biographical Archive* (see p.96), from the same publisher:

American Biographical Archive. K.G. Saur: USA, in progress. (Microfiche).
This is a cumulation of almost 400 biographical reference works. 'It will contain entries covering 250,000 individuals from the earliest inhabitants and settlers through to personages of the early 20th century.' French and German biographical archives are also in progress.

The emphasis in this section so far has necessarily been on general biographical dictionaries, national and international. There is a serious lack of biographical dictionaries devoted entirely to educationists. The only general British one is quite recent:

Dictionary of British Educationists, eds R. Aldrich and P. Gordon. Woburn Press, 1989.
It gives accounts of the lives and work of 450 British educationists no longer living who were born after 1800. There are more names from the nineteenth century than from the twentieth. The emphasis is on practice rather than theory. Politicians and educational administrators are included, and there are many lesser known figures. 'Entries contain information on their careers and their most important writings as well as other references culled from a wide range of sources'. There is also a guide to the literature of educational biography. It must be welcomed as the first British biographical dictionary (as opposed to biographical directory: see 16.3) devoted to educationists generally.

There is another British work which is more specialised but international in scope:

International Biography of Adult Education, eds. J.E. Thomas and B. Elsey, Dept. of Adult Education, University of Nottingham, 1985.

This was published with the help of funding from the MSC and UNESCO. It is 'a worldwide collection of biographies of people who have played a significant part in the development of adult education, in all its diverse forms'. Certain countries in the Third World are not represented for reasons given in the introduction. Only persons no longer living are included but the net is cast widely, e.g. Dickens and Samuel Smiles as well as Mansbridge. There are bibliographical references, sometimes in the text, sometimes at the ends of chapters. The introduction outlines 'lessons to be learned about adult education from reading the biographies.' There is a thematic index which lists the biographies under subjects (e.g. science education) and under countries. Similar works dealing with other areas are very much needed.

Only one American example can be given here:

Biographical Dictionary of American Educators, ed. J.F. Ohles. Greenwood Press: USA, 1978.
It gives signed sketches of people prominent in American education from the seventeenth century to the present. It includes living persons, but only those who were over sixty in 1975! Entries for the earlier periods are generally shorter. 'A special effort was made to include women and minority groups in the compilation.' There are references for further reading. Note the date.

Accounts of figures important in the history of education will be found in several of the works mentioned in 17.2, e.g. Bantock G.H. (see p.105) and Stewart, W.A.C. (see p.105).

Since so many of the biographical sources described in this section are concerned with the distinguished or the famous, it is refreshing to come across a book which helps to redress the balance by recording, albeit briefly, the lives and contributions of people who were little known or even unheard of:

BURNETT, J. Destiny Obscure: Autobiographies of Childhood, Education and the Family from the 1820s to the 1920s. Allen Lane, 1982.
This is an absorbing piece of educational history and affords many insights. 'It is based on an analysis of more than 800 autobiographies written by men and women born in the 19th and early 20th centuries. Most come from working people who had little formal education...Almost all are previously unpublished and came in response to appeals on radio and in the press for original material.' Sections include: Childhood; Education; Home and family, and each has a lengthy introduction.

16.3 Current biographical sources

It is often more difficult to find reliable accounts of living people than to learn about those from the past. There is one key source which must be mentioned first:

Current Biography. 11 per annum, with annual cumulation. H.W. Wilson: USA.
Each monthly issue has 16–18 several-page biographies of people in all walks of life including education. The articles are intended for the general reader and are written in a lively way. A recent portrait is usually included as well as references for further reading. The emphasis is on people well-known in America, but this is still the handiest source for short biographical sketches of those who have distinguished themselves in the contemporary world.
   The monthly issues are eventually gathered together in a handsome *Current Biography Yearbook*. Each yearbook has a cumulated index to all the articles for the last decade. Both the monthly issues and the yearbooks record the obituaries of persons previously profiled. There is also a *Current Biography Cumulative Index 1950–1985*, an invaluable guide to almost half a century of biographies.

The only comparable biographies of present-day people are the obituaries which appear in the national daily newspapers. A selection from those in *The Times* are eventually incorporated in the volumes of *Obituaries from The Times* (see p.96). The later volumes of the DNB (see p.95) are another excellent source.

If you simply require brief personal details of living persons, there are publications (see below) similar to the universally known *Who's Who* (A. & C. Black, annual), which is itself very useful for information on distinguished people connected with education. Do not forget the series *Who Was Who* for retrospective coverage from 1897.

There is now a contemporary biographical dictionary of prominent Scots:

Who's Who in Scotland. Carrick, 2-yearly
Despite its title this has no connection with *Who's Who* above. It has concise entries on about 5,000 people from all walks of life, and education is well represented. There are entries for principals of colleges and for HM Chief Inspectors for example. Most of the biographical details are supplied by the entrants themselves. Names are removed on death or retirement and new ones added. First published in 1986.

Although the coverage of *Who's Who* is not entirely limited to British figures, there are other works of this kind which are wider in scope:

International Who's Who. Europa Publications, annual
This aims 'to provide comprehensive information...on men and women who have achieved international prominence'. Entries include personal and career details with lists of publications where appropriate. The one on H.J.Eysenck, for example, consists largely of bibliographical references to his published works.

Writers Directory. Macmillan, 2-yearly.
This also provides international coverage. Entries are based on the authors' own information, and detailed bibliographies are included. There is an index of 'writing categories', e.g. under 'Education' there is a list of more than 800 writers (excluding writers of school textbooks).

There are several biographical directories of this type which are devoted to educationists and teachers:

Schools' and Colleges' Who's Who. 2nd edn. Carrick, 1990.
First published as the *Schools' Who's Who* in 1987. It 'provides a guide to key figures in secondary schools, colleges and polytechnics, and local authority education departments throughout the UK'. Professional and personal details are supplied by the persons included. There is a section for chief education officers.

Universities' Who's Who. Carrick, 1988.
Provides brief personal, professional and career information on several thousand senior staff in UK universities. There are three sections: on England and Wales, Scotland, and Northern Ireland. 'About 73% of all professors replied to the questionnaires.' There are entries for those who retired during the book's preparation.

A useful *Who's Who of Commonwealth University Vice-Chancellors, Presidents and Rectors* was issued by the Association of Commonwealth Universities for the first time in 1988.

International Who's Who in Education. 3rd edn. Melrose Press, 1987.
This is now the standard British list. The first edition appeared under the title *Who's Who in Education* in 1974. It included brief biographical details of men and women who formed part of, or were associated with, the teaching profession. Most of them were at work in the UK, but many distinguished representatives from the Commonwealth were represented. The second edition in 1981 widened the scope to include teachers, academics and administrators worldwide especially in the USA and Canada. The new title of the third edition reflects the continued change in emphasis, and illustrations are included for the first time.

There is an older British list which could still be useful:

Academic Who's Who: University Teachers in the British Isles in the Arts, Education and the Social Sciences, A.&C. Black, 1975.
Note the date. This was confined to university teachers of the rank of senior lecturer or above, or to those who had taught for five years as lecturer or assistant lecturer. Minimum essential personal, career and publication details are included, and there is a long preliminary list of abbreviations used.

Details of American educationists can be found in several biographical directories which are reasonably well known in this country:

Directory of American Scholars. Latest edn. Bowker: USA. 4 vols.
This provides concise factual biographies of American and Canadian scholars in the humanities. Each volume covers scholars in one subject area with cross references from one volume to another. Volume 4 contains a complete alphabetical index of names and a geographical index. The directory is revised every five years or so.

Leaders in Education: a Biographical Directory. **Latest edn. Bowker: USA.**
Brief biographical sketches of 'key' figures in American and Canadian education. Many educational administrators are included. There is a 'specialty' index which identifies those with particular subject interests (e.g. early childhood education) and a geographical index.

National Faculty Directory. **Gale Research Co.: USA, annual.**
An alphabetical list of teachers in universities, colleges and junior colleges in the USA and Canada. Only brief details are given.

Finally there is a volume devoted to women in contemporary education:

World Who's Who of Women in Education, **ed. E.Kay. International Biographical Centre, 1978.**
Note the date. It gives typical directory-type information but there is no introduction to explain the principles of selection or coverage. It must be accepted as it is, and it has the field to itself. However, a much more current publication: the *World Who's Who of Women* (Latest edn, Melrose Press) includes academics. The tenth edition appeared in 1990.

16.4 Indexes to biographical material

Indexes to biographical material do not themselves contain biographical articles but they provide pointers to where biographical articles can be found. If you would like to keep track of biographical material appearing in recent publications, a good source is the American:

Biography Index. **4 per annum, with annual and 3-yearly cumulations. H.W. Wilson: USA.**
It is an index to biographical items appearing in over 2,600 periodicals, and to books of biography in the English language. It is arranged alphabetically by biographee, but there is an index of persons by profession or occupation, e.g. education. A checklist of books analysed is included. The volumes go back to 1946.

There is a whole range of H.W.Wilson indexes (see 22.1) which may be worth checking for biographical information. Since they have all been appearing for many years, their value for retrospective searching is obvious.

There is no British equivalent of the *Biography Index*. However, the *British Humanities Index* (see p.155) which regularly indexes the contents of British periodicals of general interest can be used to locate biographical articles. So can *The Times Index* (see p.155) which indexes not only *The Times* but also its educational and literary supplements, and the *Sunday Times* and its magazine.

Biographical articles in educational periodicals can be traced by using the the the subject indexes to periodicals described in 22.2, e.g. the *British Education Index*, the *Education Index* (USA) and the *Current Index to Journals in Education (CIJE)* (USA). Note that all three index books as well as periodical articles.

A valuable addition to the resources for tracing biographical material is the:

BRITISH LIBRARY. *Bibliography of Biography*. **1986. (Microfiche)**
It lists over 90,000 biographical works published between 1970 and 1984 in Britain and elsewhere. Based on bibliographical records created by the British Library and the Library of Congress it takes the form of a name sequence and an author/title index.

There is a similar American publication in printed form:

Biographical Books 1950–1980. **Bowker: USA, 1980.**
A second volume covers an earlier period: 1876–1949. Both volumes have author, title, vocation, and name/subject indexes.

The massive *International Bibliography of Biography 1970–1987*. (K.G.Saur: USA, 1988 12 vols. lists over 100,000 biographies and autobiographies published worldwide.

There is a handy list of biographies (either individual or collective) of British educationists of the nineteenth century:

CHRISTOPHERS, A. *An Index to Nineteenth Century British Educational Biography.* **London University Institute of Education Library, 1965.**

This short book filled a gap when it appeared. It includes persons who were 'active in education as teachers, reformers, or organisers'. They are mainly, but not entirely, of British origin. As the compiler admits, 'a slight bias in favour of women may be detected'. References are to books only, not to periodical articles, with no foreign language material. The relevant entries in the DNB were used as a starting point. There are two parts:(1) Collective biography; (2) Individual biography, and a subject index. Note also:

LOWE, R. *Biography and Education: Some Eighteenth and Nineteenth Century Studies.* **History of Education Society, 1980.**

The author suggests that 'the time may have come for some reappraisal of biographical approaches to the study of education'. There are short chapters on selected educationists of whom Joseph Lancaster is the best known. A useful feature is the concluding select bibliography: Autobiography as a source for the educational historian, by T. Gammage. (See also the article by T.Cook in the *History of Education Society Bulletin*, no. 20, Autumn 1977, pp.46–52

Mention should be made here of the invaluable book by Matthews, W. *British Autobiographies: an Annotated Bibliography of British Autobiographies Published before 1951.* California University Press, 1955, on which Gammage's bibliography is partly based.

Finally, anyone who happens to be searching for biographies, autobiographies, memoirs, diaries, etc. of educationists from the nineteenth century and earlier should not overlook that remarkable resource: *The New Cambridge Bibliography of English Literature.* Cambridge University Press, 1972–78. Each of the first four volumes contains a chapter on education which is a mine of information. Volume 5 is the index.

17   Books of quotations; extracts; course readers

s it says in the introduction to the *Oxford Dictionary of Quotations* (see below): 'Quotations tell us of the inward thoughts of men and women...they can speak to us in ways that inspire, inform, comfort and entertain'. Books of quotations are libraries in miniature. Their compilers select the most significant observations, written or spoken, from past or present and organise them so that any one of them can be quickly retrieved, although imperfectly remembered.

To some extent the same can be said of collections of more extended extracts from writers past or present who have had something important to say on different aspects of education. Some of these collections are designed to illustrate the history of education, educational theory, or educational development. The extracts are usually placed in context so that the reader can develop a useful perspective for further study. More commonly, collections of extracts focus on a contemporary topic or theme, drawing from a range of recent books and periodical articles by specialists in the field concerned.

The Open University in particular has adopted a definite policy of producing anthologies of this kind in support of its courses on education. The have been invaluable time-savers not only to OU students but also to many taking education courses at other institutions.

The first section (17.1) describes some standard works which may be used to track down a specific quotation or to locate an appropriate quotation for a particular purpose. Although they are general works they contain many quotations which relate to education. The next section (17.2) describes some collections of longer extracts on different aspects of education. The final section (17.3) provides an extensive list of Open University course readers, any of which could be of interest to users of this guide.

17.1   Books of quotations

The quotations in most of the books desribed here are listed under authors' names, and those which are arranged by subject (in many ways a more useful arrangement) have author indexes. As already indicated they are all general books of quotations, although a few are limited by period. Two unusual but interesting compilations have been included at the end: a dictionary of biographical quotations, and an anthology of 'Western thought'.

The three best known books of quotations are all arranged differently:

***Stevenson's Book of Quotations.* 10th edn. Cassell, 1974.**
> The largest and best book of quotations for the general reader, though not the most recent. Its 70,000 entries arranged under topics, e.g. education, and teaching, make it ideal for browsing or for retrieving appropriate quotations. The very full concordance enables the reader to locate dimly remembered lines or phrases with minimum effort. There is an author index.

***Oxford Dictionary of Quotations.* 3rd edn. OUP, 1979.**
> First published ln 1941, with a second edition in 1978, this standard work was thoroughly revised and updated to meet present day needs in 1979. 'Every generation, every decade perhaps, needs its new dictionary of quotations.' About 18,000 are arranged under authors alphabetically with a full concordance. The previous editions have not been superseded and should be consulted for earlier quotations omitted from this one.

BARTLETT, J. *Familiar Quotations: a Collection of Passages, Phrases and Proverbs Traced to their Sources in Ancient and Modern Literature.* **15th edn. Macmillan, 1980.**

The fifteenth was the 125th anniversary edition of the longest established of the works described here. Over 20,000 quotations are arranged by author chronologically with an enlarged author index and the usual concordance.

The following books may be useful as additional sources:

International Thesaurus of Quotations; **compiled by R.T. Tripp. Penguin, 1970.**
A plump paperback with 16,000 quotations arranged by meaning rather than by author or key words. They have been selected 'for relevance to today's world'. There is an index of key words, and another of categories with cross-references, e.g. under 'Education' there are references to learning, scholars and scholarship, teacher training, etc. First published in the USA.

Penguin Dictionary of Quotations; **compiled by J.M.and M.J.Cohen. Penguin, 1977.**
Originally published in 1962, this paperback contains about 12,000 quotations arranged under authors (mainly European) from A–Z with an adequate concordance.

Penguin Dictionary of Modern Quotations; **compiled by J.M.and M.J.Cohen. 2nd edn., Penguin, 1980.**
'It is not only the great who make the best remarks.' This book of mainly English quotations (about 7,000 altogether) was designed as a supplement to the previous work. It is arranged in the same way.

Dictionary of Contemporary Quotations; **compiled by J.Green. David & Charles, 1982.**
This is the most current of these books of quotations. Over 7,000 are listed, the majority dating from 1945 onwards. 'Mass culture has become the dominant culture' and 'snappy one-liners have been preferred to the traditional deathless quotations embodied, one might say entombed, in the more venerable collections'. A stimulating anthology with an unusual choice of quotations. The arrangement is by topics, with an index of persons quoted.

The final two works are different in intention from those already described but may yield up items of interest to users of this guide:

Dictionary of Biographical Quotation of British and American Subjects; **eds J.Wintle and R.Kenin. Routledge; 1978.**
The ideal companion volume to the two biographical dictionaries *Makers of Modern Culture* (see p.90). and *Makers of Nineteenth Century Culture* (see p.90) It is a lively and intelligent compilation which contains quotations by and about 'those people whose contributions to British and American culture, in all walks of life, have over the years attracted most attention'. The material has been drawn 'not only from the standard lives, biographies and biographical collections, but also from anecdotes, epigrams, epitaphs, eulogies, obituaries, reminiscences, memoirs, reviews, essays critical works, letters, diaries, volumes of poetry, verse, ballads and songs, pamphlets, tracts, broadsheets, newspapers, broadcasts, institution reports, chronicles, histories, as well as from entendus, slogans, graffiti, and at least one horoscope!'. This list would serve admirably as an indicator of possible sources for biographical information in general.

Great Treasury of Western Thought: a Compendium of Important Statements on Man and His Institutions by the Great Thinkers in Western History; **eds M.J.Adler and C.Van Doren. Bowker: USA, 1977.**
The quotations in this unusual volume are longer than those in any of the preceding works. Despite its pretentious title, it is worth more than a casual investigation. In 1700 closely printed pages it includes memorable passages by distinguished authors from biblical to modern times. The arrangement is by themes. Chapter 8 is concerned with Education: its ends and means; and Teaching and learning. It is closely related to other chapters. e.g. (1) Man; (5) Mind; (6) Knowledge; (7) Language; (9) Ethics; and (10) Art, Asethetics. The high seriousness of this 'treasury' may be a little unfashionable nowadays, but it is an invaluable sourcebook.

17.2 Extracts from writers on education

Unlike the Open University readers listed in the next section the anthologies of extracts described here are not related to particular courses. However, this short lection may be helpful to students of ducation generally. It begins with llections of educational 'classics':

ASKIN, W. *Classics in Education*, **Vision Press, 966.**
> Contains extracts from more educationists and incidentally more Americans than Ulich, R. (below). There is a short biographical introduction to each extract and an attempt is made to place it in the context of the writer's work as a whole. The arrangement is alphabetical by author.

LICH, R. *3000 years of Educational Wisdom: elections from Great Documents*. **2nd edn. arvard University Press: USA, 1954.**
> Another book of extracts with brief introductions to the great educational thinkers from Confucius to Dewey. The arrangement in this case is broadly chronological.

ERSEY, S.N. *Classics in the Education of Girls nd Women*. **Scarecrow Press: USA, 1981.**
> 'Classic' is defined as 'of enduring interest, quality or style' and there is nothing at all from the twentieth century. There are brief introductions to each section starting with Ancient Greece.

ILPATRICK, W.H. *Source Book in the hilosophy of Education*. **Macmillan Co: USA, 924.**
> Note the date. An older collection of short extracts arranged by broad topics, e.g. the individual and society, socialisation, and moral education. There is an index of subjects and of authors who range from Ecclesiastes to Dewey.

A work with rather a different purpose is:

RICHMOND, W.K. *Readings in Education: a equence*. **Methuen, 1968.**
> There are thirteen sections, each designed as a study unit, covering most of the topics usually dealt with in courses for teachers. The extracts are drawn from official reports, research findings, contemporary theory, and writers from Plato to McLuhan. This is not simply an anthology with a few questions thrown in to test comprehension, but a serious attempt to help students and others to make value judgments. Unfortunately it has not been updated.

Those who would like a deeper historical erspective could profitably turn to a two-olume work which, though not strictly peaking a collection of extracts, sheds nuch light on some of the educationists

whose writings appear in the books already mentioned:

BANTOCK, G.H. *Studies in the History of Educational Theory*. **Allen & Unwin, 1980-84. 2 vols.**
Vol.1: Artifice and nature: 1350–1765. 1980
Vol.2: The minds and the masses 1760–1890. 1984
> A wide-ranging survey of historical figures from Erasmus onwards who have written about education. It aims to relate their lives to the cultural and intellectual history of their times. Vol.1 includes Erasmus, Vives, Castiglioni, Elyot, Montaigne, Bacon, Comenius, Locke and Rousseau who in the words of the author 'forms both an end and a beginning'. Vol.2 includes Rousseau, Froebel, Coleridge, Owen, Herbart, Bentham, Arnold, Marx, Nietsche and Tolstoy, with a final chapter on Dewey, Lawrence, and Eliot. There are helpful brief biographies of the main educational theorists, and an extensive bibliography and index, in each volume.

There are other useful surveys of this kind:

STEWART, W.A.C. *Progressives and Radicals in English Education 1750–1970*. **Macmillan, 1972.**
> This is 'a substantial rewriting and necessary up-dating' of *The Educational Innovators*, (1967–8, 2 vols). It is a study of progressive education in England and Wales based on the achievements of notable educators. For example there are chapters on Rousseau, Robert Owen, Pestalozzi, Kaye-Shuttleworth, Samuel Widderspoon, A.S. Neill, the Russells, Kurt Hahn and Rudolf Steiner.

Twentieth Century Thinkers on Adult Education; ed. P.Jarvis. **Croom Helm, 1987.**
> Examines the theories of thirteen major thinkers and shows how each has made a contribution to the field of adult education. In a concluding chapter the editor compares them and asks whether the study of adult education constitutes an academic discipline. Only British and American figures of the present century are included. There are useful lists of references.

The Study of Primary Education: a Source Book; compiled by C.Richards *et al.* **Falmer Press, 1985. 3 vols.**

Vol.1: No general title.
Vol.2: The curriculum: a diversity of views and official statements: aims: curriculum issues.

Vol.3: Classroom and teaching studies, roles, and relationships.
Volume 1 is concerned with primary education from a variety of perspectives. Each volume contains a varied selection of extracts from material published between 1926 and 1983, introducing teachers to 'many of the most important theoretical issues that need to be considered by practitioners and decision-makers alike'.

There is an unusual collection, not of writings but of spoken addresses, which has some general interest:

GORDON, P. *The Study of Education: a Collection of Inaugural addresses*. **Woburn Press, 1980–88. 3 vols.**
Vol.1: Early and modern, 1980.
Vol.2: The last decade, 1980.
Vol.3: The changing scene, 1988.
There is a roll-call of the century's distinguished names here from Sir John Adams (1902) onwards. The solitary nineteenth century figure is Professor J.M.D.Meiklejohn, who gave his inaugural address on Scottish education in St.Andrews University in 1876. Many of the themes are still relevant. These addresses will be useful to students and teachers who are interested in the development of educational thought and practice 'seen against a background of changes in society during the period'.

17.3   Open University course readers

The Open University has produced a wide range of 'readers' for its students to use as source books when tackling its education and education-related courses. Readers of this type have become very popular with publishers catering for the education market but few of their anthologies have the immediate relevance of those listed here. One of the earliest OU readers was:

Education in Great Britain and Ireland: a Source Book; **eds R.Bell** *et al.* **Routledge, 1973.**
It is not a reader in the conventional sense since it assembles not only official documents (cf. Maclure,

J.S. on p.42) and academic articles, but also newspaper extracts, radio discussions, political statements and the kind of documentation which 'helps to form public opinion on educational issues'.

The OU course readers and source books have been produced in association with a variety of different publishers over the years and it has not always been easy to identify them. Although the following list may not be complete it should help those who wish to check the existence of a particular title, or to locate one which may be relevant to their needs.

The great majority of the readers listed are directly concerned with education but a few from marginal areas have been included. The arrangement is by titles alphabetically. (Some titles are part of a set and appear under the general title, e.g. *Management in Education*.) Publishers are not given but dates have been added.

Achievement and Inequality in Education. 1983.
Approaches to Post-School Management. 1983.
Approaches to School Management. 1980.
Calling Education to Account. 1982.
Case Studies in Classroom Research. 1986.
Case Studies in Educational Management. 1984.
Challenge and Change in the Curriculum. 1982.
Changing Experience of Women. 1982.
Changing Policies, Changing Teachers. 1987.
Child Abuse. 1978
Children, Language and Literature. 1982.
Classrooms and Staffrooms. 1984.
Cognitive Development in the School Years. 1979.
Controversies in Classroom Research. 1986.
Culture and Power in Educational Organizations. 1988.
Curriculum and Assessment: Some Policy Issues. 1985.
Curriculum Design. 1975.
Curriculum Innovation. 1975.
Decision Making; Approaches and Analysis. 1982.
Decision Making in British Education. 1973.
Decisions, Organizations and Society. **2nd edn,** 1976.

rly Cognitive Development. 1979.
onomics and Education Policy. 1977.
ucation and the State. 2 vols, 1981.
  1: *Schooling and the National Interest.*
  2: *Politics, Patriarchy and Practice.*
ducation for Adults. 2 vols, 1983.
  1: *Adult Learning and Education.*
  2: *Educational Opportunities for Adults.*
lucation, Policy and Society. 1983.
lucation, Structure and Society. 1972.
lucation, Training and Employment. 1985.
lucational Computing. 1987.
lucational Evaluation. 1987.
lucational Worker: a Reader on Teachers'
  work. 1987.
valuating Education: Issues and Methods.
  1987.
mily, School and Society. 1988.
mily, Work and Education. 1980.
ameworks for Teaching. 1988.
dustrialisation and Culture. 1830–1914.1970.
-Service: the Teacher and the School. 1981.
nguage,Communication and Education. 1987.
anagement in Education. 2 vols. 1975.
  1: **Management of Organizations and**
    Individuals
  2: **Some Techniques and Systems.**
ledia, Knowledge and Power. 1987.
ature of Special Education: People, Places and
  Change. 1981.
arents and Teenagers. 1982.
ersonality and Learning. 2 vols, 1975–6.
ersonality, Development and Learning. 1984.

Philosophical Issues in Moral Education and
  Development. 1988.
Planning in the Curriculum. 1982.
Policy Making in Education: the Breakdown of
  Consensus. 1985.
Politics and the Processes of Schooling. 1989.
Popular Culture:Past and Present. 1982.
Popular Television and Film. 1981.
Practice of Special Education. 1981.
Pre-School Child. 1979.
Process of Schooling. 1976.
Race and Gender. 1985.
Readings in Urban Education. 2 vols. 1973.
  1: *Cities, Communities and the Young.*
  2: *Equality and City Schools.*
*Re-thinking Appraisal and Assessment.*1989.
School and Society. 2nd ed. 1977.
School in the Multicultural Society. 1981.
School Technology in Action. 1974.
School, Work and Equality. 1989.
Schooling and Capitalism. 1976.
Social and Educational Research in Action.
  1979.
Society and the Social Sciences. 1981.
Sociological Perspectives. 1971.
Standards, Schooling and Education. 1980.
Understanding School Management. 1987.
Understanding Society. 1970.
Urban Education.3 vols, 1977.
  1: *The City Experience.*
  2: *Schooling in the City.*
  3: *The Political Context.*

Bibliographies

18 Bibliographies

A bibliography is a list of books or other materials which has been arranged in a particular way for a particular purpose. Whatever the subject you are studying you need to know what relevant books and other materials are available, and what the best books on the subject are.

Perhaps the most useful bibliography for most purposes is your library's main catalogue. It will guide you to books which are readily accessible and which have been carefully selected to meet the needs of the library's own readers. However, a bibliography is usually taken to mean a list of books which is not confined to the holdings of any particular library. A good bibliography will act as a signpost to resources which may be avaiable elsewhere and which may be borrowed for you if necessary.

The usefulness of bibliographies will vary according to their scope and treatment and the purpose for which you require them. You may need to consult a national, period, author, subject or trade bibliography. It may be comprehensive, selective, annotated or evaluative, or a combination of these. Perhaps the most useful type is an evaluative one. It is also the rarest.

This chapter is concerned with sources of bibliographies and how to locate them (18.1 and 18.2); how to trace existing books and those which are currently available (18.3); how to identify new books as they are published (18.4); and where to find reliable reviews of new books (18.5). The longest section is devoted to bibliographies on different aspects of education (18.6) and this is followed by one on guides to the literature of education (18.7).

An awareness of sources of information about official publications is also desirable since important material on education often appears in them. They are now so numerous that they are described separately in chapter 19. The same applies to bibliographies of non-book materials are described in chapter 20.

18.1 Sources of bibliographies

Substantial bibliographies are normally separately published works, and even quite short bibliographies may be published as pamphlets. Most of the bibliographies described in this chapter are in book or pamphlet form, but there are other possible sources.

Bibliographies may be found in individual books: at the ends of chapters, at the end of the book, or even at the beginning of the book as a list of sources consulted by the author. Your library's catalogue will usually indicate whether a book contains a bibliography.

Bibliographies may also be found in encyclopaedias either appended to the articles or more rarely, as in *Colliers Encyclopedia* (see p.21), in a separate volume. If you consider the range of subjects covered in a major encyclopaedia it can obviously be a rich quarry for bibliographies, even on minor topics. Unfortunately the bibliographies in encyclopaedias are not always up-to-date.

Periodicals are an excellent and often neglected source of bibliographies on specific topics. If you can find an article on the topic in which you are interested quite often there will be a bibliography, or at least a list of references, at the end.

The Dewey class number for bibliographies is 016, and this is subdivided according to the main classification. For example the class number for education (see p.5) is 370, and bibliographies of education will be shelved at 016.37. Most of the bibliographies which your library has will be in the reference collection but additional copies of the most used ones may be available for loan.

18.2 Bibliographies of bibliography

'Bibliographies of bibliography' are publications which indicate what bibliographies exist, or are being published, on particular subjects. They are not as well used as they might be, since even serious students or researchers may overlook them.

There is a classic in this field which deserves honourable mention:

COLLISON, R.L. *Bibliographies: Subject and National: a Guide to Their Contents, Arrangement and Use.* **Crosby Lockwood, 1968.**
It has long been a standard work but is rather dated now and the section on education is very brief. However, it is still useful for those who wish to understand what bibliographies are all about.

The most celebrated of all works of this kind is the massive:

BESTERMAN, T. *A World Bibliography of Bibliographies.* **4th edn. Societas Bibliographica: USA, 1965–66. 5 vols.**
It lists almost 120,000 separately published bibliographies under subjects. The section on education has been extracted and published separately (see below). Note the date.

The following work was planned as a continuation:

TOOMEY, A.F. *A World Bibliography of Bibliographies 1964–1974.* **Rowman & Littlefield: USA,1977. 2 vols.**
It is based on the holdings of the Library of Congress, and lists 18,000 titles under 6,000 subject headings.

A much more recent work than either of these, which lists bibliographies published this century, is the:

Bulletin of Bibliography 1897–1987: Checklist of Bibliographies; **eds N.C-.Wood and**

P.W.Wood. Meckler: USA, 1989.

There is an invaluable key to the identification of recent bibliographies over the whole range of subjects. It is equally valuable for retrospective coverage:

Bibliographic Index. **2 per annum with annual cumulations. H.W.Wilson: USA.**
This is a subject list of bibliographies appearing in both English and foreign languages, which contain 50 or more references. It includes those published separately as books or pamphlets, and those appearing as parts of books. In addition, about 2,600 periodicals are examined regularly for bibliographical material, so that its scope is very wide.

There are several bibliographies of bibliography in the field of education which should be noted:

BESTERMAN, T. *Education: a Bibliography of Bibliographies.* **Rowman & Littlefield, USA: 1971.**
This was extracted from the parent work: the *World Bibliography of Bibliographies* (see above). Despite its date it is still a basic source.

There is an even earlier American work which you may find in some education libraries:

MONROE, W.S. and SHORES, L. *Bibliographies and Summaries of Education to July 1935: a Catalogue of More than 4,000 Annotated Bibliographies and Summaries Listed under Author and Subject in One Alphabet.* **H.W.Wilson: USA, 1936.**

Many less recent bibliographies will be found in the:

International Guide to Educational Documentation. **Unesco.**
1st edn: 1955–1960. 1963.
2nd edn: 1960–1965. 1971.
These massive compilations attempt to record the bibliographical sources (and much else) which are available for the study of education in the various countries of the world. They are out of date in many respects now, but there is no other publication which has attempted systematic international coverage in this way. Unfortunately there is no index.

Bibliographies on specific aspects of education have been published for many years a periodical which is probably unfamiliar many readers:

ulletin of the International Bureau of ducation. 4 per annun. IBE: Unesco.
From 1927–1970 it was known by its present title, and from 1970-1985 as *Educational Documentation and Information*. Each issue covers a different topic, with a survey of the resources available, including organisations and institutions as well as publications. The scope is international and the bibliographies are compiled from this viewpoint. A full list of them is given in the most recent issue.

When the periodical reverted to its former title with issue 234–5 in 1985, there was a slight change of policy. The thematic bibliographies continued, but with more substantial introductions. Each issue also contained a new section of 'abstracts of recent literature on educational policies in languages difficult to access by scholars in other countries'.

The International Bureau of Education as also produced a brief guide:

urrent Bibliographical Sources in Education. nd edn. IBE: Unesco, 1984.
It describes current bibliographies, subject indexes to periodicals and registers of research under countries alphabetically.

18.3 Books in print

t is useful to be able to identify quickly whether a particular book is in print and currently available. The publications which provide this kind of information are the rade bibliographies, which are more familiar to booksellers and librarians than they are to students and teachers. The British examples described here are general bibliographies but they will have to be used by hose looking for information about books on education. They are all issued by .Whitaker and Sons Ltd. who are better known to most readers as the publishers of *Whitaker's Almanack* (see p.53).

Whitaker's Books in Print. Whitaker, 4 vols, annual.(1) A–D; (2) E–K; (3) L–R; and (4) S–Z. (Formerly British Books in Print)

This lists by author and title in one alphabetical sequence the books which are in print and on sale in this country, with details of publisher and price and other basic information. Since a book's title often reveals the subject, it is to some extent a subject list as well. It is important to realise that WBIP includes many American books which are issued in the UK by American publishers with agencies over here. Volume 1 has a long list of publishers and their addresses although there is a separately published list: *Whitaker's Publishers in the United Kingdom and their Addresses*.

WBIP has been available since 1978 in microfiche form. Each monthly issue is a complete update of the whole work and this gives it an advantage over the printed version. Either or both versions may be available in yor library. WBIP is also the name of a database which is accessible online through *BLAISE-LINE* in the UK and from *Dialog* in America. *Whitaker's Bookbank CD–ROM Service* was introduced in 1988.

Paperbacks in Print: a Reference Catalogue of Paperbacks in Print and on Sale in the United Kingdom. Whitaker.
The extent of the paperback explosion which has been of inestimable benefit to students and teachers and to educational institutions of all kinds, as well as to the general reader, is fully apparent in this work. The earliest edition in 1964 included 5,000 titles, the 1985 edition over 70,000. Since the majority of books recommended to and bought by students are paperbacks nowadays, this is an invaluable resource. Unfortunately, Whitaker has not been updating it regularly.

Sudents and teachers may also be interested in:

Children's Books in Print. Whitaker, annual.
The books are listed under almost a hundred different categories, followed by an author, title and subject index in one alphabetical sequence. In the preliminary pages there is a list of children's book publishers and a separate list of series. There is also a section of information relating to children's books, e.g. organisations, book reviewing periodicals, awards and prizes, etc.

A very welcome addition to Whitaker's series of trade bibliographies is:

Books Now OP. Whitaker, annual.(Microfiche.)
This records details of books published in this country since 1976 which have now now been reported out of print. It is a great time-saver since previously it was not easy to discover if a title listed

in *Whitaker's Books in Print* (see above) was no longer available.

The American counterpart of *Whitaker's Books in Print* is published by Bowker, the American Whitaker. It is even larger, and the arrangement is different:

Books in Print. **Bowker: USA, annual 8 vols.**
1: Authors A–F   **5: Titles G–O**
2: Authors G–O   **6: Titles P–Z**
3: Authors P–Z   **7: Out of print**
4: Titles A–F   **8: Publishers.**
It lists over 750,000 books but government publications are excluded. Here the author and title sequences are separate. Out of print books (vol.7) and publishers (vol.8) are also listed separately. BIP is available on microfiche and CD-ROM, and is accessible online through *Dialog*.

Bibliographies which list mainly authors and titles cannot provide all the answers. Unfortunately there is no British subject guide to books in print, although there is one for recent publications (see *Whitaker's Classified Monthly Book List* on p.115). Another Bowker publication meets this need in America:

Subject Guide to Books in Print. **Bowker: USA, 4 vols, annual.**
It lists all the titles in *Books in Print* under detailed subject headings. It is therefore a valuable research tool which should not be overlooked if you are investigating an educational topic. It is a good source for compiling a bibliography on any aspect of education. There is also an annual *Books in Print Supplement* which updates both *Books in Print* (above) and the *Subject Guide to Books in Print*.

Other Bowker bibliographies are:

Paperbound Books in Print. **2 per annum, 3 vols.**
EL–HI Textbooks and Serials in Print. **Annual. (includes related teaching materials).**
Children's Books in Print. **Annual.**
Subject Guide to Children's Books in Print. **Annual.**
Books in Series in the United States. **Irregular.**
Most countries, e.g. Australia, Canada, France, and Germany have their own national trade bibliographies listing books currently available, but these are outside

the scope of the present work. It will b sufficient to mention:

International Books in Print: English Language Titles Published outside the United States and the United Kingdom. **Latest ed. K.G.Saur: W.Germany. 4 vols.**
Vols 1 and 2 list authors and titles, vols 3 and 4 contain the subject guide. This is a praiseworthy attempt to record English language titles publishe in over 150 different countries. Books, pamphlets and microfiches are included.

Many books which have been reported by publishers out of print and unobtainable will of course be available in libraries, either because libraries bought them when first published, or because they have since acquired copies in reprinted or microform editions. This applies to many periodical titles as well. Some idea of the range of formerly out of print itmes now available can be obtained by examining the following works:

Guide to Reprints: an International Bibliography of Scholarly Reprints. **Guide to Reprints Inc: USA, annual.**

Guide to Microforms in Print. **Meckler: USA. 2 vols, annual, with supplement.**

Microforms Annual: an International Guide to Microforms featuring Special Collections. **Latest edn. Pergamon Microforms.**

Another American firm, University Microfilms International, are active in this field and publish:

Books On Demand. **Latest edn. UMI: USA. 3 vols.**
This lists over 100,000 books which are available as reprints in facsimile paper reproductions although some titles are also obtainable on microfilm.

18.4   Lists of new books

Besides knowing what books are in print and available you will wish to find out what new books are being published. For this

rpose you will have to consult the current
bliographies which record the expanding
tput of publishers today. They will also
elp you to identify half-remembered
etails of books which you may have seen
entioned elsewhere. The handiest British
st, for the latter purpose especially, is:

*hitaker's Books of the Month and Books to
ome*. **Whitaker, monthly.**
This is an author, title and keyword list, in one
alphabetical sequence, of books published in the
past month, together with those due to be
published in the next two months. The entries
eventually find their way into:

hitaker's Book List. **Annual volume Whitaker.**
Formerly entitled *Whitaker's Cumulative Book List*,
this is arranged in the same way as the monthly list
(above). It records about 60,000 new books, new
editions and re-issues each year.

Both of these works are basically
uthor/title lists which do not, except
ncidentally, make it easy to identify new
ooks on different subjects. However, the
veekly *Bookseller*, also published by
Whitaker, includes a subject list of new and
orthcoming books, which cumulates every
nonth into:

Vhitaker's Classified Monthly Book List.
Vhitaker, monthly.
This is extremely useful. It lists currently published
books under selected subject headings, e.g.
education, psychology, social sciences, careers. It
also lists books in certain categories, e.g.
bibliographies, school textbooks. Anyone who wants
to keep in touch with new publications should scan
it regularly. Like all the Whitaker bibliographies, it
includes books from American publishers with
agencies in this country.

Your library will probably also have
Whitaker's *Forthcoming Books* on microfische
'2 per annum) which lists books due for
ublication in the next six months. It is
ased on the index to books advertised in
he special seasonal issues of the *Bookseller*
(see below).
Two Bowker publications giving advance
notice of new publications in the US are:

Forthcoming Books, **6 per annum. Bowker: USA**
Subject Guide to Forthcoming Books **6 per
annum, Bowker: USA.**
These are intended as supplements to *Books in Print*
(USA) (see p.000) and the *Subject Guide to Books in
Print* (USA) (see p.114). Each of the two-monthly
issues expands and updates the previous one.

All the trade bibliographies mentioned
above are compiled from publishers' trade
lists in either Britain or America. Your own
library will probably have a comprehensive
collection of publishers' catalogues. It will
include complete stocklists; subject lists;
lists of books for schools; lists of different
categories of books (e.g. reference books);
and publishers' seasonal lists containing
descriptions of new and forthcoming books.
Obviously you cannot examine all of
them, but fortunately there are the seasonal issues of the *Bookseller* which appear in
Spring and Autumn each year. These list
most of the new and forthcoming books,
with brief notes on many of them, and a
large section of publishers' advertisements.
They make pleasant browsing indeed,
although it is frustrating to be assailed with
so much information about an unceasing
flood of attractive new books most of which
you will never have time to read.
Trade bibliographies in general, although
they are indispensable for identifying books
quickly, have some disadvantages. Normally
they give only basic details about books,
and they are not comprehensive. The commercial publishers are fully represented,
others less so. For a virtually complete
listing of new books in this country, and a
fuller bibliographical description of each
one, you must turn to the:

British National Bibliography, **weekly, with 4-
monthly and annual cumulations, as well as
cumulations of classified sections and
indexes for longer periods. British
Bibliographic Services.**
This is the fullest current record of British books. It
is based on the copyright accessions of the British
Library. The arrangement is by Dewey, with author,
title, and series indexes. New books on education
will be found in the classified sequence from
370–379. The full bibliographical description

enables you to form some estimate of the quality and potential usefulness of each book.

The British National Bibliography (BNB) also contains provisional entries for books not yet published (CIP entries) but there are still complaints that the BNB is not as current as it might be. This is one reason why the Whitaker lists already described are handier for identifying very recent books. There are some categories of publications not included in the BNB but the first issue of a new periodical is recorded.

The *BNB* is certainly an invaluable bibliographical tool, and those involved in educational research especially should be aware of it and use it. Moreover, with the publication of the *Author Title Cumulation 1950-1984* on microfiche in 1986, access to its retrospective records has been helped considerably.

The online equivalent of the BNB is UKMARC. which is accessible on *BLAISE-LINE* along with LCMARC (this has records for all books acquired by the Library of Congress since 1968) and *Whitaker's Books in Print* (see p.113)

For basic coverage of American books your library will probably take the:

Cumulative Book Index: a World List of Books in the English Language. 11 per annum, with quarterly and annual cumulations. H.W. Wilson: USA.
This has two advantages. It lists books in English wherever they are published, not only in the USA. It also provides a different arrangement of entries. It is like a dictionary catalogue, with authors, titles and subjects in one sequence. American readers are used to this practice but it is unusual here. About 50-60,000 books are listed annually. *The Cumulative Book Index* has a long history going back to 1898.

Fewer books, but fuller details, appear in the:

American Book Publishing Record, monthly, with annual cumulations. Bowker: USA
Based on the *Weekly Record,* this is a well-produced guide to new books actually published. It is arranged by Dewey, like the BNB (see above) and its entries are as catalogued by the Library of Congress. The bound annual volume has cumulated entries, author/title indexes, and a subject guide. It includes books published in the US or distributed there for foreign publishers. Government publications are excluded. About 40,000 titles are listed each year. There are *ABPR Cumulative* volumes covering the years 1876–1949; 1950–1977; and 1980–1984.

The most comprehensive listing of the world's current output of books in the English language is on microfiche:

Books in English (microfiche). 6 per annum with progressive cumulation. British Library Bibliographic Services.
It provides bibliographic records of material taken from the UKMARC (British Library) and LCMARC (Library of Congress) databases. Over 100,000 titles are listed annually, with authors and titles in one alphabet. There are microfiche cumulations covering the years 1971–1980 and 1981–1985.

Unfortunately there is no separately published, up-to-date, complete listing of new books on education. You will have to look in several places, e.g. the *British National Bibliography* (see p.115) and *Whitaker Classified Monthly Book List* (see p.115) for British books and American books distributed over here; and in the *American Book Publishing Record* (see above) and the *Subject Guide to Forthcoming Books* (see p.115) for books published in America. You could also consult some of the book reviewing sources described in the next section (18.5).

Do not forget the very convenient listing of new educational publications in the *ACE Digest* which appears as an insert in the monthly *ACE Bulletin* (see p.9)

Two examples of booklists in specialised areas can be mentioned:

BACIE Bibliography of Publications in the Field of Vocational Education and Training, 6 per annum. British Association for Commercial and Industrial Education.
This was previously a supplement in the *BACIE Journal.* It now includes more periodical articles, training packs and other materials. All the items included are in the BACIE library.

The other example is the *Society for Research into Higher Education Bulletin* which includes a list of new books related to its subject.

However you should not overlook your library's own list of new additions which, if it is issued frequently and regularly, will be the most relevant list of all. It may include non-book materials, as well as books.

It may be worth consulting the accessions sts of other libraries which specialise in e field of education if they are conniently located and/or readily accessible. Even lists published by libraries in other untries may occasionally be useful to you. good example comes from the IBE in eneva:

TERNATIONAL BUREAU OF EDUCATION DOCUENTATION CENTRE. *Catalogue*. 2 per annum, E.

The list 'reflects the acquisitions policy of the Documentation Centre with its focus on educational policies, particular reforms and development trends'. The arrangement is alphabetical by author, title, etc., but there is another alphabetical listing by subject, e.g. education; educational administration; educational innovations; educational objectives; educational reform; and educational research. Much specialised material from many countries is included.

8.5 Reviews of new books

lthough the British National Bibliography ee p.115) and other sources already menoned provide adequate bibliographical escriptions of new books, quite often you ill require a fuller evaluation of a recent ork. For this purpose you will need access sources of reliable reviews. These can also e helpful if you are looking for reviews of ooks which were published some years ago.

Many people go for their reviews to the ational daily or Sunday newspapers, or to eneral or subject periodicals which often ontain book review sections. Periodicals re among the best sources for book reiews and a few of them will be mentioned ter. But there are periodicals which conist entirely of book reviews, and these upply more systematic coverage of new ooks than you will readily find elsewhere.

At present there is no British periodical f this type which is entirely devoted to eviewing new books on education. In this ountry we must rely on more general book eviewing periodicals which include some reviews of new books on education. The outstanding example has long been the:

British Books News. British Council, monthly, with annual index.

The original purpose of the *British Book News (BBN)* was to act as an aid to book selection for British Council libraries overseas. However, it soon developed into the best and most convenient guide to recent British books on all subjects, and deserves a detailed description.

Until 1987 the BBN (not to be confused with the BNB) contained short reviews by experts of about 200 books each month. It was therefore very selective, and the fact that a book was reviewed in its pages was itself a recommendation. Rather regrettably there was a change of policy from April 1987. The signed reviews which had always been a feature of each issue were discontinued and replaced by brief annotations of forthcoming books. Moreover the arrangement of the entries was no longer by Dewey (with education at 370–379) but by broad subjects (with education under the social sciences).

There has never been an annual cumulated volume, which would have been useful, but there has always been an annual index of titles, editors, series, and subjects, which your library will bind in with the year's issues. A valuable feature of the BBN is the survey (or bibliographical review) article. This surveys the literature on a particular subject or topic and occasionally it deals with some aspect of education, e.g. Higher education 1980–85 (August 1986); Computers in education (August 1986); Teaching, learning and the new technology (January 1988); and Studying schooling (April 1988). A retrospective list of these review articles is included from time to time. A section giving helpful notes on new periodical titles was introduced in 1981.

The BBN includes some annotations of bibliographies, reference books, and adult fiction. There are also notes on forthcoming school textbooks. There used to be a separate *Children's Book Quarterly* but it merged with *Books for Keeps*, the magazine of the School Bookshop Association, in 1988.

Another periodical which is entirely devoted to reviewing new books is the *Times Literary Supplement* (TLS) (weekly). The reviews are much longer on average than those which used to appear in the *British Book News*, and some are major reviews. However the TLS is essentially a literary periodical and includes only a few books on education. Note that comprehensive indexes to the TLS have been published by Research Publications PO Box 45, Reading

RG1 8HV. They cover the years 1902–1939 (2 vols) and 1940–1980 (3 vols).

Mention must also be of an American book reviewing periodical which may be found in some British libraries. It covers books on many subjects including education:

Choice, monthly. Association of College and Research Libraries: USA.
Designed primarily for librarians as an aid to book selection but worth glancing at regularly if your library has a copy. It concentrates on American books.

More particularly relevant to the student or teacher are the weekly *Times Educational Supplement* (TES) (there is a Scottish edition of this, with some overlap of material) and the *Times Higher Education Supplement* (THES). Both of them have generous book review sections. The THES naturally emphasises books in the field of higher education and it reviews more academic book titles than the TES, which includes many books at school and college level. There are special book review sections on particular subjects in the TES at fairly frequent intervals.

Both the TES and the THES have been indexed regularly in *The Times Index* (see p.155) since 1973. So has the *Times Literary Supplement* already mentioned. Book reviews will be found under the heading: 'Books (Titles and Reviews)'.

Most of the academic and scholarly periodicals have good sections at the end devoted to book reviews. An example is the *British Journal of Educational Studies* which has signed reviews by specialists. The disadvantage here is the delay in the appearance of the reviews because of the long intervals between each issue. Nevertheless, reviews in academic journals are usually more detailed, more considered, and more authoritative than those in weekly periodicals or national newspapers. The time-lag will not always reduce the reader's interest in what the reviewer has to say.

Looking for a review of a particular book can be very frustrating. You can try the monthly and annual indexes in the *British Book News* and perhaps *The Times Index* (see p.155). It is worth remembering that the *Education Index* (USA), a subject index to educational periodicals, also indexes reviews of books on education. However, there is a publication whose funcion is simply to save your time in searching for book reviews:

Book Review Digest. 10 per annum with quarterly and annual cumulations. H.W. Wilson, USA.
This is an index to reviews of current fiction and non-fiction books which have appeared in about 80 different periodicals. It tries to provide excerpts from as many reviews as are necessary to reflect the balance of critical opinion about each book. About 8,000 books each year are listed. Only a limited number are concerned with education and the emphasis is definitely on American titles, but it is the only resource of its kind which is generally available in British libraries. The main arrangement is by author, but there is also a subject and title index. There is the *Book Review Digest Author Title Index 1905–1974* (1976) 4 vols; *1975–1984* (1986), for retrospective searching.

Another example, though it will be found much less frequently in British libraries, is the:

Book Review Index. 6 per annum with annual cumulation. Gale Research Co: USA.
It is wider in scope than the *Book Review Digest* above, indexing reviews in over 200 general, specialist, and scholarly periodicals. Gale also publishes a *Children's Book Review Index* (annual).

Although, as already indicated, there is no British periodical entirely devoted to reviewing new books on education, there is a well-established one which regularly reviews new books on a closely related subject, sociology:

Reviewing Sociology: a Review Journal. 3 per annum. City of Birmingham Polytechnic, Department of Sociology and Applied Social Studies.

It contains reviews of about 1,000 words and the occasional review article of twice this length. There is a cumulated author index in the last issue of each volume.

Finally in this section, some readers may be interested in reviews of new materials appearing in microform. A useful source for his purpose is the American:

Microform Review. **4 per annum. Meckler: USA.**

Each issue carries about twenty in-depth reviews of major collections. Several articles and book reviews are also included. Retrospective coverage is provided by *Cumulative Microform Reviews*. 2 vols: (1) 1972–1976; (2) 1977—1984, from the same publisher.

18.6 Bibliographies of education

Bibliographies of particular subjects may be either comprehensive or selective. Comprehensive bibliographies can be helpful since they try to include everything published on a subject. The virtue of selective bibliographies is that by listing only the best, most useful, or most relevant works, they can save the reader's time, or help the reader who does not wish to delve too deeply.

Education is a large subject, and it is doubtful if any bibliography of education in general could ever hope to be comprehensive, even if the limits of the subject were clearly defined. Remarkably, however, a publication made its appearance some years ago which is attempting to be virtually complete in its coverage of educational publications in English and some other European languages:

BIBE: International Bulletin of Bibliography on Education. **4 per annum with annual summary volume. Coculsa Bibliografias Internacionales: Spain.**

Its intention is to cover bibliographical output on education from all countries which produce books in six specified languages: English, Spanish, French, German, Italian, and Portuguese. This is an ambitious undertaking since publications from 42

countries are involved. Coverage includes areas related to education, e.g. the philosophy, psychology, sociology, biology, anthropology, economics, politics, and history of education. Books at all levels are included. Serious efforts have been made to standardise the terminology used and this again must have been no easy task.

The first part of *BIBE* to appear was called Numero Zero (No.0). It covered the publications of a decade retrospectively in 2 vols: (1) 1971–1975; and (2) 1976–1980. Over 30,000 titles are listed in three languages: English, French, and Spanish. Moreover, only basic bibliographical details are given in these volumes. From No.1 proper onwards, i.e. the quarterly and annual issues, the contents list of each book is also given, unless it exceeds 500 words, when a summary is given instead. The annual volumes include a list of periodicals on education in the six languages covered by *BIBE*: an author index; and an alphabetical list of the most important 'classifying descriptors.'

The arrangement of *BIBE* is by the Universal Decimal Classification (UDC) 'since it is the one most used by national libraries'. However, it is not the one most easily understood by potential users and this, as well as the multilingual approach, will cause difficulties for anyone trying to use *BIBE* for the first time. The answer is careful reading of the introductory sections, patient application, and where necessary, consultation with a friendly librarian.

The aims of *BIBE* are 'objectivity, wide scope, critical discussion, international understanding, standardisation of terminology, the interdisciplinary aspect, and constant updating'. It is not a resource for the general reader.

If comprehensiveness is difficult to achieve in general bibliographies of education, it becomes a possibility in one dealing with a specific aspect:

CRAIGIE, J. *A Bibliography of Scottish Education.* **University of London Press. 2 vols. 1. Before 1872. (1970); 2. 1972-1982. (1974).**

Dr.Craigie's work is a landmark in this field. Before these volumes appeared the bibliography of Scottish education was fragmentary to say the least. Now for all practical purposes we have the essential records of Scottish educational history conveniently organised and well indexed. Items are listed without annotations, but what makes the work especially useful is that locations are given for all the entries, mainly in the National Library of Scotland but also in university, college, public, and other libraries.

There is a comparable example for England and Wales:

HIGSON, C.W.J. *Sources for the History of Education: a List of Material (Including School Books) Contained in the Libraries of the Institutes and Schools of Education, Together with Works from the Libraries of the Universities of Nottingham and Reading.* **LISE: Library Association, 1967. Supplement, 1976.**

These are unique checklists of material for research into the history of education. Some of the items are not recorded anywhere else. There are five main sections: (A) 15–17th centuries; (B) 1701–1800; (C) 1801–1870; (D) Textbooks and children's books 1801–1870; and (E) Government publications up to 1918. There is a subject index and an author index to government publications.

The undernoted work is complementary to both Craigie and Higson:

GLASGOW UNIVERSITY, DEPARTMENT OF EDUCATION. *A Bibliography of pre-1900 Education-Related Materials in Glasgow University Library,* **compiled by D.Hamilton** *et al.* **Glasgow University, Department of Education, 1983. vol.1.**

The introduction states: 'As befits its age and location, Glasgow University contains a rich storehouse of education-related materials. Some pertain to well-known authors and organisations. But there is also a dark continent of pamphlets and books that remains relatively unvisited and unexplored. This bibliography...opens up that territory'. It is arranged in four sections according to library location, each arranged alphabetically by author. Another useful but briefer bibliography also covers earlier material:

ATKINS, S.H. *A Select Check-List of Printed Material on Education Published in English to 1800.* **Hull University Institute of Education, 1970.**

It aims to give 'a balanced idea of the main themes which occupied earlier thinkers about education'. Part 1 lists the titles in author order. Part 2 lists the same titles in chronological order for those who wish to study the development of educational ideas. Many of the books mentioned are to be found in the

libraries of the institutes and schools of education. The locations are given in Higson,C.W.J. (above). Others may be found in the British Library or the Bodleian, for example.

It will become obvious that most of the remaining works described in this section are selective bibliographies. They make no pretence of being comprehensive, but many of them are annotated and may be more immediately useful to you.

There is a sense in which the printed catalogues of individual libraries can be called selective bibliographies, since all the books have been acquired to meet the needs of the readers they serve. The largest in the educational field is:

COLUMBIA UNIVERSITY. *Teachers College Library Dictionary Catalogue.* **G.K.Hall: USA, 36 vols, 1970. Supplement 1: 1971, 5 vols; Supplement 2: 1972, 2 vols; Supplement 3: 1977, 10 vols.**

This is on such a large scale that it will rarely be found in British libraries. It is a photographic reproduction of catalogue entries from a library of 400,000 books. You will look in vain here for references to recent works on education. Nevertheless its detailed listings could be useful if you are doing research. It covers education and educational systems throughout the world with particular emphasis on America. Periodicals and audio-visual materials are included. As the title indicates, authors, titles and subjects are arranged in one sequence.

Since 1979 it has been supplemented by the annual *Bibliographic Guide to Education* from the same publisher, which lists materials added to the Teachers College Library during the past year, with additional entries from the New York Public Library. It covers all aspects of education. A microfiche collection entitled *History of Education* based on the holdings of the Teachers College Library, has been published by Research Publications, PO Box 45, Reading, RG1 8HF. The collection lists 9–12,000 treatises and general works on many aspects of education.

There is a British education library catalogue which is incomparably smaller in scale:

NATIONAL UNION OF TEACHERS LIBRARY, *Catalogue.* **NUT, 1970. Supplement, 1972.**

It is very dated now, but may occasionally be useful for identifying older material. It covers the theory, aims, and methodology of education and related fields such as psychology and sociology. Textbooks are not included. The arrangement is by subject with author and title indexes.

A much more important library catalogue is concerned with a specific aspect of
education:

**LONDON UNIVERSITY INSTITUTE OF EDUCATION
LIBRARY.** *Catalogue of the Comparative
Education Library.* **G.K.Hall: USA, 1971. 6
vols. 1st supplement, 1975. 3 vols.
Vols 1 and 2: Authors, titles.
Vols 3 and 4: Subjects, divided by country.
Vols 5 and 6: Regions, subdivided by subject.**
Despite its date, this is a prime resource for anyone
wishing to investigate any aspect of comparative
education, since the collection is unique in its field.
Unusually the catalogue contains entries for
composite works, and there are references to
periodical articles.

There are also catalogues, or more correctly
union lists, of the holdings of a number of
different libraries. The work by Higson,
C.W.J. (see p.120) is a good example. The
librarians of the institutes and schools of
education have co-operated to produce a
number of bibliographies of this kind, e.g.:

ANDREWS, J.S. *Education in Germany: a Union
List of Stock in Institute and School of
Education Libraries.* **3rd edn. LISE, 1979.**

MARDER, J.V. *Education in France: a Union List
of Stock in Institute and School of Education
Libraries.* **LISE, 1971.**

Another example on a more specific topic
is:

CAMPBELL, A.G.D. *Novels and Plays with a
Background of School: a Union List of Books in
the Stock of Education Libraries in British
Universities.* **2nd edn. LISE, 1979.**

There is a similar list from a Scottish
education library:

STIRLING, M. *Novels about Teachers and Teaching.* **Jordanhill College of Education Library,
1972.**

It may be helpful at this stage to provide
brief notes on some of the bibliographies
which are available on different aspects of
education. They vary in size and importance, and also in their up-to-dateness.
It is always advisable to check the publication date of bibliographies. Several of
those included here are standard works.
Others, particularly in the last group, are
in pamphlet form.

BANKS, O. *The Sociology of Education: a
Bibliography.* **Batsford, 1978.**
A guide for students rather than for those involved
in serious research. The emphasis is on British
material but relevant American works are included,
and a limited amount of foreign material. There
are no annotations, but each section has a brief
introduction.

BARON, G. *A Bibliographical Guide to the
English Educational System.* **3rd edn. Athlone
Press, 1965.**
Although this edition was published in the mid-
sixties it remains a useful starting point for further
investigation, expecially of the historical
development in all its aspects.

BLAUG, M. *Economics of Education: a Selected
Annotated Bibliography.* **3rd edn. Pergamon,
1978.**
A substantial work with very helpful annotations.
Items are listed chronologically to show the
development of the subject since 1945. Each section
has an introductory survey of the key texts.

CLARKE, J.L. *Educational Development: a Select
Bibliography with Particular Reference to
Further and Higher Education.* **Kogan Page,
1981.**
'Educational development is a term which covers
the application of technology to education and,
more broadly, the use of new teaching strategies,
evaluation methods and curriculum development
designed to improve the quality of teaching and
learning. Its aim is to facilitate the adaptation of
educational institutions to the changing demands
of society.' This is a straightforward international
bibliography with only a brief introduction and no
annotations. There is a list of relevant periodicals
at the end.

*Select Bibliography of Adult Continuing
Education.* **5th edn. Eds J.H. Davies and J.E.
Thomas. National Institute of Adult
Continuing Education, 1988.**
The 4th edition (1984) by Thomas,J.E. and
Davies,J.H. was itself an extension of earlier works
by Kelly,T. *A select bibliography of adult education in*

Great Britain, published in 1952, 1962 and 1974. This new edition 'reflects new interests and emphases in scholarly research and practical experiments'. Its scope is international though it is limited to English language sources.

Those requiring a more exhaustive bibliography are referred to the NIACE Databank, i.e. computer databases of research. Database 1 covers adult continuing education, and Database 2 adult basic education. They provide access to reviews of research and resource materials. The desriptors used are based on the *Eric Thesaurus* (see p.18). Briefer bibliographies on adult education are described later in this section.

STAGG, S. and ERAUT, M. *A Select Bibliography of Educational Technology.* **2nd edn. Council for Educational Technology,1975.**

The first edition in 1975 was annotated, but the editors had to 'face up to one of the inevitable consequences of working in so rapidly an expanding field of education' and the annotations were omitted from this edition. Not surprisingly perhaps there has been no updating since.

On a related topic there is *Distance Education in Western Europe: a Selective Annotated Bibliography of Current Literature* (CEDEFOP:HMSO, 1986)

WHITE, J.N. and BURNETT, C.W. *Higher Education Literature: an Annotated Bibliography.* **Oryx Press: USA, 1981.**

There is a strong American emphasis in this work, which has only a page and a half on British higher education. Otherwise it is well produced and usefully annotated. The main sections cover the historical background and the nature and scope of American education; community and junior colleges; organisation and administration; and comparative systems of higher education. There is a brief section on higher education as a field of study. There are numerous appendices, e.g. an annotated bibliography of relevant professional journals (all American).

YOO, Y. *Soviet Education: an Annotated Bibliography and Readers' Guide to Works in English, 1893–1978.* **Greenwood Press: USA, 1980.**

Another straightforward bibliography, arranged under topics alphabetically, e.g. administration, supervision, vocational education. There are author and title indexes.

Two American publishers, Garland and the Greenwood Press, are very active in this field and have produced a number of substantial bibliographies on different aspects of education (see pp.125–6).

There is an unusual and rather special ised bibliography which may be include here:

Bibliography of Policy Related Education Documents in Selected Countries in Africa, Asia, the Caribbean and the Pacific, compiled by D.Clayton and E.Jamieson. 2nd edn. Overseas Development. Administration: University of Leeds School of Education, 1988 2 vols.

Designed for overseas students on advanced education courses in this country to help them trace source material for their dissertations. It is restricted almost entirely to official publications of the countries concerned. Locations are given in institute and school of education libraries.

A variety of bibliographies on more spe cific educational topics are described below Most of them are much briefer than thos already mentioned:

BUCKLE, E. *et al. The Young Student in School, College and Work: a Bibliography.* **HERTIS, 1982.**

First published in 1977 as *The Young Student in Further Education and the Sixth Form.* There are references to periodical articles as well as books, and brief introductions to each section.

GOLDSTEIN, S. and FARRAR, D. *Giftedness: an Annotated Bibliography.* **Bath University Schools of Education, 1982.**

An extended version of a work originally compiled in America. It is designed to help educators and researchers in both countries. The annotations are an important feature. The arrangement is by topics with author and title indexes.

HAYWOOD, P.G. *Comparative Adult Education and Lifelong Education: a Bibliography.* **Nottingham University Library, 1979.**

A list of material in Nottingham University Library the School of Education Resources Centre, etc. Arrangement: General and international; Africa; the Americas; Asia; Europe: general; specific countries. There is a subject index at the beginning.

HAYWOOD, P.G. *A Bibliography of Adult Teaching, Psychology and Research: a Source Book.* **Nottingham University Department of Adult Education, 1983.**

'A source book of references for research students to use in their work' by the same author. The two works were designed to be used together. All the items listed are available in the Nottingham University Library system. Other bibliographies from Nottingham are concerned with literacy; community education; correspondence education; and basic education.

MANNING, A.J. et al. Contraction Management n Schools and Colleges: an Annotated Bibli- graphy. Sheffield City Polytechnic, De- partment of Education Management, 1982.
Material is mainly from British sources, dealing with frustration in education at different levels, staffing and financial implications, health aspects, etc. (see also the title by Watson,L.E. below).

MORRISON, C.M. An Annotated Bibliography of Adult Education. Scottish Council for Research in Education, 1980.
This is more an evaluative commentary than bibliography and mentions a number of key works in the field.

NATIONAL BOOK LEAGUE. Moral Education; compiled by W.M.Doeser and H.J.Blackham NBL, 1976.
Note the date. One of the numerous pamphlet bibliographies from this source. It is aimed at teachers and parents and has helpful annotations. It extends an earlier list which appeared in 1971.

PARKER, J.H. A Select Annotated Bibliography of Text Books in Education. Keele University Library, 1972.
The aim here is to show the reader 'the diversity of topics on which any meaningful consideration of the text books must be based'. Most of the entries are taken from periodical literature. Note the date.

RICHARDS, C. Curriculum Studies: an Intro- ductory Annotated Bibliography. 2nd edn. Falmer Press, 1984.
Twice the size of the first edition in 1978. The bibliography retains its British emphasis. A third edition is anticipated. The arrangement is by topics with an author index. There is a brief list of journals concerned with the curriculum, and another of official publications.

SKINNER, A. Disaffection from School: Issues and Interagency Responses: an Annotated Bibliography and Literature Review on Absenteeism and Disruption and on the Responses of Schools and other Agencies to These and Allied Issues. National Youth Bureau, 1983.
The subtitle gives some idea of the problems the compiler had in deciding what to include. The

literature review examines five subject areas of interest and concern with full introductions to each of them. There is an area/project/source index, also author and subject indexes. The thrust of the work is towards school-based problems.

TEATHER, O.C.B. Staff Development in Higher Education: an International Review and Bibliography. Kogan Page, 1979.
Separate chapters review the situation in Australia, Britain, Canada, Denmark, East and West Germany, India, the Netherlands, New Zealand, Sweden, Switzerland and the United States. Key documents on staff development are reprinted and there is a list of centres and associations. The references and bibliography occupy 30 pages. Note the date.

TURNER, E. Criterion Referenced Assessment: an Annotated Bibliography. Stirling University Department of Education, 1980.
Aims 'to provide a comprehensive collection of references on criterion-referenced assessment and related fields.' Most of the 900 references come from America and date from the 1970s. Full abstracts are usually given. A significant number of articles on mastery learning are included. There is an index of authors and topics.

WATSON, L.E. The Management of the Further Education College: an Annotated Bibliography. Sheffield City Polytechnic Department of Education Management, 1981.
Covers British publications on the internal manage- ment and administration of FE and technical colleges. It is arranged alphabetically by author.

Two of the *Guides to Sources in the History of Education Series* published by Lancaster University in association with the History of Education Society should be noted:

HURT, J.S. Education and the Working Classes from the Eighteenth to the Twentieth Centuries. 1985. (No.8)

SZRETER, R. The History of Education in Non- Education Related Journals: an Annotated Bibliography of References. 1986. (No.9)

It may be of interest to include a few examples of bibliographies which are con- cerned with the history of educational in- stitutions:

SILVER, H. and TEAGUE, S.J. *The History of British Universities 1800–1969: a Bibliography.* **Society for Research into Higher Education, 1970.**

This 'grew out of an awareness of the immense gaps in the historical material on British universities and of the difficulty of tracing and using many of the likely sources'. It covers British universities excluding Oxford and Cambridge. There is no attempt to include unpublished materials. The largest section has entries for individual universities arranged alphabetically. Materials are grouped under standard headings, e.g. foundation documents, official publications, university magazines, histories, periodicals, with brief notes where required. There is a useful section on 'academic biographies of significance in British university history'. An index of authors is provided. This was an important pioneering bibliography.

BERRY, M. *Teacher Training Institutions in England and Wales: a Bibliographic Guide to their History.* **Society for Research into Higher Education, 1973.**

'Although there is an impressive volume of literature about teaching and teachers, there is a peculiar lack of published material about the institutions responsible for their training.' It is fortunate that this gap has been at least partially filled since many of the institutions mentioned have now disappeared or been amalgamated with others. Each section has a brief introduction but no annotations are provided. There are indexes of authors and institutions.

BARR, B. *Histories of Girls' Schools and Related Biographical Material: a Union List of Books in the Stock of Education Libraries in British Universities.* **Librarians of the Institutes and Schools of Education, 1984.**

This has only a short introduction and no annotations. There are four parts; Part 1: Schools, general works; Part 2: Schools listed in alphabetical order of name; Part 3: Biographies: collective works; and Part 4: Biographies and autobiographies. There are geographical and name indexes, and a brief list of references. There is another short list of school histories in the *History of Education Society Bulletin*, no.30 , Autumn 1982, pp.55–7. Note also:

STEPHENS, B. and UNWIN, R.W. *Materials for the Local and Regional Study of Schooling 1700–1900.* **British Records Association, 1987. (Archives and the user).**

As an excellent, comparatively recent example of the history of an individual institution we have:

HARTE, N. *The University of London 1836–1986: an Illustrated History.* **Anthlone Press, 1986.**

'All universities are different, but some are more different than others. The University of London is the most different of them all.' A well-produced overview of the development of a complex institution, enhanced by the illustrations. It was written to celebrate the 150th anniversary.

This is probably the most appropriate place for a bibliography which can usefully be linked with a few of the preceding works:

GOSDEN, P.H.G.H. *Museum of the History of Education: Catalogue.* **Leeds University, 1979**

The importance of the collection lies in its 'uniqueness and potential rather than its present size' for it was the first of its kind in the country. 'It has as its twofold aim the documentation and illustration of the history of education in England, and the promotion of research and publication in the history of education.' The catalogue consists mainly of lists of textbooks and children's exercise books arranged by curricular subjects, ' but an interesting collection of science teaching apparatus is also recorded'.

There is another bibliography from the same source: Cunningham,P. *The Local History of Education in England and Wales* (1976), and an associated periodical: the *Journal of Educational Administration and History* (2 per annum).

Several of the bibliographies on the history of education mentioned at the beginning of this section are relevant here. The standard bibliographies of British history should also be consulted.

The search for material need not be limited to bibliographies of education. One example should be enough to illustrate this:

BARROW, M. *Women 1870–1928: a Select Guide to Printed and Archival Sources in the United Kingdom.* **Mansell, 1981.**

This invaluable source book contains several sections relevant to the study of female education during the period. The contents are divided into archives; printed works; non-book material; and libraries and record offices. The section on archives includes a description of the Emily Davies Collection at Girton College, Cambridge, and the papers of Frances Mary Buss at the North London Collegiate School for girls. The section on printed works has information on relevant official publications. It also has brief biographical notes, with references, on about 50 women prominent in all fields including education, e.g.Dorothy Beale and Rachel and Margaret Macmillan. This is much more than a bibliography and will repay close study. Those who are interested in this field will find that the periodical *Women's Studies International Forum* (6 per annum, Pergamon), is worth looking at regularly.

Another bibliography on a topic only marginally covered in this guide deserves a place as an excellent example of a comprehensive bibliography:

RIEDLANDER, J. *Early Reading Development: a Bibliography.* **Harper & Row, 1981.**
'A survey of English language literature on the subject up to the age of seven. It includes all relevant material published during a period of about fifty years from the 1920s to mid-1979.' The references cited are 'periodical articles, books and relevant sections of books, conference papers, theses, government and other institutions reports...General and sectional introductions help to make the book accessible to students as well as to researchers.' It would be the ideal starting point for any research project on the subject. There is also an extensive list of periodical titles and their abbreviations which is itself a conspectus of sources for information on reading development. The book is beautifully printed and presented. A new edition would be welcomed.

The above work illustrates very well how comprehensiveness may be achieved within a strictly defined and limited topic. It is when the scope of the subject widens that the problems begin to arise. The next work is on quite a different scale. Although it is not strictly concerned with education it includes many references to it:

International Bibliography of the Social Sciences. Vol.1: Sociology. **Tavistock Publications, annual.**
This is one of the four annual volumes of the *International Bibliography of the Social Sciences* which was launched in 1952. It is one of the major publishing ventures of its time. The *Sociology* volume like the others is in bilingual form (English/French). Despite the impressive range of titles included it is 'selective rather than comprehensive'. This is because the editors in their wisdom have applied rigorous standards for inclusion.

There are sections on both education and psychology. Periodical articles are covered as well as books, and particular attention is paid to official publications. There are author and subject indexes and also a list of periodicals consulted. Despite a time-lag in publication of about two years, this is a valuable resource for the serious reader because of its worldwide coverage, both recent and retrospective: the volumes now stretch back for almost 40 years. The work is prepared by the International Committee for Social Science Information and Documentation (ICSSID).

Finally in this section, there are a number of substantial bibliographies of American origin which have been published (or announced for publication) in recent years. The first two series come from the firm Garland:

Garland Bibliographies in Contemporary Education

DIEM, R.A. *Computers in Education: a Research Bibliography.* **Garland: USA, 1988.**

GRAMBS, J.D. *Sex Differences in Education: a Select Bibliography.* **Garland: USA, announced.**

HINES, E.R. and MCCARTHY, J.R. *Higher Education Finance: an Annotated Bibliography and Guide to Research.* **Garland: USA, 1984.**

LEMING, J.S. *Contemporary Approaches to Moral Education: an Annotated Bibliography and Guide to Research.* **Garland: USA, 1983.**

LESTER, P. *Teacher Job Satisfaction: an Annotated Bibliography and Guide to Research.* **Garland: USA, 1988.**

POWELL, M. and BEARD, J.W. *Teacher Attitudes: an Annotated Bibliography and Guide to Research.* **Garland: USA, 1986.**

POWELL, M. and BEARD, J.W. *Teacher Effectiveness: an Annotated Bibliography and Guide to Research.* **Garland: USA, 1984.**

RUSS-EFT, D.F. *et al. Issues in Basic Adult Education: an Annotated Bibliography and Guide to Research.* Garland: USA, 1981.

SILVERSTEIN, N.A. and DERIVAN, W.J. *Prevention Education and Substance Abuse: a Guide to Research.* Garland: USA, announced.

WOODWARD, A. *et al. Textbooks in School and Society: an Annotated Bibliography and Guide to Research.* Garland: USA, 1988.

Garland Reference Books on International Education

ALTBACH, P.G. *et al. Education in South Asia: a Select Annotated Bibliography.* Garland: USA, 1987.

BEAUCHAMP, E.R. and RUBINGER, R. *Education in Japan: a Source Book.* Garland: USA, 1988.

BRICKMAN, W.W. *Education in Russia from the Middle Ages to the Present: a Bibliography.* Garland: USA, 1986.

EL SANABARY, N. *Education in the Arab Gulf State: a Select Annotated Bibliography.* Garland: USA, announced.

PARKER, F. and PARKER, B.J. *Education in the People's Republic of China, Past and Present: an Annotated Bibliography.* Garland: USA, 1986.

RUST, V.D. *Education in East and West Germany: a Bibliography.* Garland; USA, 1984.
    Another Garland bibliography: Sternlicht M. and Sternlicht,M. *Special Education: a Sourcebook* is described in 26.1 (Handbooks of research) (see p.000).

The last few bibliographies are from another American publisher on topics which are not too well covered already:

KARNES, E.L. *et al. Discipline in Our Schools: an Annotated Bibliography.* Greenwood Press: USA, 1973.

KARNES, E.L. and BLACK, D.D. *Teacher Evaluation and Merit Pay: an Annotated Bibliography.* Greenwood Press: USA, 1986.

LEMIN, J.S. *Foundations of Moral Education: an Annotated Bibliography.* Greenwood Press: USA, 1983.

WEINBERG, M. *The Education of Poor and Minority Children: a World Bibliography.* Greenwood Press: USA, 1986. Supplement 1979–1985, 1987.

18.7 Guides to the literature of education

A guide to the literature is more than straightforward bibliography. The best one are comprehensive surveys, often in narra tive form, of the resources availabe for th study of a particular subject. Their purpos is to map out the ground for the studen and research worker so that they can fin their way more confidently through th literature.

Not all of the guides described in this sec tion have, or achieve, this objective. Som are more ambitious than others. Never theless they are, in general, among th most useful of the publications in th present work. (Other useful titles are des cribed in 25.3: Organising the literature.)

HUMBY, M. A *Guide to the Literature of Education.* **3rd edn. London University Institute of Education, 1975.**
    Note the date. When it was published this was the best British survey of the resources available for the study of education, and it is a pity that no subsequent edition has appeared. However it contains information that is not included in any other work of its kind. It is not designed for continuous reading, since it is essentially a well-organised list of sources with full and helpful annotations. The arrangement is by types of sources, not by topics. It may possibly be too detailed for the average student, but those doing educational research in any form would be well advised to refer to it. For other than current information it is unlikely to be superceded.

ibliographical Aids and Reference Tools for the iterature of Education: a Guide to Works *elating to Education held by Southampton* *Jniversity Library. Latest-edn. Southampton* *Jniversity Library.*

Designed primarily as a user's guide for students and staff. It covers, much more briefly, some of the same ground as Humby,M. (above) but frequent revisions have kept it up to date. There are short introductions to each section, and most entries have brief annotations. This is a practical guide well calculated to assist the beginning student or researcher.

RICHMOND, W.K. *The Literature of Education: a Critical Bibliography.* **Methuen, 1972.**

The approach here is quite different from that of the two works already mentioned, which are both concerned with types of sources. Richmond adopts a subject approach. It is an ambitious work in that it tries to outline, in fewer than 200 pages, the key writings in all the main areas of education, with supporting bibliographies. It is nevertheless lively and readable and most students would gain something from it. Although many years have passed since it was published there is no other work which is directly comparable.

HAYWOOD, P. and WRAGG, E.C. *Evaluating the Literature.* **Nottingham University School of Education, 1978.**

This one of the *Rediguides* series (see p.167). It is a convenient signpost to the use of education literature for the beginning researcher. It contains much practical advice in its thirty-odd pages.

There is an excellent short chapter on the literature and sources of education in Roberts,N. *The use of Social Sciences Literature* (Butterworths, 1977). It was written by D.J.Foskett, then Librarian of London University Institute of Education, but note the date. Your attention is drawn to a similar, but much more recent, American source:

WEBB, W.H. et al. *Sources of Information in the Social Sciences: a Guide to the Literature.* **3rd edn. American Library Association, 1986.**

This is a 'thorough updating' of Carl M. White's standard work. It provides a review of the general social science literature and also of particular areas, e.g. education, psychology, and sociology. 'Representative monographic publications and necessary reference tools are described for the distinct research areas within each field.' This work is strongly recommended despite its American emphasis. The section on education is an excellent short survey.

A praisewothy attempt to provide a more stimulating introduction to the literature of education than can be obtained from the printed page was made by:

HOOTON, J.P. A *Guide to the Literature of Education.* **1980. (Tape/Slide)**

This introduces the most essential bibliographical tools, and consists of 80 slides with an accompanying booklet. Media productions, of course, date as quickly as books, and need to be revised just as frequently.

Most of the works already described are concerned with the literature of education in general. The remaining works in this section deal with particular areas or aspects of education:

BRISTOW, T. and HOLMES, B. *Comparative Education Through the Literature: a Bibliographic Guide.* **Butterworths, 1968.**

A sensible, straightforward guide which filled a gap when it appeared. It does not aim to be comprehensive- a difficult task in this field. The chapter headings are: (1) Teaching comparative education; (2) Imaginative writing and comparative education; (3) National area studies; (4) Cross-cultural and case studies; and (5) Library tools and research in comparative education. Note the date.

DIBDEN, K. and TOMLINSON, J. *Information Sources in Education and Work.* **Butterworths, 1981.**

'Intended to help students and their advisers during all stages of education. The first and major part puts the literature in the context of the needs at various levels of education; a bibliography, which is directly related to each chapter, forms the second part.' There is also a list of information sources for careers advisers. The book is clearly written and contains much useful advice. A new edition would be welcome.

HARTNETT, A. *The Social Sciences in Educational Studies: a Selective Guide to the Literature.* Heinemann, 1982.
Provides 'bibliographical maps to the literature in 21 areas that are important in educational studies'. Among the topics covered are: language and education; the curriculum; the sociology of classrooms; women and education; sociology and special schooling; and sociology and curriculum innovation. Contributors are from the UK and the USA. A few final pages by J.Vaughan give concise advice on searching the literature and keeping up to date.

HARTNETT, *A Sociology of Education: an Introductory Guide to the Literature.* Liverpool University School of Education, 1975.
Although this is fairly brief and now rather dated it is worth including as an example of a guide to one specialised area of education.

PETERS, A.J. *A Guide to the Study of British Further Education: Published Sources on the Contemporary System.* National Foundation for Educational Research, Pergamon, 1967.
Note the date. A companion to the same author's *British Further Education* published in the same year. The main sections are: Further education considered as a whole; its branches; its services; and its future. there are two appendices: (1) A list of abbreviations; and (2) A list of reports mentioned which are commonly known by chairman's name.

TOMLINSON, S. *Ethnic Minorities in British Schools: a Review of the Literature 1960–1982.* Gower, 1987.
Undertaken as a preliminary to a Policy Studies Institute/University of Lancaster Research Project investigating factors associated with success in multi-ethnic schools. It brings together much of the scattered literature on the subject, and there is an author bibliography at the end.

If allowance is made for their American emphasis two guides published by Jossey-Bass could be of interest:

Key Resources on Higher Education, Governance and Leadership: a Guide to the Literature; ed. M.W. Peterson. Jossey-Bass: USA, 1987.

Key Resources on Teaching, Learning, Curriculum and Faculty Development: a Guide to the Literature; eds. R.J.Menges and C.Mathis. Jossey-Bass: USA, 1988.

The Open University has been particularly active in producing literature guides on aspects of education. They have usually been designed as integral parts of OU courses, and appear in the attractive format of the course units. Earlier examples include:

DALE, S. *The Control of Education in Britain: Using the Literature.* Open University, 1979. (Course E222.)

DALE, S. *Management and the School: Using the Literature.* Open University, 1981. (Course E323)

DALE, S. *Special Needs in Education: Using the Literature.* Open University, 1983. (Course E241.)

HARRY, K. *Schooling and Society: Using the Literature.* Open University, 1977. (Course E202.)

MORRIS, K. *The Curriculum: Using the Literature.* Open University, 1983. (Course E204.)
Students taking courses at other universities or colleges would benefit if they had similar guides. Each one has a useful introduction on the use of books and libraries and a convenient outline of library search procedure. These are followed by descriptions of essential bibliographical tools and lists of relevant organisations, etc. Much basic information is presented in an inviting way.

Other OU guides of this type, in areas of related interest, are concerned with *Ageing Population* (1977, course P252), and *Reading Development* (1977, course PE231). Sheila Dale, the author of the first three guides mentioned above, is the joint-author of another excellent work:

DALE, S. and CARTY, J. *Finding Out About Continuing Education: Sources of Information and their Use:* Open University Press, 1985.
It deals with the literature of adult and continuing education and appears in a more conventional paperback format. It is not linked to a specific OU course. The information is presented clearly and informally and would be very useful to anyone who is interested in this area. It has two especially helpful chapters: on using libraries, and on literature search procedure, which could be used by

those studying education in a wider context. There is no index.

There are two other OU literature guides which are singled out for special mention here because they deal with areas particularly relevant to students and teachers not covered in the present guide:

OPEN UNIVERSITY, CHILDREN. LANGUAGE AND LITERATURE TEAM. *Finding Out About Children's Books: an Information Guide for Teachers*, **S.Dale et al. Open University Press, 1982.**
'This is an integral part of the study pack *Children, Language and Literature,* and aims to provide a checklist of sources of information for teachers on children's literature'. Sections include: About children's literature; selecting and tracing children's books; storytelling: non-book materials; organisations and associations. Well produced and clearly presented in the format of the OU course units.

OPEN UNIVERSITY, CHILDREN, LANGUAGE AND LITERATURE TEAM. *Children, Language and Literature,* **M.Hoffman et al. Open University Press, 1982.**
Another excellent guide 'intended primarily for teachers of children 5–16 who want to be well-informed about children's literature'. Contents: (1) The role of literature; (2) Literature in the classroom; and (3) Choosing children's books. It is a mine of useful suggestions, help and advice for those fortunate enough to discover it.

Both of these guides were produced as part of the OU's INSET programme at the OU Centre for Continuing Education. They are strongly recommended not only to teachers but also to anyone who has an interest in children's literature.

If you are interested in literature guides to other subjects, you could refer to:

A Literature Guide to Literature Guides. **Manchester Polytechnic, Department of Library and Information Studies, 1980.**
There are two parts: (1) Introducing literature guides (which explains their nature and functions); and (2) A bibliography of literature guides, arranged by subject, e.g. education, psychology, social sciences. A new edition is needed.

Guidance on literature searching generally will be found in Gash,S. *Effective Literature Searching for Students* (Gower, 1989).

19 Official publications

This chapter should be read in conjunction with chapter 2 which deals in some detail with official reports and documents on education, how to identify them and how to find information about them. This one describes some of the standard guides to official publications (19.1); some general catalogues and lists (19.2); and finally educational lists, which include inspection reports on schools and colleges (19.3).

The range of official publications is very wide, from the latest report on some aspect of education to the Highway Code. There are two main categories: Parliamentary Papers, which relate to the legislative process in Parliament, and Non-Parliamentary Papers, which are issued by Government Departments.

The majority of official publications in this country are issued by HMSO, but a surprising number are not (see the *Catalogue of Official Publications not Published by HMSO* on p.132). It is not generally appreciated that HMSO is the largest publisher in the UK, so that tracking down official publications can often be a formidable task.

Some libraries have extensive collections of official publications. In the *HMSO Annual Catalogue* (see p.132) there is a list of academic and public libraries where sizeable collections of HMSO publications may be consulted by research workers and students. Quite often they have specialist staff to organise the collections and answer enquiries. There is a useful *Directory of Specialists in Official Publications* by V. Nurcombe (2nd edn, Standing Committee on Official Publications (SCOOP), 1988).

The emphasis here is on official publications of British origin, but for readers who have occasion to consult those issued by other countries or international organisations brief mention is made of relevant sources.

19.1 Guides to official publications

There is insufficient space here to describe all the different types of official publications and how to trace them. However, there are some very helpful guides which already do this. The first, and briefest, is itself an official publication.

HMSO Books: Guide to Publications and Services. Latest edn. Publicity Department, HMSO Books, St. Crispin's, Duke Street, Norwich, NR3 1PD.

This attractive booklet describes the publishing and bibliographic activities of HMSO, and how to trace and obtain HMSO publications. It includes guidance on official publications not obtainable from HMSO.

The other guides are more substantial and more detailed:

BUTCHER, D. *Official Publications in Britain.* Bingley, 1983.

'Examines the nature and organisation of official publishing in Britain, the adequacy of bibliographical control and the treatment of these publications in libraries.' References to education are minimal.

RICHARD, S. *Directory of British Official Publications: a Guide to Sources.* Mansell, 2nd edn, 1984.

Lists some 1,300 organisations that issue official publications themselves rather than through HMSO. There are sections on England and Wales; Northern Ireland; and Scotland.

RODGERS, F. *A Guide to British Official Publications.* H.W.Wilson:USA, 1980.

An annotated list of selected publications issued by British government departments and related agencies, official and quasi-official bodies, and many of the committees, boards and councils active as publishers. There is a chapter on 'Education and libraries'. Note the date.

A more recent survey of different categories of official publications in this country will be found in:

Whitehall and Westminster: Proceedings of a seminar on British Official Publications, ed. J.Nurcombe. **Standing Committee on Official Publications (SCOOP), 1985.**

For official publications in the countries of the EEC we have several guides, all from the same publisher:

HOPKINS, M. *European Communities Information: its Use and Users.* **Mansell, 1984.**

JEFFRIES, J. *A Guide to the Official Publications of the European Communities.* **2nd edn. Mansell, 1981.**

Official Publications of Western Europe, ed. E.Johansson. **Mansell, 1984 –8. 2 vols.**
Vol.1: **Denmark, Finland, France, Ireland, Italy, Luxembourg, Netherlands, Spain and Turkey, 1984.**
Vol.2: **Austria, Belgium, Federal Republic of Germany, Greece, Norway, Portugal, Switzerland and the UK, 1988.**

American government publications are covered in:

McILVAINE, B. *A Consumers, Researchers and Students Guide to Government Publications,* **H.W.Wilson:USA,1983.**
Explains 'what government publications are; why they are useful; where they can be found; how to find and use indexes that direct you to government publications; and how to locate information on such topics as education and statistics'.

There are two excellent short guides to government publications on education in this country:

ARGLES, M. and VAUGHAN, J. *British Government Publications Concerning Education during the 20th Century.* **4th edn. History of Education Society, 1982.**
Concise but informative, this gives the essential background as well as detailed listings. It has useful

sections on Scotland and Northern Ireland. There is a helpful appendix: Some reports with their popular names and official designations, which goes back much further than the one in the present guide (see 12.1).

ARGLES, M. *British Government Publications in Education During the 19th Century.* **History of Education Society, 1971.**
This 20-page pamphlet has a brief introduction which is followed by sections on guides and indexes; indexes of 19th century Parliamentary Papers; Departmental reports; other handbooks and guides; and Hansard. There is a chronological list of some important reports and finally, references for further reading.

The same authors produced a short general guide to official publications on education which is now rather dated:

ARGLES, M. and VAUGHAN, E. *British Government Publications Concerning Education: an Introductory Guide.* **Liverpool University Institute of Education, 1969.**

19.2 Lists of official publications

One of the main problems in locating British official publications until recently was the lack of a complete list of those currently in print to make searching easier. There is still no printed list of this kind, but we now have:

HMSO in Print on Microfiche. **4 per annum, HMSO.**
It gives up-to-date information on over 35,000 titles currently available from HMSO's Publications Centre, so it is an invaluable reference source. It includes all types of parliamentary, and most non-parliamentary, publications but international organisations publications are excluded. Many titles appear under several headings, e.g. author, title, government department, chairman.

HMSO's bibliographic database is accessible on Blaise-Line (updated monthly), and on Dialog (see 26.7) from 1990. There is also a CD-ROM version:

Catalogue of United Kingdom Official Publications (UKOP). **HMSO: Chadwyck-Healey. (CD-ROM).**

Compiled from the HSMO database and the *Catalogue of Official Publications not Published by HMSO* (see below). It contains 160,000 records from 1980 to date and is updated quarterly.

Until *HMSO in Print on Microfiche* appeared, it was necessary to consult a variety of catalogues and lists, in particular the so-called *Sectional Lists,* to find out which HMSO publications were currently in print. Most of the sectional lists give details of the publications of particular government departments, e.g. those of the DES (see p.134). Other sectional lists give information about publications on particular subjects. The lists are regularly updated. Note that the SED sectional list (no. 36) has been discontinued, and that other sources must now be consulted (see p.135).

By far the most convenient and informative listing of new official publications is the:

HMSO General Catalogue. HMSO.
First issued in 1989–90. It covers new and forthcoming books with a selection of the more popular titles from a massive back list.
Arrangement is within broad subject categories. The great virtue of the catalogue is that it has concise annotations of the great majority of items listed, including those issued by major international organisations. The section on education is invaluable. HMSO also issues seasonal annotated lists of New Books.

Basic information about new British official publications appears in the *Daily Lists,* and later in the *Monthly* and *Annual Catalogues* issued by HMSO. They should be available in most libraries.

The *Daily Lists* are issued every day except Saturdays, Sundays, and public holidays. Your library may get them in weekly batches. The titles are also listed on Prestel (see 14.17) usually on the day of publication, or in the case of international organisations publications on the date they are on sale from HMSO. The details are displayed on Prestel for one week. Information about HMSO publicity leaflet, sectional lists, telephone numbers, etc. is also given.

The *Monthly Catalogue* has two main sections: Parliamentary Publications listed numerically by series, and Non-Parliamentary Publications listed under the Departments which issued them. It also has a useful insert: the Monthly Selection, which gives short descriptions of publications which are likely to be of general interest. From 1987 the indexes have been cumulative throughout the year.

The *HMSO Annual Catalogue* is arranged in the same way as the monthly catalogue, with an index of authors, chairman, title and subjects. Five-yearly indexes of HMSO publications are also issued, e.g. 1976–1980.

Note that the publications of international organisations for which HMSO is the agency are included in the *Monthly Catalogue* but are omitted from the *Annual Catalogue.* This is because there is a separate:

HMSO Agency Catalogue. HMSO, annual.
This replaced the *International Organisations Catalogue* (last issued in 1985). It lists all the items which are sold by HMSO for British, European and International organisations, including periodicals. Check the index under 'Education' for relevant titles. The first issue covered the publications of 1986 and 1987.

The *Annual Catalogues* since 1894 have been re-issued by Chadwych-Healey in reduced facsimile reprints. Excellent eyesight and considerable patience are required to use them:

Catalogues and Indexes of British Government Publications 1920–1970. **Chadwyck-Healey, 1974. 5 vols.**
Vol.1: Consolidated indexes 1936–1970.
Vol.2: Annual catalogues 1920–1935.
Vol.3: Annual catalogues 1936–1950.
Vol.4: Annual catalogues 1951–1960.
Vol.5: Annual catalogues 1961–1970.

nual Catalogues of British Official and
rliamentary Publications **1984–1919.**
hadwyck Healey, 1975. 2 vols.
ol 1.: 1894–1909.
ol 2.: 1910–1919.

The United States Historical Documents
stitute has also issued a cumulative index
the annual catalogues for 1922–1972 as
art of its microform reprint of HMSO
blications for the period. It merges
venty-five separate annual and quinquen-
al indexes into one sequence of author
nd subject entries. It was published by
arrolton Press (USA) in 1976.

One could be forgiven for thinking that
ll official publications in Britain are issued
y HMSO but it is certainly not the case.
or adequate proof of this, reference can be
ade to the:

atalogue of Official Publications Not
ublished by HMSO. **6 per annum with annual**
umulations. Chadwyck-Healey.
It lists the publications of over 400 organisations
including government departments, nationalised
industries, research institutions, and other official
bodies, e.g. the Central Office of Information. 'A
number of well-known organisations are not
included in the catalogue either because they do
not publish or because they only publish through
HMSO.'

Items are listed in alphabetical order under
their publishing body, e.g. the DES, with full
bibliographical information, the price, and the
source from which it can be obtained. Inspectorate
reports on schools are included. Each entry has a
code number, and also a microfiche number, since
microfiche editions of almost all the items are
available. Periodicals are listed separately. There is
an alphabetical index of authors and subjects; and
there are indexes to sources of publications and to
microfiche identification numbers. The annual
volume is a handsome production which is a
pleasure to use.

This seems an appropriate place to in-
lude a publication that filled a definite gap
n its first appearance in 1981:

ritish Reports, Translations and Theses.
lonthly, with indexes cumulated annually.
iritish Library Document Supply Centre.

BRTT, as it is known, is a monthly bibliography of
material received by the British Library DSC which
falls into the category of 'grey literature' : semi-
published items that can be difficult to identify and
locate. Its aim is to increase awareness of what has
been issued and to promote its wider use.

BRTT lists British report literature and
translations produced by government organisations, industry, universities, and learned
institutions; and most doctoral theses accepted by
British universities and polytechnics since 1970. It
also covers reports and unpublished translations
from the Republic of Ireland, and selected British
publications of a report nature that are not
published by HMSO.

Arrangement is by subject using a special
coding system, e.g. Humanities, psychology and
social sciences (05); Education and training (05P);
Psychology (05Q); Sociology (05R). This is the
SIGLE classification (see below). A keyterm index
is supplied with every monthly part. Author, report
number, and keyterm indexes are provided on 48x
com fiche in March, June, September and
December. They are cumulated in printed form
annually. All the documents listed in BRTT are
available to registered users through the British
Library DSC Loan/Photocopy Service.

BRTT is a major contributor to SIGLE (System
for Information on Grey Literature in Europe). All
the material listed in BRTT excluding translations
is included in the SIGLE database which can be
accessed in the UK using Blaise-line.

Not many students or teachers will auto-
matically think of periodicals or 'serials' in
connection with official publications, but
another British Library list will help them
to appreciate just how many there are:

Checklist of British Official Serial Publications.
Latest edn. British Library Reference
Division.
This is arranged alphabetically by periodical titles
with the name of each issuing body added. It
includes annual reports but excludes items of local
interest. There is a list of discontinued and changed
titles at the end.

So far we have been concerned mainly
with British official publications. As already
indicated many of those issued by international agencies or overseas organisations
are recorded in the *Monthly Catalogue* and
later in the annual *HMSO Agency Catalogue*
(see p.132).

The Office for the Official Publications of the European Communities issues an annual *Catalogue: Part A. Publications*. It takes the form of a classified index (1701 is Education and Training) which lists monographs, series and periodicals under each heading but there are no annotations.

The *Unesco Publications Catalogue* is also published annually, and is much more informative. A brief section on general reference books and bibliographies is followed by a longer section on education with notes on new and selected titles, then a complete list. Unesco series on education are also listed.

Unesco has also issued retrospective bibliographies which may be of interest.

***Bibliography of Publications Issued by Unesco or Under its Auspices: the First Twenty-Five Years: 1946–1971.* (1973.)**

***Unesco List of Documents and Publications.*
1972–1976. 2 vols, 1979.
1977–1980. 2 vols, 1984.
1981–1983. 2 vols, 1985.**

It should be noted that all current and out-of-print Unesco documents and publications exist on microfiche.

19.3 Lists of official publications on education

References to official publications on education appear in many of the catalogues and lists already mentioned, notably the new *HMSO General Catalogue* (see p.132) which provides detailed descriptions of mainly recent publications. However, there are some specifically educational lists, several of which may already be familiar to you. One of the *HMSO Sectional Lists* (see p.132) is particularly relevant:

DEPARTMENT OF EDUCATION AND SCIENCE *(Sectional list no.2)*. **Latest edn. HMSO.**

This includes only titles published by HMSO, not those issued separately by the Department. Out-of-print titles are excluded, but recent issues of periodicals are recorded. Items not published by HMSO are included in the *Catalogue of Official Publications Not Published by HMSO* (see p.132).

The DES has begun a very convenient annual bibliography of its new publications

***DES Publications: a List of Publications and Selected Press Notices Compiled by the DES Library.* DES, annual.**
First published in 1986, this replaced the *DES Annual Report* (see p.32) but serves quite a different purpose. It lists all the significant publications on education issued during the year by the DES and HM Inspectorate; parliamentary publications on education; and educational legislation proposed or enacted. Publications of independent bodies funded by the DES are not included, but their addresses are given inside the back cover.

Titles are entered under more than one heading and can be traced in several ways. Those of a particular type are grouped together, e.g. Acts, circulars, HM Inspectors' reports, etc. Some titles are entered under the series name, e.g. Building Bulletins, Curriculum Matters. Others are listed under the names of the bodies which issued them. e.g. Assessment of Performance Unit. Some appear under subject headings, e.g. Curriculum, Education Law. Sources for obtaining publications are indicated.

The DES Library operates a Public Enquiry Unit which dealt with over 70,000 enquiries in 1989. The number has been rising substantially in recent years. It recently started issuing a series of information sheets, e.g. lists of LEAs, universities, grammar schools, which may be faxed on request.

HMSO publish a number of catalogues and leaflets describing selected HMSO and international organisations' publications in particular areas. They concentrate on more recent items. Relevant examples are: *Education; Books for Schools; Statistics;* and *Journals.* They are free from the Publicity Department, HMSO Books, St. Crispin's Duke Street, Norwich, NR3 1PD.

The DES issues an annual list of government circulars:

DEPARTMENT OF EDUCATION AND SCIENCE. *Index to Circulars and Administrative Memoranda Current on 1st January 19—.* **HMSO, annual.**

The full text of recent government circulars will be found in:

DEPARTMENT OF EDUCATION AND SCIENCE. *Circulars and Administrative Memoranda issued in 19 —*. annual.

There are handy lists of recent DES circulars, etc. in the *Education Year Book* (see p.57). For older Board of Education circulars in England and Wales consult:

VAUGHAN, J.E. *Board of Education Circulars: a finding List and Index*. History of Education Society, 1972.
'Now and again, to be sure, circulars of the Board of Education achieve fame, or have it thrust upon them.' (Quoted from E.T. Campagnac in the *Teachers World.* Jan.26, 1926.) The list is arranged in numerical order of circulars with a subject index. Locations are given in Institute and School of Education libraries, but 'the only known almost complete collection of these documents exists at the DES Library'.

Official publications on education in Scotland used to appear in:

SCOTTISH EDUCATION DEPARTMENT *Sectional list no. 36*. HMSO. (Ceased publication.)
The sectional lists are now being rationalised and this one has been discontinued. (Like the DES one above, it included only currently available titles.) However, there is now a sectional list on *Scotland* (no.71) which includes SED publications which are still in print.

This is updated by a *Scottish Office Publications List* issued annually by the Scottish Office Library, but it does not include circulars. For these we must consult:

SCOTTISH EDUCATION DEPARTMENT. *List of Departmental Circulars and Memoranda Current on 30 June 19—* SED, annual.

More recent SED circulars are included in the *Scottish Office Circulars List* (Annual) issued by the Scottish Office Library. Older circulars may be found in the *SED Annual Reports* (see p.33) where they were listed separately.

As most people are aware, HM Inspectors' reports on schools and colleges in this country are now being published for general information, and they are available free of charge. A convenient general listing is provided in:

HMI Reports List and KWIC Index. DES Library, annual.
The first index covered reports issued in 1983–85. It is estimated that about 250 reports are published each year in England, 150 in Scotland, and 80 in Wales. There are 2 parts: (1). A numerical listing of the reports; (2) A subject index in KWIC. form which enables the reader to identify a report from significant words in the title.

Directory of HMI Reports for England, Wales and Scotland; ed. J.Howson. A.P. & R.Baker Ltd, annual, with 3 quarterly supplements.
Formerly published by Education Data Surveys. This lists HMI reports by local authority; by reference number; by type of institution; and by subject area. It was first published in 1984. A useful feature is a list of articles based on the reports.

A list of each year's HMI reports also appears in *DES Publications* (Annual, see above), and more frequently in the *Catalogue of Official Publications Not Published by HMSO.* (6 per annum), see p.132. They are also noted in the *ACE Digest* (see p.9). Reviews of HMI reports issued during a particular period, or covering particular types of schools, are contained in a series of HMI publications *Education Observed*. Notes and/or comments on recent HMI reports can usually be found in the weekly *Times Educational Supplement* and its Scottish edition.

Lists of inspection reports in Scotland appear in the *HMI Reports and KWIC Index;* the *Directory of HMI Reports for England, Wales and Scotland;* the *ACE Digest* (see above); and the annual *Scottish Office Publications List* (see above). A non-official view of some inspectors' reports on Scottish schools is given in:

SCOTTISH PARENT TEACHER COUNCIL. *HM Inspectors' Reports; a Guide for Parents*. SPTC, 1985.
Looks at reports published from 1983 and attempts to explain some of the jargon used, for the benefit of bemused parents. The address of the Council is Atholl House, 2 Canning Street, Edinburgh, EH3 8EG.

20 Non-book materials

An increasing flood of non-book materials is being produced to meet the demands of the new approaches to teaching and learning in universities, colleges and schools. Most of these items are published commercially, but more and more institutions are producing their own materials to meet the particular needs of their own staff and students.

The first step in finding out what is immediately available is to consult your library's catalogue which should include a complete listing of A-V materials held. There may also be A-V bibliographies to highlight holdings in particular subject areas. New acquisitions should be included in your library's general list of additions.

Once you have become familiar with your own library's resources, you will wish to find out what other A-V materials are available. This is more difficult than in the case of books. At present, for example, there is no legal deposit for A-V materials, as there is for books, and no national bibliography covering all types of materials. However, the British Library in recent years has been assuming a more positive role in improving bibliographical control in this field.

No attempt will be made to provide a comprehensive survey of all the bibliographies, catalogues and lists of A-V materials. They vary considerably in their quality and usefulness, and they tend to date more quickly than corresponding records of printed materials. However, an effort has been made to include the main sources which could be helpful to students and staff in universities and colleges, and to teachers in schools.

Those who wish to survey the bibliographical territory of educational and information technology generally should consult:

MADDISON. J. *Information Technology and Education: an Annotated Guide to Printed Audio-Visual and Multimedia Resources.* **Open University Press, 1982.**

There is a useful short article *Audio-Visual Aids in Education* by P.Wicks in *British Book News.* May 1988, pp.340–3.

20.1 Guides to A-V catalogues and producers

Tracking down A-V materials of all types will involve you sooner or later in consulting the catalogues of individual publishers and producers. A good selection of these should be available in the A-V section of your library. There is a convenient guide which makes a good starting point for further investigation:

Distributors: the Guide to Film and Video Sources for Education and Training. **Latest edn. British Universities Film and Video Council.**
> This appeared in 1990 as a thoroughly revised and updated version of the *BUFVC Distributors' Index* which it replaced. It includes indexed and annotated details of over 600 distributors of films and videos (and their catalogues) suitable for higher education, including open learning.

An older, reasonably comprehensive, list may still be useful for reference.

AVSCOT Checklist of UK Audiovisual Software Producers, **compiled by G.Geddes and T.MacKechnie. AVSCOT, 1981.**
> This was prepared on behalf of the Scottish Branch of the Audiovisual Group of the Library Association. It is a straightforward alphabetical list of producers' names and addresses. Future editions were promised, with more information, and subject and media indexing.

There is a very convenient handbook which has been used in schools and colleges for many years to locate teaching and learning resources:

Treasure Chest for Teachers: Sources Available to Teachers and Schools. **Teacher Publishing Company, 3-yearly.**

The emphasis is on materials for practical classroom use. The contents include lists of societies and associations, embassies and tourist offices, etc. which provide services to teachers and schools; information about where to find material on different countries; lists of industrial, commercial and nationalised concerns which provide services; details of museums, art galleries and other places for schools to visit; lists of suppliers and manufacturers of educational equipment; and lists of publisher and publications. There is a classified index, which lists all these sources of information under subject headings.

One of the virtues of the *Treasure Chest for Teachers* from the consumer's point of view is that many of the materials produced by the organisations listed can be obtained at minimal cost. There is another book whose specific aim is to review resources of this kind:

MASON.R.S. *Free and Cheap Resources for Schools: a Survey and a Guide.* **Library Association, 1984.**
    'The author surveys the many sources of free and inexpensive material...and discusses and assesses the material itself.' Types of material include books, pamphlets, leaflets, worksheets, periodicals, wallcharts, posters, maps, postcards, films, kits and samples. There are chapters on different subject areas, as well as several appendices, one of which lists low cost periodicals and another sources of free 16 mm films.

There is a standard American guide on quite a different scale from any of those already mentioned.

Audio Video Market Place: a Multimedia Guide. **Bowker: USA, annual.**
    This is a directory for the A-V industry in America. The main section is a list of producers, distributors and services arranged geographically, then alphabetically, with a classified index. Formerly the *Audiovisual Market Place*.

Reference may also be made to the *Educational Media and Technology Yearbook* (see p.31), another American work, which includes a list of media-related organisations worldwide, and a list of producers and publishers.

Many of the catalogues described in the next two sections (20.2 and 20.3) have indexes of distributors and/or producers.

20.2 General catalogues of A-V materials

Catalogues of AV materials may be divided into general catalogues which list all or most types of those which list only one or two, e.g. film and video materials. An effort has been made to maintain these divisions in the following sections but it has not always been possible.

Catalogues may also be divided into those which list commercially produced materials and those which list materials produced by educational institutions. This will become apparent in the present section which is concerned with general catalogues, and the next, which describes film and video catalogues.

The current output of British books is recorded in the *British National Bibliography* (see p.115) but until more recent years there was no corresponding record of non-book materials. The gap appeared to have been filled by the:

British Catalogue of Audio-Visual Materials: a Subject Catalogue of Audio-Visual Materials. **1st experimental edn. British Library Bibliographic Services Division, 1979. Supplements 1980, 1982.**
    This was an impressive achievement. The first edition was based on records of items held in the former Inner London Education Authority (ILEA) Central Library Resources Service Library (now transferred to London University Institute of Education Library as the Curriculum Resources Collection, and still open to all inner London teachers.' The ILEA film and video collection was transferred to the London Borough of Greenwich. In the *British Catalogue of Audio-Visual Materials* (BCAVM) supplements the scope was wider.

The information about the items was supplied by their publishers. The catalogue listed A-V materials available for purchase or loan in the UK. Records and audiotapes were omitted as they were adequately covered elsewhere. The arrangement is by Dewey with a detailed subject index. There is also an index of titles, series, people, and organisations responsible for the creation of the materials.

The long-term future of the BCAVM is uncertain. Moreover, in the absence of statutory legal deposit for A-V materials, the record cannot be as complete as it is for books. However, the information contained in BCAVM is accessible through BLAISE (the British Library Automated Information Service).

There is an older series of catalogues which once held their own as guides to the range of conventional A-V materials for use in school:

EDUCATIONAL FOUNDATION FOR VISUAL-AIDS.
Subject Catalogues of A-V Materials. **EFVA, various dates.**
These catalogues of filmstrips, slides, kits and OHPs are probably familiar to most teachers, but some of the contents are now dated. There is a separate catalogue of wallcharts. All the catalogues have been revised from time to time.

The American firm Bowker produced several worthwhile handbooks in the 1970s:

Bowker A-V Guide: a Subject Guide to Audiovisual Educational Material, **ed. M. Koenig. Bowker: USA, 1975.**
Designed for teachers, lecturers and librarians. It lists audiovisual and visual only materials produced in the USA, the UK and Europe.

Core Media Collection for Schools, **eds. L.G.Brown and B.McDavid. 2nd edn. Bowker: USA, 1979.**
A carefully selected list, covering a wide variety of subjects and ability levels. Some of the items are obtainable in this country. There was also a *Core Media Collection for Elementary Schools* (Bowker, 1978).

It seems likely that these handbooks have now been superseded by the databases of A-V materials more recently established by Bowker: the *Textbook Database*, which lists books and non-book materials 'from kindergarten through first year of college' and includes kits, maps, and other teaching aids; and the *Audio Visual Software Database.* A new *Video Database* is in preparation.

An ambitious project has been launched at the University of Southern California in Los Angeles. Here the National Information Center for Educational Media (NICEM) has created the world's largest computer-based system for A-V learning materials. There are many different indexes in the system and new data is constantly being added. The information is available in printed and microfiche formats and is also accessible through *A-V Online* from Silver Platter Information Ltd.

However, increasingly institutions of higher education in this country are producing their own teaching and learning materials to support the courses they offer. Some of these have been published because they may be useful to staff in other institutions and other items are available for loan. The outstanding list is the:

BUFVC Catalogue, **eds J.Ballantyne and O.Terris. British Universities Film and Video Council, annual. (Microfiche.)**
First published in 1983, this superseded the well-known printed catalogues from the same source: *Audio–Visual Materials for Higher Education* (4th edn, 1979. 4 vols. Supplement 1981–82); and the *Higher Education Learning Programmes Information Service (HELPIS) Catalogue* (6th edn, 1980).
The current *BUFVC Catalogue* lists A-V materials for use in higher education. It includes films, videos, sound recordings, tape-slide programmes, slide sets which have substantial booklets, and filmstrips. Computer software and videodiscs have now been added. The catalogue is in three parts: the classified list, a title index, and a subject index. All subject areas are covered, and material appraised by subject specialists has been clearly indicated. Distributors' addresses are given in the printed booklet which accompanies the catalogue. Some of the items are held for preview at the BUFVC offices at 55, Greek Street, London.
The booklet also provides instructions on the use of the catalogue. The database from which it is compiled is available online and forms part of the British Library's BLAISE-LINE service under the title HELPIS. There are no restrictions by language, date, or country of publication, except that all the material listed is available in the UK. The *BUFVC Catalogue* is updated in Autumn each year. HELPIS is updated monthly.

The BUFVC launched a new in-house database AVANCE at the end of 1989. It has been developed with a grant from the ES. It records details of films, videos, etc. as well as information about producers. The CELPIS programme records were downloaded early in 1990.

There are older catalogues of materials produced by educational institutions which were pioneering efforts in their time and are mentioned here mainly for historical reasons:

Colleges of Education Learning Programmes Information Service (CELPIS): a Second List of Some Audio-Visual and Other Materials Made by Colleges and Departments of Education and Teachers' Centres. **Council for Educational Technology, 1976.**

The first CELPIS catalogue was issued in 1973. Both catalogues list materials for teacher education and training over the whole range of subjects, including education. The arrangement is by subjects alphabetically. There are no indexes. Inevitably much of the material is now dated and will no longer be available.

The same can probably be said of another catalogue of more localised interest. It was compiled by the librarians of four colleges of education in the West of Scotland:

Western Region Working Group on Educational Technology. Instructional Materials Catalogue: a Union List of Teaching and Learning Materials Produced in Four Colleges of Education in Scotland. **Craigie College of Education, Ayr, 1973. Supplement, 1976.**

Both the original catalogue and the supplement are arranged in classified sequence with title and subject indexes.

Individual institutions often produce catalogues listing A-V (and other) materials available for purchase outside or loan. A good example is *The Jordanhill Catalogue: a Range of Educational Materials.* Latest edn. Jordanhill College, Glasgow.

There is a catalogue of distance learning and independent study materials which has proved useful:

Open Learning Directory 1983: a Catalogue of Distance Learning and Independent Study Materials : Basics to A Level, **compiled by S.Yelton et al. Great Ouse Press : Nelson and Colne College.**

It was designed to help tutors and course organisers in open learning systems. The items come from colleges and commercial publishers. Many conventional printed materials are included. The compilers have provided ' a more extended description of each item than is usual in a catalogue of this kind'. There is a lengthy bibliography of articles and materials written about distance learning.

Many Teachers' Centres and Curriculum Development Centres have produced catalogues of their holdings and the items may be available for loan or reference. In the Strathclyde region of Scotland, for example, Glenpark and Robertson Centres, in the Renfrew Division, have each issued substantial catalogues of A-V materials most of which can be borrowed.

There is a useful source book which can help to pinpoint the existence and location of A-V collections:

Archival Collections of Non-Book Materials: a Preliminary List Indicating Policies for Preservation and Access. **British Library Research and Development Department, 1984. (Also on microfiche.)**

It lists organisations in the UK which have archives of non-book materials (i.e. films, sound recordings, photographs, etc.) in a broadly classified arrangement. Details given include functions, coverage, and availability.

This may be an appropriate point to mention several guides to collections of photographs, which still have a variety of uses:

Picture Sources UK; **ed. R.Eakins. Macdonald & Co, 1985.**

More than 11,000 collections of photographs, prints, etc. in the UK are described. Sources include: commercial agencies, public libraries, specialist photographers, museums and galleries, trade associations, manufacturers, government agencies, historical societies, universities, publishers, etc. Arrangement is by broad subject, with collection and subject indexes. There are introductory sections on pictures and the law, and on picture research.

***Picture Researcher's Handbook: an International Guide to Picture Sources – and How to Use Them,* compiled by H. and M. Evans. Latest edn. Van Nostrand Reinhold International.**
'This is a practical guide, with a single primary purpose: to help you find illustrations, and to do so as quickly, easily and effectively as possible'. Ultra-specialist sources are omitted, and so are sources which 'we have reason to believe we do not give a satisfactory service'. The entries are arranged in 3 groups: General; Regional; and Specialist, with a subject index. Collections from many different countries are included.

***Directory of British Photographic Collections,* compiled by J. Wall. Heinemann for the Royal Photographic Society, 1977.**
Designed for anyone who needs to consult, use, or reproduce photographs. Records over 1,500 collections 'ranging from small assemblies of rare Victorian prints to the resources of a modern news agency or a public institution'. Arrangement is by subject divisions, e.g. Society and Human Relationships, which includes education. There are indexes of subjects, owners, titles, locations, titles, and photographers, and a select bibliography.

A National Survey of Slide Collections, **by R.McKeown and M.E.Otter was published as a British Library research paper in 1989.**

20.3   Film and video catalogues

Films and videos are becoming an indispensable resource in support of teaching and learning at all levels, and there is now a wide range of catalogues which list the items available. In this case there is a well-established national record:

***British National Film and Video Catalogue: a Record of British and Foreign Films and Videocassettes which have Recently been made Available for Non-Theatrical Recording in Britain.* 4 per annum with annual cumulation. British Film Institute.**
Started as the *British National Film Catalogue* in 1983.

There are two main sequences, one for non-fiction the other for fiction films and videocassettes. The former are arranged by UDC (see p.5) and items o education will be found at 37. The entries are usefully annotated. Almost a quarter of the items originated as TV programmes. Foreign items are included. There are indexes of subjects and titles and a list of distributors' addresses. The British Film Institute (BFI) collects material through the National Film Archive by voluntary deposit and purchase. However, its acquisitions are by no mear comprehensive.

The BFI also produces a catalogue of *Films and Videos for Schools,* the contents of which are drawn from the *British National Film and Video Catalogue.* It lists several thousand films and videos which are available on free loan or hire.

For video materials only there is the:

***Penguin Video Source Book.* 3rd edn. Penguin, 1983. Update, 1984.**
Originally compiled by the National Video Clearin House Inc. in the USA, where the two earlier editions appeared, it is designed for 'educators and others'. The arrangement is by titles alphabetically but there are several indexes including a subject category index, and a videodisc index.

Another sourcebook of American origi on the grand scale is the:

***Educational Film and Video Locator.* Latest edn. Bowker: USA. 3 vols.**
The 1990 edition indexes 51,000 film and video titles which are available from the Consortium of College and University Media Centres.

There are several other sources of information about film and video materials which are available for sale, loan, or reference, as the case may be. Good examples are the catalogues of the film library services, which are of interest to teaching staff in universities, colleges and schools:

***Higher Education Film and Video Library Catalogue.* Latest edn. British Universities Film and Video Council.**
The Library provides 'an outlet for visual materials recommended for degree level use which would not normally be available from other sources'. The actual distribution of films is handled by the Scottish Film Library. The catalogue is arranged under broad subject headings, e.g. education, and

psychology, then alphabetically, with an index of titles. There is a historical section of films which have
dated because of the presentation or the age of the
print. Many of the items are available for purchase.

FL Vision: Film and Video for Education and General Interest. Concord Film and Video Council, annual.

Formerly known as the *Central Film Library
Catalogue*. It contains titles for the classroom and
lecture theatre in school and further and higher
education, and some of more general interest.
There is a separate catalogue: *Film and Video for
Industry*, which could be useful to some educational
institutions. The Central Film Library is not just a
lending library. Many of the titles in this catalogue
may be purchased. The subject and title indexes at
the end give some idea of the range of topics
covered in the catalogue.

The corresponding Scottish service is
provided by the;

SCOTTISH CENTRAL FILM AND VIDEO LIBRARY (SCFVL). Various catalogues, Scottish Central Film and Video Library.

Opened in 1939, as the Scottish Central Film
Library, it is now administered by SCET (see
p.174). It 'offers the widest range of educational
and cultural subjects available in Great Britain'.
There are many films from overseas, and an
increasing number are for sale as well as for hire.
The SCFVL no longer issues a complete catalogue.
The present policy is to issue subject and topic lists
which are helpfully annotated, e.g. *Video and Film for
Primary Schools* (1988) and *Training Materials on Film
and Video* (1988). Other lists on careers guidance,
computers, etc. are much briefer.
    Mention should also be made of the *Scottish Archive
Film for Education Project* established by the Scottish
Film Council in 1985. It is producing videotape
compilations of extracts from archive film for use
in both formal and informal educational contexts.

There are other agencies which issue
substantial catalogues of films and videos
for educational purposes.

BBC Enterprises Film and Video Catalogue. Latest edn, with supplements. BBC Enterprises Ltd.

A rich collection of material which has been shown
on BBC television. Many of the programmes are
available for hire as well as for purchase. The
arrangement is by UDC, so that the section on the
social sciences includes education. The items listed

under this heading are mainly Horizon
programmes, e.g. The Gifted Child.

BRITISH FILM INSTITUTE. Films and TV Drama On Offer. Latest edn. BFI.

There are three sections: Feature film listings; TV
drama listings; and Short film listings. Coverage is
international. Bookings can be made only by film
societies and institutions which are registered
members. Factual TV programmes are excluded
since they are listed in the *British National Film and
Video Catalogue* (see p.140).

CONCORD FILM AND VIDEO COUNCIL. Catalogue of 16 mm Films and Videos. Latest edn, with supplements.

Started as the Concord Films Council in 1959. The
catalogue lists documentaries, animated films and
feature-length productions concerned with
contemporary issues at home and abroad. The
Council also distributes films for many other
bodies. All the items are available for hire. Films
are listed alphabetically by title but there is a
subject index. This is one of the best sources for
educational films.

EDUCATIONAL FOUNDATION FOR VISUAL AIDS. 16 mm Films in the National Audio-Visual Aids Library. Latest edn. EFVA, Paxton Place, Gipsy Road, London, SE27 9SR.

The Library serves teachers and local authorities.
The catalogue lists a large amount of commercially
produced material, most of which may be hired or
purchased. The arrangement is by subject with a
title index. Unfortunately the catalogue has not
been kept up to date.

Granada Television Catalogue. Latest edn. Granada Television International Ltd.

This lists material on videocassette and standard
16 mm film taken from more than twenty-five
years' television output. Subject catalogues are
planned.

GUILD SOUND AND VISION. Film and Video Programmes. Latest edn. Guild Sound and Vision.

Guild distributes non-theatrical film and news
programmes 'which are designed to educate, train,
instruct and inform'. It also operated recording
schemes on behalf of Channel 4 TV and the Open
University. However, these schemes had to be re-
negotiated following the new Copyright Act (see
p.50) and Channel 4 decided to withdraw. The new
scheme provides access to all the undergraduate
programmes of the OU (see p.50). The catalogue is
arranged by broad subject areas, e.g. educational

studies, social studies. OU films are listed in a separate section.

NATIONAL AUDIO-VISUAL AIDS LIBRARY. *Film Library for Teacher Education Catalogue.* **Latest edn, with supplements. EFVA.**
Lists 16 mm films currently available for loan to institutions which are members of the Film Library for Teacher Education. Sections: (1) Child development; (2) Aspects of psychology and sociology; (3) The educational system and its history: comparative education; (4) Methodology. Arrangement is chronological within each section. A synopsis of each film's contents is given. There is an alphabetical index of titles.

RICHARD PRICE ASSOCIATES LTD. *Film and Television Catalogue.* **Latest edn.**
Lists those programmes from London Weekend, Channel 4, Trident and Grampian Television companies which are especially suitable for educational use. They cover a wide range of subjects.

YORKSHIRE TELEVISION. *Educational Videos.* **Latest edn. YTV.**
Lists pre-recorded videos at primary, secondary, college and university level. One of the more useful catalogues.

Two valuable guides to tracking down film and video materials appeared in the early 1980s:

Researcher's Guide to British Film and Television Collections. **Latest edn. British Universities Film and Video Council.**
Documents the film and television materials held in archives throughout the UK, which are are normally available for viewing outside the premises in which they are held. Coverage is from national archives to specialised collections. There are sections on film research and copyright in films, and some useful appendices. See also *Archival Collections of Non-Book Materials* (p.139).

Researcher's Guide to British Newsreels. **Latest edn. British Universities Film and Video Council (BUFVC), 2 vols.**
A companion work to the one above. It aims 'to illustrate the history and development of newsreels and cinemagazines...and at the same time serve as a practical reference work for...researchers'. The main part is a series of abstracts in chronological order from 1901 (vol.1 includes a chronological wallchart for easy reference). There are also lists of newsreel organisations, libraries and archives, and

documentation centres.

A Television Researcher's Guide compiled by BBC Television Training is available through BUFVC. It contains many useful tips and advice on doing TV research and 900 contact addresses.

There is an older catalogue of archive material which may be of interest:

NATIONAL FILM ARCHIVE. *Catalogue of Viewing Copies.* **British Film Institute, NFA, 1971.**
The NFA has a collection of 20,000 titles going back to 1895. The catalogue lists 3,000 duplicate copies of selected titles for internal viewing only. They include fiction and non-fiction films, and newsreels. There are indexes of directors, subjects, and persons.

Another older catalogue which deserves mention is the *Index of Documentary Films About Children,* issued by the National Children's Bureau, 8 Wakley Street, London, ECIV 7QE.

The catalogues of individual institutions should not be overlooked. Basic details of videotapes and audiotapes produced by the Open University are given in the catalogue *Undergraduate Course Material* (see p.65). Note also:

BRUNEL UNIVERSITY, AUDIO-VISUAL CENTRE. *Catalogue of Videotapes and Films.* **Latest edn.**
Lists videorecordings produced at Brunel and other universities which are held in the Centre's stock. Those made at Brunel are available for purchase but not for loan.

Again, regional or local authorities teachers' centres, etc. are possible sources of information about materials which may be available for previewing or borrowing.

For those who wish to keep up-to-date with new developments in this field there is the:

Video Education Magazine. **3 per annum. Video Education Magazine Ltd. (Videocassette.)**
'A new venture in publishing on videocassette for all interested in educational matters.' Each video is an

hour long and includes an education news bulletin, and reviews of materials and other items concerned with curricular innovation and special developments in school and college, etc.

This section would not be complete ithout mention of a remarkable publishing ɛnture which gives us a vision of how in-ɔrmation may be presented to us in future:

omesday Project. **British Broadcasting orporation, 1986. (Videodisc.)**
This is a unique information source on two videodiscs. It gives immediate access to an immense collection of facts which have been assembled and organised under the supervision of the BBC working with government and professional organisations, research teams from the universities, and other experts. It includes national statistics, research surveys, maps, pictures, specialist descriptions and video sequences. 'Using the Domesday system' it is claimed 'requires no computer literacy, no programming. It is like having a research library on your desk, with high technology systems to do all the searching for you'.
    The *National DISC* concentrates on official and research information, including over 9,000 sets of data from a wide variety of sources. There are four sections: Culture; Economy; Society; and Environment. The *Community DISC* contains some 23,500 photographs, 10,000 sets of statistical data, contemporary articles and reports, etc. This time the information is organised in relation to Ordinance Survey maps. The user moves from map to map, either across country or between maps of different scales. The whole system is interactive, requiring the use of a videodisc player, a micro, and a monitor. It has been called 'the first electronic reference system'. There is a useful account in an article by Gove,P.S. BBC advanced interactive video and the Domesday Disks in *Aspects of Educational Technology*. vol. 21, 1988, pp.152 –7.
    Those who would like up-to-date information on interactive video should consult the *Interactive Video Yearbook* (Kogan Page). The same publisher issues *Interactive Video: a Generic Courseware Catalogue*, which claims to list all the items currently available in the UK. The yearbook and catalogue are distributed by Kogan Page on behalf of the National Interactive Video Centre.
    The Department of Teaching Media at Southampton University has published *Inter-active Media in Higher Education* (1989) which examines the current 'state of the art' and future potential of interactive video.

20.4 Computer software

A work of this kind must take into account the rapidly expanding volume of computer software which is being produced to meet educational demands. Although the range of materials is still inadequate to meet instructional or training needs over the whole range of subjects, numerous guides have already appeared to help users to evaluate existing resources, and new items as they become available. Not all of these guides are British. The most generally useful guide to available software is:

M & E Educational Software Directory, **by J.Arthur and T.Russell. Macdonald & Evans, 1985.**
> It is designed 'to provide all types of educational establishment – primary, secondary and beyond - with up-to-date factual and concise information on educational software'. The arrangement is by subject or application, then alphabetically by title. Suitability for age groups is indicated wherever possible and prices are given. Lists of books and periodicals on computing and computer education have been included. There is a list of computer organisations and associations, and another of software suppliers, as well as a 'jargon-free' glossary.

The Chest Software Directory. **Latest edn. Hewlett-Packard.**
> Contains details of 700 software products available to the UK academic community at special discounts. It includes a section on education and training.

Other recommendable guides include:

BLAISE.D. *Evaluating Educational Software.* **Croom Helm, 1986.**
> One of the best surveys currently available. It provides teachers and educational researchers with practical guidelines for the selection and evaluation of educational software. The last two chapters, on choosing and using software, are particularly relevant. There is an appendix which summarises software selection criteria, and a bibliography.

Parents' Guide to Educational Software for Computers at Home and in the School, **ed. W.Tagg. Telegraph Publications, 1985.**
'Written and compiled by a team of some of Britain's leading figures in computer education' this combines common sense and professional guidance on the selection and use of software. It includes descriptions of 75 of the best educational programs.

SELF.**J.** *Microcomputers in Education: a Critical Evaluation of Computer Software.* **Harvester Press, 1985.**
Argues that the quantity of educational software is counter-productive and that quality is lacking. The book provides a critical survey of existing software and the methods used to produce it, and indicates likely developments.

Which Software Guide. **Latest edn. Hodder for the Consumers' Association.**
Over 1,000 computer programs arranged alphabetically in nine subject areas, including educational programs. Each item is briefly described, with an indication of the computer on which it runs, age suitability, etc. There are indexes of software publishers and computers.

The American guides are much more ambitious, and more up to date, than any of these:

Software Encyclopedia. **Bowker: USA, 2 vols, annual.**
It includes over 25,000 programs from about 3,000 producers. All the items are annotated and indexed 'to enable the user to find, compare and evaluate software options'. Bowker also publishes:

Software for Schools. **Bowker: USA, annual.**
Arrangement is by titles; also under nine computer systems; then by grade levels. There are introductory essays dealing with computer usage in schools.
Bowker's main *Microcomputer Software Database* contains detailed information on many thousands of microcomputer software packages. Related databases cover hardware manufacturers, software producers and distributors.

Index to Computer-Based Learning, **ed. A.Wang Entelek: USA , 1984. 2 vols.**
Compiled in the Computer Based Learning Department of the University of Wisconsin which acts as a national centre for information retrieval

and dissemination in the USA. There is a large section on education, and each entry contains a full program description. All the materials are cross-referenced in six ways. Programs are arranged by serial numbers, but can readily be identified by using the indexes.

Other American guides which may be encountered are:

Tess: the Educational Software Selector. **Latest edn. Teachers College Press: USA.**

TRUETT.**C.** and GILLESPIE.**L.** *Choosing Educational Software: a Buyer's Guide.* **Latest edn. Libraries Unlimited: USA.**

SpecialWare Directory: a Guide to Software Sources for Special Education. **Latest edn. Oryx Press: USA.**

More practically useful than any of these is *Evaluating Educational Software: a Guide for Teachers,* by H.N. Sloane *et al.* Prentice-Hall International: USA, 1989.

Reviews of new computer programs will be found in most of the periodicals concerned with educational computing, but they are too numerous to mention here. There are two additional sources which may be noted:

Educational Computing Programmes Information Exchange. **6 per annum. P.H. Educational.**
This provides member schools and colleges with useful information on currently available software, and classified lists covering CAL, computer studies and school administration.

Small Computer Program Index. **ALLM Books, 21 Beechcroft Road, Bushey, Watford, Herts WD2 2JU.**
An index to thousands of program listings in books and magazines, including educational programs.

Campus 2000 and NERIS (see 14.17) provide access to lists of computer programs nationwide. Teachers and others in Scotland are fortunate in having a National Software Centre located in SCET (see

174) at Downanhill in Glasgow. It was set p as part of the Scottish Microelectronics Development Programme (SMDP). Computer packages are made available through fourteen regional distribution centres. A publications list is obtainable on request.

Finally, since programmed learning materials are not dealt with elsewhere in this guide, it may be helpful to mention that a handy list of those currently on the market has appeared at intervals in the *International Year Book of Educational and Training Technology* (see p.31).

20.5 Sound recordings

The value of sound recordings not only of music but also of poetry, drama, documentary and instructional material and so on, has been appreciated by libraries for many years and many of them have built up substantial collections.

Improvement in the quality of tape cassettes encouraged libraries to concentrate as far as possible on this medium. Now they are having to meet the increasing demands of those who prefer the superior sound reproduction offered by compact discs.

Until recently the major organisation with a role for the collection of sound recordings was the British Institute for Recorded Sound. However, no complete catalogue of its holdings was ever published. The Institute's collection was taken over by the British Library in 1983 and was renamed the British Library Sound Archive. It has since joined forces with the Mechanical Copyright Protection Society to develop a national discography. The first phase of the project is due for completion in 1990, and the discography will then be extended retrospectively. A computerised database is being established with all its associated advantages.

The Archive has already completed a *Directory of Recorded Sound Resources in the*

United Kingdom, (compiled and edited by L. Weerasinghe and J. Silver. British Library, 1989), which should make it easier to locate material in specialised collections. It is pleasing to note that access is being granted to the Archive for research purposes. A full account of projected developments will be found in the *Library Association Record* for March 1986.

Meantime, all lovers of music and the spoken word are greatly indebted to General Gramophone Publications Ltd whose series of catalogues have greatly eased the problems of identifying and obtaining sound recordings generally. The company is building up a cumulative database which will eventually be expanded retrospectively to include all items from 1923 when the *Gramophone* library began.

However, this section on sound recordings is concerned with the spoken word and not with music. More particular mention must be made here of the:

Gramophone Spoken Word and Miscellaneous Catalogue. General Gramophone Publications Ltd, annual.

Unlike the *Gramophone* music catalogues this appears only once a year. It contains detailed information on sound recordings in specific categories such as drama, languages, documentary, instructional, entertainment, and so on. It is a prime source for schools and other educational institutions, and a rich treasure for the intelligent listener. See also *On Cassette* and *Words on Tape* (below).

Despite the protestations of the record companies about unauthorised copying, the issue of new records, tape cassettes and compact discs continues undiminished, and keen users need a reliable guide to make choices. The indispensable periodical in this field is the:

Gramophone Magazine. Monthly. General Gramophone Publications Ltd.

Each issue contains reviews of new and re-issued records, cassettes, and compact discs by a regular team of contributors. Reviews of spoken word recordings are included, and there are sections on trade shows, equipment reviews, etc. The *Hi-fi News* and *Record Review* (Monthly. Link House Magazines Ltd) covers much the same ground, and maintains comparable standards.

It is regrettable, if understandable, that the invaluable series of *Penguin Guides* to records, cassettes and compact discs are devoted entirely to music and do not include spoken word recordings. There is a gap here waiting to be filled.

On quite a different scale two impressive guides to spoken word recordings have appeared in America:

On Cassette: a Comprehensive Bibliography of Spoken Word and Audio Cassettes. **Bowker: USA, annual.**
Over 11,000 titles are listed, described and cross-indexed. All kinds of fiction and non-fiction books on tape are included, as well as speeches, interviews, plays, poetry readings, seminars, etc.

Words on Tape: an International Guide to the Audio Cassette Market. **Meckler: USA, annual.**
A *Books in Print* (see p.113) approach to the literature recorded on cassettes. It includes fiction, non-fiction, poetry, etc. listed by author, title, and subject.

Anyone using these works may also be interested in the remarkably comprehensive *International Index to Recorded Poetry* (H.W.Wilson: USA, 1983) which is really outside the scope of the present guide.

Details of support cassettes and audiotapes produced by the Open University are included in *Undergraduate Course Material* (see p.65)

There is an interesting brief survey of spoken word recordings in *British Book News* (October 1985, pp.585–7).

20.6 Radio and TV programmes

Much of the basic information about radio and television broadcasting will be found in the standard annual handbooks issued by the:

BRITISH BROADCASTING CORPORATION: *Annual Report and Handbook.* **BBC Publications, annual.**

INDEPENDENT BROADCASTING AUTHORITY. *Guid to Independent Television and Independent Radio.* **Independent Television Publications annual.**

Fuller details of BBC Schools Programmes are given in:

BBC RADIO FOR SCHOOLS AND COLLEGES. *Annual Programme.*
BBC TELEVISION FOR SCHOOLS AND COLLEGES. *Annual Programme.*
The BBC Schools Broadcasting service currently offers a wide range of radio series and TV series covering most subjects in the curriculum. They cater for all stages of school life from infants to students of 19 in school or college. Information about all the broadcast series and the materials provided to accompany them are included in these annual programmes which are published each Spring for the following year.

Independent Television provides a comparable service to schools. Details are give in the:

INDEPENDENT TELEVISION FOR SCHOOLS AND COLLEGES. *Annual Programme.*

Many radio and TV programmes offe learning opportunities for adults. Viewer and listeners can send for packs of materia or booklets relating to the programmes some free, some modestly priced. The include further information, reading list and local contacts, and often sugges follow-up activities. The material can be used by classes and groups as well as b individuals.

Information about these publications i given on air during or at the end of a broadcast, and is printed in the *Radio Time* and *TV Times* which provide details of th actual programmes. In addition a full list o BBC network education programmes i given on CEEFAX on the day of trans mission. ITV has its own information ser vice on ORACLE.

Other relevant publications are the *BBC ntinuing Education Newsletter; Training Re- rces for Adults on ITV and Channel 4* (IBA); */ Take-up* (ITV); and *SEE 4,* which appear gularly. They provide further details of rthcoming programmes which offer portunities for learning.

Many programmes which appear on TV e subsequently made available for pur- ase on videocassette, and many may also hired. Some catalogues of items on offer ve already been described in 20.3. e.g. e *BBC Enterprises Film and Video Catalogue* ee p.141) and the *Guild Catalogue* (see 141). For the recording of TV program- es other than those produced by the OU elow) see 13.3 (Copyright and education).

Open University radio and TV broad- sts, which are of interest to many general ewers as well, are detailed in the *Radio imes.* Information about videos and diotapes produced by the OU are given the catalogue *Undergraduate Course Mater- l* (see p.65). Educational institutions ishing to record OU television program- es should obtain a licence from Guild und and Vision (see p.50). Off-air cences for recording OU radio program- es are not available.

Special reference must be made here to e BBC's new *Education Programme* which arted in 1987. It is designed to offer 'a ajor platform for education in the UK'. he programme provides news, infor- ation and opinion on current issues. It btains the views of consumers as well roviders on what is happening 'at grass oots level'. It is dealing with such topics as e assessment of pupils and teachers; life ills teaching; private v. state education; CSE; new methods of open learning; iberal and vocational education; and so on. upporting fact sheets are issued. The rogramme should certainly help viewers to eep up to date with current developments.

20.7   Reviews of A-V materials

Undoubtedly one of the main problems in choosing non-book materials for institu- tional or personal use is obtaining reliable evaluations of their content and quality. The best source for reviews of current ma- terials was the periodical *Visual Education* which appeared monthly from 1950 to 1980 but unfortunately ceased publication. The weekly *Times Educational Supplement* continues to review non-book materials of all kinds, including computer packages, but not in a systematic way. It also reviews new equipment.

One of the best sources at present for keeping abreast of new publications in the A-V field is the:

Viewfinder: the BUFVC Magazine. **3 per annum. British Universities Film and Video Council.**
Apart from the diary section, and information about conferences and courses, it has a section called Subject News, which gives details about new items on specific subjects. It also has notes on new equipment. Issue no. 9 (May 1990) has a select list of interactive videodiscs for education and another of videodisc distributors and their addresses.

Reviews of new A-V bibliographies, and much else, appear in another periodical:

Audio-Visual Librarian. **4 per annum. Audio- Visual Groups of ASLIB and the Library Association.**
This has steadily improved since it first appeared in 1973. Although obviously intended for librarians it would be useful to anyone who wishes to keep up to date with current developments in the field. Apart from news of activities it contains longer reports on projects, conferences, courses, and A-V materials, as well as articles treating aspects of the subject in greater depth.

Other sources for reviews of computer software and sound recordings will be found in the appropriate sections (20.4 and 20.5 respectively).

It is of course impossible to exploit A-V or media resources fully unless adequate good quality equipment is available. Reviews of new A-V equipment will be found in the *TES* and *Viewfinder* (see above) but a comprehensive overview is needed at regular intervals. There was an excellent guide which fulfilled this purpose some years ago:

HENDERSON.J. and HUMPHRIES.F. *The Audio-visual and Microcomputer Handbook: the SCET Guide to Educational and Training Equipment.* **4th edn. Kogan Page, 1983.**
> It provided basic information for those responsible for purchasing and using A-V equipment, as well as microcomputers, in industry and education. It contained advice on the use of media and had an extensive products directory covering equipment, software, and production services. The microcomputer supplement was an important feature. Another edition, or another work of similar quality, would be very welcome.

There are some useful lists of educational hardware in some recent issues of the *International Yearbook of Educational and Training Technology* (see p.31). The *Audio Visual Directory* (Annual), and the periodic both from Maclaren Publishers, may also be consulted for advice about A-V equipment, materials, and services.

Periodicals

21 Periodicals

Periodicals are often underexploited by students, teachers and readers generally. They are important because they are usually more up to date than books and because much of the material in them never appears in books at all. They are valuable for information on specific topics, and for keeping in touch with new developments in education and related subject fields. Indeed, regular use of periodical literature is probably the best way of keeping up to date that there is.

The better known weekly periodicals such as *The Listener* and *New Society,* and monthly ones such as *Encounter* should not be overlooked as possible sources for educational articles. However, there are many periodicals devoted specially to education or to different aspects of it. General lists of periodicals are described in 21.1, lists of educational periodicals in 21.2. and sources of information about new periodicals in 21.3.

Most students and teachers will have access to the *Times Educational Supplement* (and/or its Scottish edition) and to the *Times Higher Education Supplement,* which are published weekly in newspaper format. Periodicals published at longer intervals may provide an added perspective or a fuller understanding or particular topics. Scottish readers, for example, may scan the *Scottish Educational Review,* issued by the Scottish universities, or *Education in the North,* issued by the Northern College.

In exploring the range of periodicals in a fair-sized education library you may be discouraged by the number on display. As with the general periodicals, any one of them might contain articles that could be of interest to you – the problem is knowing where to look. However, by using the subject indexes to periodicals (see 22), and the periodical abstracting services (see 23) you can exploit their contents more readily than you imagine. Moreover there is a current awareness service: *Contents Pages in Education* (see p.158) which enables you to scan the contents pages of over 500 educational periodicals on a continuing basis.

The more important periodicals received by your library will be filed and eventually bound or kept on microfilm. As the years pass, the once current issues will acquire added value for research purposes. As most researchers are already aware, much of the most relevant material is to be found in periodicals rather than in books, and many of the articles they require will have to be borrowed from other libraries (see 24).

However, the use of periodicals should not be confined to serious research workers. Anyone who is investigating a topic for an essay, assignment or project will at some stage find it helpful to examine the periodical literature available.

21.1 General lists of periodicals

Most readers will probably be reasonably satisfied with the range of periodicals immediately available in the library which they are using. Those who are doing more serious research, or have particular interests of their own, will also wish to find out what other periodicals exist. There are several excellent guides to help them:

***Willings Press Guide: a Guide to the Press of the United Kingdom and to the Principal Publications of Europe, the Americas, Australasia, the Far East and the Middle East.* Willings, annual.**
This is the most familiar guide to periodicals and newspapers. It is a handy size in a flexicover binding. About 20,000 titles are listed, including directories. It now has separate lists of new and discontinued periodicals, a useful feature. Reliable though it is, *Willings* is not the best source of information about academic or specialised periodicals. However, it has a classified index which lists periodicals in subject groups, e.g. education: psychology and psychiatry; and sociology.

Benn's Media Directory. **Benn's Information Services Ltd. 2 vols, annual.**
Has a large format but covers much the same ground as *Willings* in more detail. There is also information on media organisations, etc. It was formerly called *Benn's Press Directory.*

In both these guides the emphasis is on trade periodicals, i.e. those commercially published. There is a higher proportion of scholarly and academic periodicals in:

Current British Journals: a Bibliographical Guide; **ed. D.P.Woodworth and C.M.Goodair. Latest edn. British Library Document Supply Centre.**
Arranged by UDC (see p.5) with an index of periodical titles and subjects. In many cases brief annotations are given. This is now the standard general list of British periodicals, though it cannot be as up to date as annuals like *Willings* and *Benn's.*

There is another important British list in a more limited subject field:

Walford's Guide to Current British Periodicals in the Humanities and Social Sciences, **ed. A.J. Walford with J.M. Harry. Library Association, 1988.**
A selective list. Relevant areas covered besides the social sciences (which includes education) are philosophy, psychology and biography. The general arrangement is by subject. Details of abstracting, indexing, and online services are given for each subject, with notes on available directories, etc.

The largest of all general lists of periodicals is American:

Ulrich's International Periodicals Directory : a Classified Guide to Current Periodicals, Foreign and Domestic. **Bowker: USA. 2-yearly. 3 vols. Supplemented by *Ulrich's Quarterly.***
Total coverage is impressive although the information is given in abbreviated form. The arrangement is by broad alphabetical subject headings. If a periodical is included in an indexing or abstracting service this is indicated. There used to be a separate volume for irregular serials and annuals but they are now interfiled in the main sequence. Other new features are: descriptive annotations for 10,000 leading serials, file-names for titles available online, and information on 200 titles available on CD-ROM. The quarterly supplement lists new periodicals published since the main directory appeared, and also 'cessations'.

A more recently established list on an equally impressive scale serving much the same purpose is the *Serials Directory: an International Reference Book.* Latest edn. EBSCO Publishing: USA, 3 vols. EBSCO also publishes an *Index and Abstract Directory* (see p.161).

Full lists of current periodicals are issued by firms specialising in the supply of periodicals to libraries worldwide. Minimal information is given, but they will help you to check the existence of titles quickly, and they are frequently updated. A good example is:

Blackwell's Catalogue of Periodicals and Continuations. **Latest edn.**
A compact title list of the journals most frequently ordered by academic libraries, with their subscription costs. Continuations, i.e. monographic series and serials in book form, are listed separately.

None of the publications mentioned so far make any attempt to evaluate the periodicals listed in their pages. The following work will therefore be very useful, despite its American emphasis:

KATZ. B. and KATZ, L.S. *Magazines for Libraries.* **Latest edn. Bowker: USA.**
This handsome book provides intelligent assessments of most of the periodicals, which have also been carefully selected. The arrangement is alphabetical by subject, e.g. education, psychology, sociology. The proportion of British titles is limited. The sixth edition appeared in 1989.

Individual libraries' lists of periodicals and union lists of the periodicals held by groups of libraries, can be helpful in identifying unfamiliar titles (see 24).

Serious students and researchers will wish to know which periodicals are available in microform. There is an annual publication which meets this need:

Serials in Microform. **University Microfilms International (UMI) : USA, annual.**
A large paperbound volume which lists, by title and subject, periodicals (more than half of them current) which are available through the UMI

Serials Subscription Service. The copies are
supplied at a fraction of the cost of the paper editions. The arrangement here is by title and subject.

They may also wish to know which
periodicals are available in translation:

**Journals in Translation: a Guide to Journals in
Translation. Latest edn. International
Translations Centre. Delft, and the British
Library Document Supply Centre.**
Over 1,000 titles from all subject fields are listed
alphabetically. There is a 'keyword in context'
subject index, and a list of publishers/distributing
agents. Those titles held by, and available from, the
British Library DSC are clearly indicated.

21.2 Lists of educational periodicals

There are numerous sources for information on educational periodicals. However, the only separately published British
list is:

**VAUGHAN, J.E. British Journals Concerning
Education: a List for Research Workers and
Others. British Educational Research
Association, 1983.**
Lists about 200 titles, giving basic information
including editors' names. *Willings Press Guide* (see
p.151) was used in its compilation. It includes
periodicals on the teaching of particular subjects.
Revised and updated editions were anticipated.

There is a shorter list of the same kind in
the *Education Year Book* (see p.57) which
should be available in academic and public
libraries. The list will probably be adequate
for the needs of most readers. It is also up
to date.

The current issue of the *British Education
Index* (see p.156) contains a full title list of
the periodicals regularly indexed by the
service. The annual cumulation gives their
publishers as well. Again, periodicals on the
teaching of individual subjects are included.

A fuller, international list will be found in
the latest issue of *Contents Pages in Education*

(see p.158) which is a current awareness
service. It gives details of over 500 journals
covered by the service. There is an even
longer list of 850 journals (mainly American)
in the latest issue of the *Current Index to
Journals in Education (CIJE)* (USA) (see
p.157).

Useful current lists of periodicals on
various aspects of education are included in
each issue of the education abstracting
services described in 23.2. A much less
recent list of educational pereiodicals will
be found in Humby, (see p.126).

There is a convenient short list of American educational periodicals at the beginning of each issue of the *Education Index*
(USA) (see. p.157) However, the standard
American list is a separately published
work:

**CAMP, W.L. and SCHWARK, B.L. Guide to
Periodicals in Education and its Academic
Disciplines. 2nd edn. Scarecrow press, 1975.**
The fullest, though unfortunately not a very
current guide to educational periodicals in the US.
There is no British equivalent on the same scale.
Over 600 titles are listed in an alphabetical subject
arrangement, with subject and title indexes. A new
edition is badly needed. Meanwhile, a welcome
must be given to *Education Journals and Serials: an
Analytical Guide*, by M.E. Collins (Greenwood Press :
USA, 1988)

Finally, there are two separately published international lists which should be
mentioned:

**INTERNATIONAL BUREAU OF EDUCATION. List of
Periodicals. Latest edn. IBE: Unesco.**
This has introductions in English and French. The
arrangement is alphabetical by title. Basic details
and indications of the IBE's holdings are given.
There are several indexes: one of institutions;
another of periodicals under their countries of
origin; and a subject index based on keywords used
in the *Unesco: IBE Education Thesaurus* (see p.19).

**World List of Specialised Periodicals: Sciences of
Education. Maison de Sciences de l'Homme
Service for the Exchange of Scientific
Information, 1974.**
Note the date. However, this may still be useful for
occasional reference. It includes 'scientific'

periodicals only, i.e. those giving the results of new research or original studies, and excludes those on the teaching of particular subjects. A similar list on psychology was published in 1967.

21.3   New periodicals

Despite the unpredictable life histories of periodicals and their high mortality rate, new ones are appearing all the time. Indeed, it is often easier to learn of their arrival in the world than of their departure from it.

Perhaps the most convenient source of information on new and discontinued periodicals is now *Willings Press Guide* (see p.151) which has separate lists of them. *Ulrich's International Periodicals Directory* (see p.152) performs a similar service in America.

The first issue of a new periodical is likely to be recorded in the weekly *British National Bibliography* (see p.115), although this could be some time after publication. There is an equally authoritative source:

Serials in the British Library. 4 per annum with annual cumulations. British Library Bibliographic Services.

This not only records new titles but also gives location for them in selected libraries. It includes British serials received through legal deposit. It also notes serials which have ceased publication. Arrangement i alphabetical by title, with a subject index derived fron keywords in each title. It is cumulated continuously each year on microfiche. It updates *Current Serials Received* (see p.163), a complete list of periodicals taken by the British Library.

There is a very brief list of new period icals on various subjects, with evaluativ notes, in each monthly issue of the *Britis Book News* (see p.117).

Advertisements for new periodicals ar often inserted in academic journals. Im portant new titles should be available in good education library soon after publica tion. Your own library may provide occasio al lists of new titles added, with brie annotations. However, in the present econc mic climate, most libraries are having t adopt a more stringent acquisitions polic and to rely more heavily on the resources o the British Library Document Suppl Centre.

22 Subject indexes to periodicals

Although much can be achieved by scanning current issues of periodicals the real keys to their contents are the subject indexes and the abstracting services.

Most periodicals have their own indexes. Occasionally they have cumulated indexes covering many years, which make searching for articles much less tedious. Even more useful are the general indexes which regularly index the contents of a large number of different periodicals (see 22.1). They enable you to find relevant articles in periodicals which you would not have thought of consulting in the first place.

There are subject indexes of this kind which are devoted almost exclusively to educational periodicals (see 22.2) and these are the ones which will be most used by readers of this guide. The periodical abstracting services offer further advantages and they are fully described in chapter 23.

22.1 General subject indexes to periodicals

There are numerous subject indexes which, although not directly concerned with educational periodicals, may help you to retrieve articles of educational interest. The first of them should be known to all students and teachers since it is a basic tool for locating articles on a very wide range of subjects:

British Humanities Index. 4 per annum with annual cumulation. Library Association Publishing Ltd.

It indexes, by subject and author, articles in about 300 British periodicals of general interest such as *The Listener, New Society* and *Encounter,* which often contain articles on education. It also indexes articles in several newspapers, e.g. *The Times* and *The Guardian* (but not *The Scotsman* or the *Glasgow Herald*). It started life in 1916 as the *Subject Index to Periodicals,* so its value for retrospective searching is obvious.

The BHI is now complemented by the *Applied Social Sciences Index and Abstracts* (see p.160). Unlike the BHI it is international in scope, but since it is a combined indexing and abstracting service it is described in 23.2.

Another British subject index covers a very limited range of periodicals but they are all widely read and used:

The Times Index. Monthly, with annual cumulations. Times Newspapers.

Formerly an index to *The Times* newspaper only, it now covers all the newspapers and periodicals emanating from Printing House Square:

The Times
The Sunday Times (including the magazine)
The Times Educational Supplement
The Times Scottish Education Supplement
The Times Higher Education Supplement
The Times Literary Supplement

It is therefore a very important source for current information on education and other topics. Again it becomes increasingly useful as time goes on for retrospective searching. Entries are usually, but not always, made under specific rather than general subject headings, e.g. under universities rather than education. Personal names are included.

Until recent years, The *Times Index* was issued quarterly, but monthly publication has improved its currency and therefore its value. If your library keeps back issues of *The Times* and its weekly supplements (probably on microfilm) you will be glad to have this index at your disposal.

There are several well-known American subject indexes which may be worth consulting if they are available in your library. They are published by the H.W.Wilson Company:

Readers' Guide to Periodical Literature. 18 per annum with quarterly and annual cumulation. H.W.Wilson: USA.

This is the best known and most used of the H.W.Wilson indexes. It covers a broad range of general interest periodicals, mainly American (almost 200 in all). Authors and subjects, as in all Wilson publications, are in one alphabetical sequence. Retrospective volumes are available from 1900.

There is also an *Abridged Readers' Guide to Periodical Literature* (9 per annum with quarterly and annual cumulations). It indexes about a third of the titles in the parent work. Retrospective volumes are available from 1960.

If you find the *Readers' Guide* useful, you may be interested to known that there is now a *Readers' Guide Abstracts,* which gives a summary of each article indexed by the main work (see p.159).

Essay and General Literature Index. 2 per annum including the annual cumulated issue, with five-yearly cumulations. H.W.Wilson : USA.

Indexes English language essay collections and anthologies with the emphasis on the social sciences. Retrospective volumes are available from 1900. There is a separately published *Essay and General Literature Index: Works Indexed 1900–1969.*

Humanities Index. 4 per annum with annual cumulations. H.W.Wilson : USA.

Indexes articles in about 300 periodicals in this field. Annual volumes go back to 1974. Before this it was part of the *Social Sciences and Humanities Index,* now discontinued.

Social Sciences Index. 4 per annum with annual cumulations. H.W.Wilson : USA.

This was formerly part of the *Social Sciences and Humanities Index* but became a separate publication in 1974. It indexes about 300 English language periodicals, including some on subjects related to education, e.g. psychology, sociology, and women's studies.

All of the H.W.Wilson indexes (ten of which are described in the present guide) are now available in the form of databases for online searching through WILSONLINE. 'This gives access to more than half a million articles in the 3,500 periodicals that Wilson indexes annually, and to the more than 60,000 books catalogued each year.' There is a simplified version of WILSON-LINE called WILSEARCH, a new personal computer software package for use by the general reader and by schools.

22.2 Subject indexes to educational periodicals

The most essential subject index to periodicals on education, for British users, is the

British Education Index. 4 per annum with annual cumulations. BE1, Leeds University.

It indexes by subject and author 'articles of permanent educational interest in about 250 British periodicals concerned with education and teaching, including the teaching of particular subjects'. A list of the periodicals indexed appears at the beginning of each issue, along with an explanation of how to use the *British Education Index* (BEI). Publication details are given at the end of each annual volume.

Not every periodical is fully indexed. Many are indexed on a selective basis only, with the emphasis on those articles likely to be of continuing interest. The main body of the work lists articles under topic headings. There is a detailed list of headings at the front to help you to pinpont articles on different aspects of education. It is preceded by an author list.

The BEI was issued three times a year from 1954 to 1971. Since then it has appeared quarterly with an annual cumulation. From 1976 to 1985 it used précis indexing, which was less easy for the layman to understand. Since 1986 the BEI has been published by Leeds University instead of the British Library, as formerly. The précis indexing system has been replaced by a 'flexible system based on a natural language' devised in consultation with educationists. A separate thesaurus (see p.19) has been published which includes both subject definitions and cross-references, and this is the key to the use of the BEI.

The thesaurus is also the key to the contents of the database, for the BEI has been accessible online through BLAISE-Line since 1982, and through Dialog in America since 1988. With the change in publisher a review of the titles indexed was undertaken and about 40 titles were replaced.

The present BEI database contains records of articles indexed since 1976, and since in its printed form the BEI goes back to 1954, it opens up a very wide range of information. It is one of the basic tools in education and should be known to, and used by, all students and teachers. Those with access to a good education library will find that many of the articles indexed are immediately available.

There is an American equivalent of the BEI:

ducation Index. **10 per annum, with uarterly and annual cumulations. I.W.Wilson : USA.**
It is not so directly useful to British users since many of the 350 or so periodicals indexed are American, and your library will take a much smaller proportion of them. However, it is always worth consulting as an extra resource. Although it is primarily an index to periodicals, it also indexes other material including the contents of year books. At the end of each issue there is an index to reviews of new books on education, again mostly American. The arrangement is quite different from that of the BEI. Author, title and subject entries are in one sequence. A list of the periodicals indexed appears at the front of each issue. Changes are made from time to time in response to the requirements of users.

The other important American index is the:

urrent Index to Journals in Education (CIJE). **Monthly, with six-monthly cumulations. Oryx Press : USA.**
This is the largest of the three indexing services mentioned so far. The *CIJE* is issued by ERIC (see p.190) and indexes articles in almost 800 educational and education-related journals. The indexing is impressively thorough. The terms used as headings are derived from the *ERIC Thesaurus* (see p.18). The main section lists periodical articles under their titles and the majority have annotations. There are also subject and author indexes, and a journal contents index which lists the contents of recent issues of periodicals. Again, it must be said that many of the periodicals indexed by *CIJE* may not be in your library, but the issues or articles you want may be borrowed for you.
The *CIJE* had annual cumulations until 1975, when they became semi-annual because of their increasing size. A cumulated author/title index covering 1969–1984 appeared in 1985. The contents of *CIJE* are accessible online through DIALOG and are also available on CD–ROM (see p.157).

Less frequently found in this country, but worth consulting if it is available, is the:

Australian Education Index. **3 per annum with annual cumulations. Australian Educational Research Association.**
It indexes by subject, and by author, articles in over 80 periodicals, as well as books, reports, theses, etc. published in Australia. Unfortunately many of the items indexed will not be available in British libraries. Articles are listed under broad subject categories which are outlined at the beginning. A more specific subject index records articles by their titles. The descriptors (terms) used are selected from the *Thesaurus of Education Descriptors*, an Australian work based on the *Thesaurus of ERIC Descriptors* (see p.18). There is also a:

Canadian Education Index. **3 per annum with annual cumulation. Canadian Education Association.**
This is an author/subject index to selected periodicals, books, pamphlets, and reports concerning Canadian education.

One must regret the demise of two British publications which are not, strictly speaking, subject indexes but rather current awareness services:

Hertis Education Review: a Fortnightly Review of the Press and Literature Covering Further and Higher Education. **26 per annum. Hertis. The Hatfield Polytechnic. (Ceased publication)**
Its aim was 'to provide a fast service for current topics of discussion' in education. It covered the field of further and higher education fairly widely, and included references not only to books and periodical articles but to newspaper articles, press releases, speeches by MPs, questions asked in Parliament and so on. Entries were arranged alphabetically under about thirty topics, e.g. environmental education, polytechnics, and teacher training, and they were briefly annotated. It was obviously more up to date than the other indexes already mentioned, but since it did not cumulate and there were no indexes its value for retrospective searching was, and is, very limited.

Higher Education Current Awareness Bulletin. **26 per annum. University of Aston-in-Birmingham Library. (Ceased publication.)**
The aim here was to cover all aspects of higher education, although its average issue was about ten pages. It indexed selected periodical articles, books, conference papers, news items and so on. The general arrangement was by subject. Occasionally it included a list of periodicals indexed. It first appeared in 1968.

The DES library used to issue free: *Current Titles:* a monthly selection of about 500 periodical articles related to the work of the DES and HM Inspectorate, but its circulation is now restricted. However, the Library still issues monthly and annual indexes to press notices released by the DES.

Mention of current awareness services is a reminder that your own library may provide a service of this kind. If so, it will have the advantage that it is geared to the needs of the students and staff it actually serves. Some libraries even provide a personalised current awareness service, based on user profiles, for individual members of staff and research students. If so you should take full advantage of them and ensure that your profile is kept up to date.

There was an important development in 1986 when a 'computer-based international current awareness service' in education was introduced by Carfax, publisher of many periodicals in the educational field. The service, which met a long-standing need, is both a current awareness service and a subject index:

Contents Pages in Education. Monthly, with 6-monthly, annual and 3-yearly cumulations. Carfax Publishing Co.

Although it is intended primarily for researchers and librarians it could be just as useful to students and teachers generally. It regularly shows the contents pages of over 500 of the world's educational journals and fully indexes them by author and subject. There is also a detailed directory of all the periodicals covered by the service. The contents pages are arranged alphabetically by the title of the periodical. A unique identifier is given to each contents page. By checking the subject index you can use the identifiers to scan the titles of articles in relevant periodicals and note those which interest you.

23 Periodical abstracting services

The subject indexes described in the previous chapter enable you to locate articles in education and related topics. Normally they do not provide any further information about the articles, although the CIJE (see p.157) is one exception. Periodical abstracting services go a stage further by providing précis or short summaries of articles. An abstract should help you to decide whether it is worth obtaining and reading the original article. Often it will be sufficient for your immediate purpose.

Abstracting services for theses, dissertations and current research projects are described in 26.3 and 26.4.

23.1 General abstracting services

There are several general abstracting services which could be useful to those who are seeking information on current and less recent developments in education. The first should already be familiar to all students and teachers:

Keesings Record of World Events. **Monthly. Longman. (Loose-leaf, with annual binder)**
Universally known as *Keesings Contemporary Archives* until the title changed in 1987. It is an invaluable record digested from news agencies and official sources worldwide. Since 1931 it has provided incomparably detailed coverage of political, social and economic events. Full texts or summaries of major treaties, agreements, speeches, parliamentary debates, etc. are given. Each issue now starts with a monthly review. Indexes cumulate throughout the year. Topics are listed alphabetically under countries and there is a name index.

The full text of speeches made in parliament are of course contained in the *Weekly Hansard* published by HMSO. Not all education libraries will take this, but they may acquire copies of individual *Daily Issues* following important educational debates.

The American equivalent of *Keesings* is the:

Facts on File Yearbook: Complete World News Digest for 19— (Annual bound volume containing all the weekly issues.) Facts on File : USA.
The most important news events are presented in considerable detail. The index has over 50,000 entries, and this will give some idea of the scope of the yearbook. It was first published in 1940. There is also a *Facts on File 5-Year Index to World News Affairs*, which provides a chronology of world events.

A good example of a general periodical abstracting service which started publication in 1986 is the:

Readers' Guide Abstracts. **8 per annum with cumulations. H.W.Wilson : USA.**
This was the first of the numerous H.W.Wilson indexes to produce an abstracting service. It has the same coverage as the *Readers' Guide to Periodical Literature* (see p.155).

23.2 Education abstracting services

Unfortunately there is no abstracting service which covers education as a whole, if we except the American *Resources in Education* (ERIC) which is unique in its scope and is therefore given a section to itself (26.6) in the chapter on educational research. There is also *Research into Higher Education Abstracts* (see p.186) which gives summaries of current research projects. The periodical abstracting services described below are of more general interest. Each of them covers a particular area or aspect of education. Perhaps the best known is:

Sociology of Education Abstracts. **4 per annum. Carfax Publishing Co.**
> Provides abstracts from over 350 periodicals and also from books. Coverage is international but the abstracts are always in English. The main arrangement is by author, but there is a subject index in two parts: Educational Study Areas, and Sociological Study Areas. A cumulated author index has been published from vol. 3 onwards.

Other abstracting services include:

Educational Administration Abstracts. **4 per annum. Sage Publications : USA.**
> Provides abstracts from about 160 mainly American periodicals. The abstracts are classified by subject (see the contents list) with an author index. A detailed subject index would have been helpful. As usual with abstracting services, there is a time-lag in publication. First published in 1966.

Educational Technology Abstracts. **4 per annum. Carfax Publishing Co.**
> Started in 1985, this covers about 180 relevant journals. Arrangement is under subject headings: design and planning; teaching methods; instructional media; instructional resources; learning; assessment and evaluation.

Multicultural Education Abstracts. **4 per annum. City of Birmingham Polytechnic.**
> Based at the Polytechnic's International Centre for Multicultural Education. It endeavours 'to provide a key to the substantial amount of difficult to locate material being written in this field'. About 420 journals, and relevant books, are scanned for material. A cumulated author and subject index appears in the final issue of each volume. Started in 1982.

School Organisation and Management Abstracts. **4 per annum. Carfax Publishing Co.**
> Also launched in 1982, this is an 'international current awareness service for the busy practitioner and scholar'. It scans about 170 educational journals and relevant books, as well as conference papers, reports and theses. A cumulated author and subject index is included in the last issue of each volume.

Technical Education Abstracts. **4 per annum. Carfax Publishing Co.**
> A well-established service which is designed for 'all those concerned with scientific, technical and further education including education for industry and commerce at all levels'. The abstracts are drawn from a wide range of sources, including periodicals and separately published works. The last issue in each volume has cumulated indexes. First published in 1961.

There are two abstracting services in areas related to education which deserve mention here:

Psychological Abstracts: Nonevaluative Summaries of the World's Literature in Psychology and Related Disciplines. **Monthly. American Psychological Association : USA.**
> Each monthly issue has '16 major classification categories' most of which have subsections. For example, educational psychology has subheadings for curriculum; progress and methods; special and remedial education; and so on.
>
> *Psychological Abstracts* is only one of a family of related services called *Psychinfo* which provides access to the world's literature in psychology and related behavioural and social sciences. Full details are given inside the front cover of each issue.

Child Development Abstracts and Bibliography. **3 per annum. Chicago University Press : USA.**
> Includes abstracts from professional journals and reviews books related to the growth and development of children. Each issue has two sections: Abstracts, and Book Notices. There is an associated journal called *Child Development* (6 per annum).

An important new combined indexing and abstracting service in the social sciences appeared in 1987. Its scope and coverage, and its British origin, make it especially useful to readers in this country:

Applied Social Sciences Index and Abstracts. **6 per annum with annual cumulation. Library Association.**
> It provides 'international coverage of the whole range of applied social sciences...from criminology, geriatrics, immigration and unemployment to dyslexia, AIDS, race relations, and inner city problems'. Over 500 English language journals from 23 countries are scanned. It will obviously yield many items of interest in areas related to education, e.g. work and leisure. It is hoped that the service will become available online.

Finally attention is drawn to a publica-
on which provides details of indexing and
bstracting services, in all subject fields, in
his country:

TEPHENS. J. *Inventory of Abstracting and
Indexing Services Produced in the United
Kingdom.* **Latest edn. British Library.**
It lists over 400 services covering documentary
material published as journals, printed lists or
cards, in microform, or machine-readable form.

About a dozen services relating to education are
included.

Serious educational researchers will find
a fuller list of abstracting services in education in *Ulrich's International Periodicals
Directory* (see p.152). Another American
source is *The Index and Abstract Directory*
(EBSCO Publishing, 1989). This is a companion to the *Serials Directory* (see p.152)
from the same publisher.

24 Location lists of periodicals

Your library will have its own periodicals list. However, it cannot take all the educational periodicals likely to be required by its readers for serious study or research, and it will have to draw on the resources of other libraries to supplement its own. In order to do this it will use union lists of periodicals. These are really location lists, since they record the holdings of a number of libraries either in the same geographical area or in related subject fields. Application can then be made directly on your behalf to the library which holds a file of the periodical required.

If relevant union lists are not available your library may have the individual periodicals lists of neighbouring libraries or of libraries further afield. However, the majority of requests for periodicals (or more commonly periodical articles) nowadays are met from the resources of the British Library Document Supply Centre at Boston Spa in Yorkshire. Its catalogue of *Current Serials Received* (see p.163) will give some idea of the extent of its holdings.

The next two sections describe some of the standard sources for locating periodicals in which you are interested. One of the advantages they have over the general lists of periodicals (described in 21.1) is that they also give information about periodicals no longer published.

24.1 Union lists of periodicals

The standard union list of periodicals, not confined to education, is the:

British Union-Catalogue of Periodicals: a Record of the Periodicals of the World from the 17th Century to the Present Day in British Libraries, ed. J.Stewart *et al*. Butterworths, 1955 - 58. 4 vols. Supplement to 1960. 1962.

These five volumes record the holdings of a number of British university libraries. BUCOP, as it is known, was kept up to date by the quarterly issues of *New Periodical Titles*, which cumulated in bound volumes up to 1980. This has now been discontinued and replaced by *Serials in The British Library* (see p.154).

The location of periodicals on education has been made much easier over the years by the existence of two union lists, one for England and Wales, the other for Scotland:

Union List of Periodicals Held in Institute and School of Education Libraries. Latest edn. **Librarians of the Institutes and Schools of Education.**
A comprehensive finding list for the periodical holdings of education libraries in England and Wales. The titles are listed alphabetically. A symbol against each title indicates the library or libraries in which copies will be found. Details about back numbers held are also given. Many of the titles in this list are not in the Scottish one, and vice-versa, so that they usefully complement each other.

Union List of Periodicals Held on the Libraries of the Scottish Colleges of Education. Latest edn. **Craigie College of Education, Ayr.**
A straightforward list of all the periodicals, not only educational, held in the libraries of the Scottish colleges, now reduced in number (see p.70). It does not include the holdings of University Departments of Education in Scotland.

24.2 Library periodicals lists

Many libraries issue lists of their periodical holdings in printed form. A good example in the educational field is the one issued by *Jordanhill College Library* in Glasgow, which is revised annually. It is an alphabetical title list, and includes periodicals on other subjects.

Although Jordanhill is the largest college of education library in Britain and its periodical holdings are extensive, it should be appreciated that other specialised educa-

on libraries will have fuller holdings in
articular areas. For example, the *London
niversity Institute of Education Library* (see
121) is very strong on comparative educa-
on titles.

Your library may have copies of such lists.
should also have copies of those of neigh-
ouring libraries if they have not already
een amalgamated in a union catalogue
ee p.162). Even if they have, individual
brary lists are usually more up to date
nan a union catalogue.

The periodicals lists of larger general
braries may also be held. The most useful
f such lists is:

**BRITISH LIBRARY, DOCUMENT SUPPLY CENTRE.
Current Serials Received. Annual.**
The DSC's holdings embrace all subjects including
the humanities and the social sciences. It exists 'to
provide a loan/photocopy service to libraries in the
UK prepared to abide by the regulations relating to
registered users. The service is also extended to
libraries abroad'. All the titles are available for
supply by photocopy within the provisions of the
British copyright law. The list is updated by the
quarterly issues of *Serials in the British Library* (see
p.154).

The Document Supply Centre (DSC) also
produces a quarterly *Keyword Index to Serial Titles
(KIST)* (on 48x microfiche) which is an alphabetical
list of all significant words in the periodicals' titles,
and thus provides a form of subject access.

The latest production of the DSC is *Boston Spa
Serials* on CD-ROM. A single compact disc, updated
twice yearly, contains over 360,000 serial titles as
well as annuals, newspapers and journals in many
languages.

Another substantial list which should be
found in Scottish libraries at least is the
Current Periodicals List issued by the National
Library of Scotland, although its holdings
are available for reference only.

Educational research

25 Research in general

The next two chapters are concerned with educational research. They are designed to help you if you are undertaking more serious research into some aspect of education for an advanced essay, thesis, or dissertation.

Many of the works already described will be very helpful, indeed indispensable, to the serious researcher, e.g. educational thesauri, educational reports and documents, subject indexes to periodicals, and abstracting services. However the following sources will be used more by serious researchers than by others.

There are at least two exceptions to this. The sections on bibliographical references (25.4 and 25.5) have relevance for all students and teachers, who must know how to record details of books and periodicals, and how to compile a bibliography. They have been included here because they fall naturally into the subject matter of the chapter.

25.1 Introductory guides to research

Before undertaking research of any kind the postgraduate student in particular may find it helpful to look at a few publications which evaluate the experiences of those who have already been involved in research activity:

WELSH, J.M. *The First Year of Postgraduate Research Study.* **Society for Research into Higher Education, 1979.**
Sets out to look at the ways in which students approach research and the problems which they encounter as postgraduates. It also reviews previous work on the subject. Both J.M.Welsh and E.Rudd (below) have useful comments on the relationship between student and supervisor.

RUDD, E. *A New Look at Postgraduate Failure.* **Society for Research into Higher Education, 1985.**

'Examines the reasons why postgraduate students drop out or are inordinately slow to complete their studies.' It makes interesting reading, not least on the reasons why students undertake postgraduate study at all, and why theses seem to increase in size as the years go by.

EGGLESTON, J. and DELAMONT, S. *Supervision of Students for Research Degrees: with Special Reference to Educational Studies.* **British Educational Research Association, 1983.**
Main sections: (1) Rules and procedures for the administration of students for higher research degrees; (2) The supervision of postgraduate students: a necessary isolation; and (3) A study of postgraduate research students in education.

There are numerous guides which will be of more immediate practical assistance to the beginning researcher. Priority must be given to a very convenient series of booklets:

Rediguides: Guides in Educational Research. **Nos 1-29. Nottingham University School of Education, various authors and dates.**
The titles are set out below. It should be obvious from the range of topics covered that they are a boon to any beginning researcher. They have been written in a very concise and practical way. Their small format and their emphasis on particular aspects of research make them much less forbidding than some of the more ambitious handbooks on educational research:

1. *Planning Educational Research.*
2. *Evaluating the Literature.*
3. *Research Strategies.*
4. *Sampling.*
5. *Attainment and Diagnostic Testing.*
6. *Testing Reading Ability.*
7. *Attitude Assessment.*
8. *Characteristics of the Learner.*
9. *Using Personal Constructs.*
10. *Constructing Tests.*
11. *Conducting and Analysing Interviews.*
12. *Designing and Analysing Questionnaires.*
13. *Designing an Experiment.*
14. *Classroom Interaction Research.*
15. *Historical Research.*
16. *Research and the Curriculum.*
17. *Community Research.*
18. *Sociometric Techniques.*
19. *Computer Usage.*
20. *Statistical Strategies.*
21. *Descriptive Statistics.*

22. *Embarking upon Research.*
23. *Writing Research Reports.*
24. *Organisational Research.*
25. *Presenting Research Results.*
26. *Case Study.*
27. *Researching Adult Education.*
28. *Essential Empirical Concepts.*
29. *Analysis of Variants.*

BERRY, R. *How to Write a Research Paper.* **2nd edn. Pergamon, 1986.**
This is still a reliable introduction to writing extended essays or research papers. It is brief, clear and provides basic but essential information, with advice on using libraries and making bibliographical references.

EVANS, K.M. *Planning Small-Scale Research: a Practical Guide for Teachers and Students.* **3rd edn. NFER-Nelson, 1984.**
The best short book on planning a not too ambitious piece of research. It describes the different types of research; how to devise tests and questionnaires and carry out the investigation; and how to write it up for an article or thesis. There is a bibliography.

TURABIAN, K.L. *A Manual for Writers of Research Papers, Theses and Dissertations.* **Revised British edn. Heinemann, 1982.**
It is good have a British edition of this standard American guide. The changes are minimal but help to meet the needs of British users. One of the appendices is a brief guide to proof correction. A fifth American edition was published by Chicago University Press in 1987.

The following books are more geared to the needs of educational researchers:

BELL, J. *Doing your Research Project: a Guide for First-time Researchers in Education and Social Science.* **Open University Press, 1987.**
'A guide to good practice for those new to research, whether students or professionals, undertaking an investigation.' It aims to help them 'to avoid some of the pitfalls and time-wasting false trails that can eat into their time, and to establish good research habits'. Note also:

LEWIS, I. and MUNN, P. *So You Want to Do Research: a Guide for Teachers on How to Formulate Research Questions.* **Scottish Council for Research in Education, 1987. (Practitioner mini-paper)**

For the more ambitious there is:

PHILLIPS, E.M. and PUGH, D.S. *How to Get a Ph.D: Managing the Peaks and Troughs of Research.* **Open University Press, 1987.**
Adopts a practical and realistic approach. Both authors have experience of research and supervision. There is advice on how *not* to get a Ph.D and how to manage your supervisor.

There are two other publications which it may be useful to mention at this stage Both are from the same source:

PEDEN, H. and HILLS, P. *Sources of Funding for Research and Publication.* **Primary Communications Research Centre, Leicester University, 1983.**

DIXON, D and HILLS, P. *Talking About Your Research.* **Primary Communications Research Centre. 1981.**

25.2 Research methods in education

There is no shortage of books to help with the general approach to educational research and with research methodology. The following book covers both traditional and new approaches and should be known to all researchers:

COHEN, L. and MANION, L. *Research Methods in Education.* **3rd edn. Routledge, 1989.**
'This introductory text was written to cover the whole range of methods currently employed by educational researchers.' It is written in a clear and lively way and should help students and teachers to master the principles and practices of research. It should also be useful to consumers of research.

Several books look at research from the teacher's point of view:

HITCHCOCK, G. and HUGHES, D. *Research and the Teacher: a Qualitative Introduction to*

chool-Based Research. **Routledge, 1989.**
Should help teachers and student teachers to
develop an understanding of the background
assumptions, issues and techniques of social and
educational research.

OPKINS, D. *A Teacher's Guide to Classroom
esearch*. **Open University Press, 1985.**
Aims to help students and teachers to carry out
small-scale research in their own classrooms on
problems of their own choosing, using qualitative
rather than quantitative data techniques. The
various methods of data collection and analysis are
described. The material is well presented at an
appropriate level.

IUSTLER, D. *et al*. *Action Research in
:lassrooms and Schools*. **Allen & Unwin, 1986.**
For teachers at all levels who are aware of problems
in their practice and would like to set up an
enquiry. It considers the underlying principles
involved and how to develop a plan of action.
Sections: (A) General issues; (B) Six small case
studies; (C) Three large-scale projects.

VALKER, R. *Doing Research: a Handbook for
Teachers*. **Methuen, 1985. (Re-issued by
Routledge. 1989.)**
The emphasis is on applied research in an
educational context. Aimed at teachers
undertaking educational research for the first time.
Too often, as the author says, 'research tends to be
very effective in providing answers to questions no
one is asking'.

Other books which may be helpful are
Case Studies in Classroom Research and *Con-
roversies in Classroom Research,* both edited by
M.Hammersley and published by the Open
University Press in 1986.

The following book is unusual in focusing
on research from the consumer's rather
than the researcher's point of view:

BORG, W.R. *Applying Educational Research: a
Practical Guide for Teachers*. **2nd edn.
Longman: USA, 1987.**

There are other books on research
methods in education which could be useful
if they are available in your library. Some
are American, and most are comparatively
recent:

ARY, D. *et al*. *Introduction to Research in
Education*. **3rd revised edn. Holt, Rinehart:
USA, 1985.**

BEST, J.W. *Research in Education*. **J.V. Kahn.
6th edn. Prentice-Hall: USA, 1989.**

BORG, W.R. and **GALL, M.D.** *Educational
Research: an Introduction*. **4th edn. Longman:
USA, 1983.**

BURGESS, R.G. *Field Methods in the Study of
Education*. **Falmer Press. 1985.**

BURGESS, R.G. *Issues in Educational Research:
Qualitative Methods*. **Falmer Press, 1985.**

BURGESS, R.G. *Strategies of Educational
Research: Quantitative Methods*. **Falmer Press,
1985.**

CHARLES, C.M. *Introduction to Educational
Research*. **Longman: USA, 1988.**

EICHELBERGER, R.T. *Disciplined Inquiry:
Understanding and Doing Educational
Research*. **Longman, 1989.**

*The Enquiring Teacher: Supporting and
Sustaining Teacher Research,* eds **J.Nias** and
S.Groundwater-Smith. Falmer Press, 1988.

FRAENKEL,J. and **WALLEN,N.E.** *How to Design
and Evaluate Research in Education*. **McGraw-
Hill: USA, 1990.**

HEGARTY, S. and **EVANS, R.** *Research and
Evaluation Methods in Special Education*.
NFER-Nelson, 1985.

MACMILLAN,J.H. and **SCHUMACHER,S.** *Research
in Education: a Conceptual Introduction*. **Scott-
Foresman: Eurospan: USA, 1989.**

*Qualitative Research in Education: Focus and
Methods,* eds **R.R.Sherman** and **R.B.Webb.
Falmer Press, 1988.**

SHIPMAN, M. *Educational Research: Principles,
Policies and Practices*. **Falmer Press, 1985.**

SLAVIN, R.E. *Research Methods in Education: a Practical Guide.* **Prentice-Hall: USA, 1984.**

VERMA, G.K. and BEARD, R.M. *What is Educational Research?: Perspectives on Techniques of Research.***Gower, 1981.**

WIERSMA,W. *Research Methods in Education: an Introduction.* **Allyn & Bacon: USA, 1986.**

WINTER, R. *Learning from Experience: Principles and Practice in Action-Research.* **Falmer Press, 1989.**

Special mention must be made of a new handbook which is much more ambitious than any of these:

Educational Research, Methodology and Measurement: an International Handbook, ed. **J.P. Keeves. Pergamon, 1988.**
This derives from the *International Encyclopedia of Education* (see p.23). It is a collection of articles on educational research methods, filling almost 1,000 pages. Sections are: (1) Methods of educational enquiry; (2) Knowledge, policy making and educational enquiry; (3) Measurement in educational research; and (4), Research techniques and statistical analysis. A number of specially commissioned articles take account of recent developments.

Most of the foregoing books are about research methods in general. Examples of books on more specific topics are:

BELL, J. *et al. Conducting Small-Scale Investigations in Educational Management.* **Harper & Row, 1984.**

POWNEY, J. *Interviewing in Educational Research.* **Routledge, 1987.**

Do not forget the excellent series of *Rediguides* from Nottingham University School of Education (see p.167). There is another guide designed primarily for psychologists which could be equally useful to educational researchers:

HARRIS, P. *Designing and Reporting Experiments.* **Open University Press, 1986.**
One of a series of 'open guides' to psychology. It describes the whole procedure for setting up and reporting practical work in psychology.

There is an Open University course: Research Methods in Education and the Social Sciences (DE304). Those unable to take the course would find a reading of the course units helpful. Most academic libraries should have sets of OU course units for reference or borrowing. See also the book by J.Bell (p.168).

For more experienced researchers, the OU offers a taught MSc course in *Advanced Educational and Social Research Methods* which will be offered for the last time in 1991.

References to recent books on educational research methods are included in a valuable review article by Burgess,R.G 'Research methods in the Social Sciences' in *British Book News,* April 1987, pp.172–5.

25.3 Organising the literature

The present guide includes the main types of material which you may need to consult. However, the works described in this section should give you a wider view of the literature of education and some useful perspectives. Other relevant sources are described in 18.7 (Guides to the literature of education).

FOSKETT, D.J. *How to Find Out: Educational Research.* **Pergamon, 1965.**
Although this was written twenty-five years ago, it is still worth reading. Some of its references to educational publications are now dated, but it offers very sound advice on the approaches to sources of information.

BURKE, A.J. and M.A. *Documentation in Education.* **Teachers College Press: USA, 1967.**
Note the date. This is still the most comprehensive publication of its kind. Despite its American emphasis it is an excellent survey of the types of material available for research purposes.

BERRY, D.M. *A Bibliographic Guide to Educational Research.* **2nd edn. Scarecrow Press: USA, 1980.**
A 'concise guide to assist students in education courses to make effective use of the resources of the library of their college or university'. It lists over

500 reference sources by types of material with annotations for each entry. Useful for American works which could not be included in the present guide.

OODBURY, M. *A Guide to Sources of Education-Information.* **2nd edn. Information esources Press: USA, 1982.**
Larger and more detailed than D.M.Berry and slightly more recent. Its introductory notes to each section provide much more guidance on the use of bibliographical resources. Again the emphasis is on American publications.

There is a much briefer British work hich could be useful in this context. It is y Haywood,P. and Wragg,E.C. *Evaluating e Literature* (no.2 in the *Rediguides* series) see p.167).

25.4   Bibliographical references

Normally when you write a thesis or extended essay you will be expected to provide a bibliography or list of references onsulted. This will include all the significant items which you have used, including periodicals as well as books, pamphlets, eports, etc. Nowadays it may even include non-book materials.

The bibliography should be appended to he thesis or essay and start on a fresh page. The items will normally be arranged alphabetically by author's surname (or in he case of official publications by the name of the issuing organisation or department). In some cases, e.g. encyclopaedias, year books and annuals, the title may be used as the heading. The items should be numbered in sequence, and these numbers can then be used in the text to indicate sources of information and ideas. References to specific pages of a work may be given in a footnote.

You will find it helpful to keep a record of the books and other materials you consult as you are preparing and writing you thesis or essay. This is best done on standard 8 x 5 or 5 x 3 cards so that they can easily be rearranged for your final bibliography. (The larger size is required if you wish to make detailed notes on particular items.) Certain basic details are required so that books and periodical articles can be readily identified:

(a) Books

Author (surname first, followed by initials). Title (followed by subtitle if explanatory). Edition if not the first. Publisher (preceded by place of publication if not British). Year of publication. Indent from second line onwards if preferred. Example:

BURGESS, T. and SOFER, M. *The School Governor's Handbook and Training Guide.* **2nd edn. Kogan Page, 1986.**
The information should be taken from the title page of the book, not its cover. You may need to refer to the back of the title page for the edition and the date of publication. If several places of publication are given, e.g. New York, London, Sydney, etc. take the first as being the country of origin.

(b) Periodical articles

Author (surname first, followed by initials). Title of article. Volume no., issue no., month, year (for a weekly periodical give date only), inclusive page nos. Indent from second line onwards if preferred. Example:

ZEICHNER, K.M. and LISTON, D.P. Teaching student teachers to reflect. *Harvard Educational Review,* vol.57 no.1, 1987, pp.23–45.

A specimen bibliography showing entries for books and periodicals is given in 25.5.

There are other ways in which bibliographical details may be recorded. For example, it is quite common to put the year of publication in brackets immediately after the author's name. However, some institutions have their own rules or regulations for the presentation of theses, including a preferred form for bibliographical references, and you should certainly follow their instructions. For fuller guidance you should consult:

FOSKETT, D.J. *Notes on Compiling Bibliographies for the Guidance of Students Preparing Reports and Theses in the Field of Education.* 3rd revised edn. London University Institute of Education, 1977.
> The scope of this pamphlet is wider than the title suggests. It has sections on the use of libraries; bibliographical sources; theses; periodicals; other specialist guides; related fields; note-taking; cross-references; compiling notes; method of citation; form of citation; and lay-out of the bibliography. There are some useful abbreviations, and selected references.

A number of British Standards may also be consulted:

Recommendations. Bibliographical References (BS 1629:1976). (Guidance on the presentation of references to books and other separately issued publications, serials, etc. with examples.)

Recommendations for Citing Publications by Bibliographical References (BS 5605:1978). (Guidance for authors and editors on the preferred method of arranging lists of references in books and journals. Includes methods of making attribution within the text.)

Recommendations for Citation of Unpublished Documents (BS 6371:1983).

Specification for Abbreviation of Title Words and Titles of Periodicals (BS 4148:1985).

Recommendations for Citation of Published Sound Recordings (BS 6098:1981).

Specific advice on the form, layout, and bibliographical presentation of theses is given in:

Recommendations for the Presentation of Theses (BS 4821:1972 (1986)).

Those who are preparing text for printing should also be familiar with:

Recommendations for Preparation of Typescript Copy for Printing (BS 5261 Part 2:1975 (1983)).

Specification for Typographic Requirements. Marks for Copy Preparation and Proof Correction, Proofing Procedure (BS 5261 Part 2:1976).

Recommendations. The Preparation of Indexes to Books, Periodicals and Other Publications (BS 3700:1976 (1983)).

The British Standards Institution issue new Standards and revises existing ones as required. The *BSI Yearbook* should be checked for any amendments.

There is a large-scale American work *Periodical Title Abbreviations* (Latest edn Gale Research Co: USA, 2 vols) which has very full lists of titles in their full and abbreviated forms. There are inter-edition supplements.

25.5 A specimen bibliography

A specimen bibliography is set out below. Books and periodicals have been kept separate for easy reference. Where there are more than two authors, only the first is named, and 'et al' is added:

(a) Books

BELL, G.H. *Developing Teacher Education in the European Communities: a Case Study.* 2nd edn. Dept. of Educational Studies, Tees-side Polytechnic, 1980.

COBURN, P. *et al. Practical Guide to Computers in Education.* Reading, Massachusetts, Addison-Wesley,1982.

HARGREAVES, A. and WOODS, P. (eds) *Classrooms and Staffrooms.* Open University Press, 1984.

HER MAJESTY'S INSPECTORS OF SCHOOLS. *Teaching and Learning in the Senior Stages of the Scottish Secondary School: a report.* HMSO, 1983.

HOOVER, K.H. *The Professional Teacher's Handbook: a Quick Guide for Improving Instruction in Today's Middle and Secondary*

hools. 3rd edn. Boston, Allyn & Bacon
82.

ATIONAL SOCIETY FOR THE STUDY OF EDUCA-
ON. *Policy Making in Education: 81st
arbook of the NSSE. Part 1*, eds A.Lieberman
d M.W.McLaughlin. Chicago, NSSE, 1982.

XON, J. *A Teacher's Guide to Multicultural
ducation*. Blackwell, 1985.

AVITCH, D. *The Troubled Crusade: American
ducation 1945-1980*. New York, Basic Books,
83.

COTTISH EDUCATION DEPARTMENT. *The
eachers' Superannuation (National Salaries)
cotland) Regulations, 1982*. HMSO, 1982.

ONEY, F.M. and SCOTT, V.M. *Careers
uidance in Colleges and Polytechnics: a Study
Practice and Provision*. NFER-Nelson, 1984.

OLSTOY, L. *Tolstoy on Education: Tolstoy's
ducational Writings 1861-62*; selected and
dited by A.Pinch and M.Armstrong. Athlone
ress, 1982.

NIVERSITY GRANTS COMMITTEE. *A Strategy for
ducation into the 1990s: the UGC's Advice*.
MSO, 1984.

) Periodical articles

AKER, T.A. and LINDQUIST, M. 25 ideas, for
ore interesting in-service. *Education
anada*, vol.24, Winter 1984, pp.28–33.

ONKLIN, R.C. Teacher competency
esting:the present situation and some
oncerns on how teachers are tested. *Journal
f Curriculum Studies*, vol.17 no.1, Jan-Mar
985, pp.1–15.

UKE, D.L. What is the nature of educational
xcellence and should we try to measure it?
hi delta kappan, vol.66 no.10, June 1985,
p.671–4.

LYN, T. Contexts for independent learning.
ducational Psychology, vol.5 no.1, 1985,
p.5–15.

RACE, G. Judging teachers: the social and
olitical contexts of teacher evaluation.
ritish Journal of Sociology of Education vol.6
o.1, 1985, pp.3–16.

AUFFMAN, D. and LAMKIN, C. Designing

schools for tomorrow's technology. *Education
Digest*, Mar 1985, pp.54–7.

MARDLE, D. *Education and Leisure: a
Reappraisal. Westminster studies in education*,
vol.7, 1984, pp.77–88.

MOORE, A. Changes in Scottish education.
BACIE Journal, vol.40 no.2, Mar-Apr 1985,
pp.47–8.

POWELL, J.P. and ANDRESEN, L.W. Humour and
teaching in higher education. *Studies in
Higher Education*, vol.10 no.1, 1985, pp.79–90.

WALSH, K. *et al.* Staffing the secondary
school. *Oxford Review of Education*, vol.11
no.1, 1985, pp 19–31.

WARNOCK, M. Teacher teach thyself. *The
Listener*, vol.113, no.2902, 28 Mar 1985,
pp.10–14.

YOUNG PEOPLE, EMPLOYMENT AND OTHER
MATTERS (theme of whole issue). *Compare*,
vol.14 no.2 1984, pp.123–214.

25.6 Organisations concerned with research

No attempt will be made to describe all the organisations concerned with research in this country, but some of the best known ones involved directly or indirectly in research have been included. Others will be found in the *Education Year Book* (see p.57), and there are full accounts of a number of them in Butcher,H.J. and Pont,H.B. (see p.180) although this now requires updating.

The best evaluation of the main British research organisations is a chapter by Taylor,W. The organization and funding of educational research in England and Wales, in the *World Year Book of Education*, 1985, pp.42-67. The whole volume is a mine of information about the structure of educational research in different countries, and it has valuable bibliographies.

The Department of Education and Science and the Scottish Education Department are involved in promoting, funding and supporting research. Much of it has a practical emphasis and relates to current educational needs. Each of them produces an annual report listing current research projects (see pp.186,187)

In England we have the:

National Curriculum Council (NCC). 15–17 New Street, York YO1 2RA.

Established under the Education Reform Act 1988, along with a Curriculum Council for Wales. It replaced the School Curriculum Development Committee (SCDC). Its functions include advising the Secretary of State on, and carrying out as required, programmes of research and development, and publishing and disseminating information on the curriculum. There is an *NCC News*.

School Examinations and Assessment Council (SEAC). 15–17 New Street, York YO1 2 RA.

Replaced the Secondary Examinations Council following the Education Reform Act 1988. Its functions include advising the Secretary of State on, and carrying out as required, programmes of research and development, and disseminating information on matters associated with school examinations and assessment. There is a newsletter, the *SEAC Recorder*.

The bodies now superseded, the SCDC and the SEC, themselves replaced the well-known Schools Council in 1983-84. It was an independent body which was financed jointly by the DES and the education authorities. Its function was to undertake research and development work in the curriculum, teaching methods, and examinations in schools in England and Wales.

The Schools Council issued an impressive range of publications, including the *Schools Council Project Files and Index* (see p.187), which was taken over by the SCDC, and an annual report. Many of them were issued by commercial publishers. Some education libraries may still have a copy of the Schools Councils's own publications list, otherwise the best approach is probably through your library's catalogue. For a committed account of the Schools Council during the twenty years of its existence (from 1963–1983) see Plaskow,M. *The Life and Death of the Schools Council* (Falmer Press, 1985).

Assessment of Performance Unit. DES, Elizabeth House, York Road, London, SE1 7PH.

The APU is part of the Department of Education and Science. Its terms of reference are to promote the development of methods of assessing and monitoring the achievements of children at school and to try to identify the incidence of under-achievement. It produces full reports on each survey, short reports by teachers on the main findings, discussion documents, an *APU Newsletter*, and occasional papers. The latter normally appear under the authors' own names, and represent personal views. There is also a series of DES publications which present some of the main survey findings in a digestible way to a wider audience. A full list of APU publications used to be given in the *DES Annual Report* (see p.32) which is no longer published. They are now noted in *DES Publications* (see p.134).

The best known research organisations in England and Wales are the:

National Foundation for Educational Research in England and Wales. The Mere, Upton Park, Slough, Berks, SL1 2DQ.

The NFER is an independent organisation which carries out research in education and educational psychology, constructs tests, and provides information and advice on research developments. Most education libraries will have standing orders for NFER publications, which are now very numerous. There will probably be a series entry for them in your library's catalogue. In particular the NFER produces the *Register of Educational Research in the United Kingdom* (see p.186), *Research Papers in Education* (a series of in-depth research reports), the well-known termly journal *Educational Research*, and a new loose-leaf journal *Topic: Practical Applications of Research in Education*.

Society for Research Into Higher Education University of Guildford, Surrey, G42 SXH.

The SRHE aims to encourage and co-ordinate research into all aspects of higher education. It arranges national meetings and conferences, and membership extends to all parts of the world. It is wholly independent and issues a number of publications useful to researchers including: *Research into Higher Education Abstracts* (see p.186) and the *Register of Research into Higher Education* (see p.186). It publishes various monographs and research reports; a *Bulletin* (2 per annum) of news and information: an *International Newsletter* (6 per annum), and an annual report. It is also responsible for the *Leverhulme Programme of Study into the Future of Higher Education* which has produced a number of interesting volumes. The Society maintains a register of members' research interests which is kept up to date. Its object is to put researchers in touch with colleagues who are working on similar or related projects.

British Educational Research Association (BERA). 11 Serpentine Road, Selly Park, Birmingham.

The broad aim of the BERA is 'to encourage the pursuit of educational research and its applications for both the improvement of education and the general benefit of the community'. It is particularly concerned to ensure that educational research findings are communicated to all those who are interested in the theory and practice of education. Membership is open to anyone who has an interest in educational research.

Economic and Social Research Council (ESRC). 1 Temple Avenue, London, EC4 0BD.

Formerly the Social Science Research Council, which was established by Royal Charter in 1966. The name was changed in 1982. Its concern with educational research is not extensive but it exercises an important influence. Its functions are to encourage and support research in the social sciences; to make grants to students for postgraduate instruction in this field; to carry out its own research; and to provide appropriate research services, including advice and the dissemination of knowledge about the social sciences. It publishes a list of *Research Supported by the ESRC* (see p.187) and an annual report.

Further Education Unit (FEU). DES, Elizabeth House, York Road, London, SE1 7PH.

Formerly the Further Education Curriculum Review and Development Unit, it was set up in 1977 to act as an advisory, intelligence and development body for further education. Since 1983 the FEU has been an independent limited company based at the DES. Although research is not its main function, it publishes a wide range of documents in areas such as vocational preparation, special needs in FE, adult education, the new technology, staff development, multicultural education, and study skills. It is concerned with curriculum development generally, and also has an interest in TVEI and YTS. It issues a newsletter.

A list of current FEU research projects is included in the FEU *Annual Report*. Fuller details will be found in *FEU Research Projects: Current or Completed*. New projects are listed in *Project Information Bulletins*. Out-of-print publications are available on microfiche from Chadwyck-Healey.

Further Education Research Network. Fern Centre, Leicester Polytechnic, Scraptoft Campus, Scraptoft, Leicester, LE7 9SU.

An independent self-financing charity which was established by teachers in order to equip themselves with the knowledge and techniques relevant to contemporary changes in further and higher education. It supports a wide variety of investigations which are normally initiated by members. It publishes the *Fern Journal* (2 per annum) and the *Fern Newsletter* (3 per annum).

National Institute of Adult Continuing Education (NIACE). 196 De Montford Street, Leicester, LE1 7GE.

The NIACE 'provides a means of consultation and co-operation between all the forces in adult education, and a service of information and advice on all relevant aspects. It conducts researches, surveys and enquiries, organises conferences and seminars, and publishes material relevant to its field. It possesses a reference library and operates a computerised database of bibliographical information which is available to all interested bodies.' Among its publications are a year book (see p.71) and the periodicals *Adult Education* (4 per annum) and *Studies in the Education of Adults* (2 per annum).

National Council for Educational Technology for the United Kingdom, (NCET). 3 Devonshire Street, London, W1N 2BA.

NCET was formed from a merger of the Council for Educational Technology (CET) set up in 1973 and the Microelectronics Education Support Unit. It is the central organisation for promoting the application and development of educational technology throughout the UK. NCET 'defines desirable advances, shows how these can be achieved, at what cost and with what effect'. It maintains a *Register of Research on Information Technology in Education* (see p.187). Its publications include a series of working papers which have been particularly influential. It issues the *British Journal of Educational Technology* (3 per annum) and a termly *NCET News*, as well as an annual report.

The Scottish equivalent of the National Curriculum Council is the:

Scottish Consultative Council on the Curriculum (SCCC). Gardyne Road, Broughty Ferry, Dundee, DD5 1NY. (Information and Maketing Services)

The SCCC incorporates the former Consultative Committee on the Curriculum (CCC) and the Scottish Curriculum Development Service (SCDS). Schools, further and higher education, industry and parents are all represented, and it works closely with the Scottish Examination Board. It has primary and secondary executive committees (PEC and SEC) but is also establishing 'deliberative' committees which undertake forward thinking on broad areas of policy, e.g. School and Community (COSAC), Special Educational Needs (COSPEN) and Scottish Education/Industry (SEIC). The old CCC issued many influential working papers, reports, curriculum papers and bulletins over the years, and the new SCCC is continuing this policy. An attractive set of brochures has been produced to mark twenty-five years of the CCC/SCCC and it includes an impressive publications list. There is an *SCCC News* (2 per annum).

The National Foundation for Educational Research has its Scottish counterpart in the:

Scottish Council for Research in Education (SCRE). 15 St. John Street, Edinburgh, EH8 8JR.

SCRE aims to conduct, sponsor and co-ordinate educational research in Scotland; to publish the results of research; to maintain registers of current and completed research; and to make grants to research workers. Scottish education libraries at least will have standing orders for all their publications and will acquire additional copies of the more important ones. SCRE has issued a long series of monographs on many aspects of Scottish education over the years. Its *Annual Report* includes details of current research projects, and there is also an informative *SCRE Newsletter* (2 per annum, formerly *Research in Education*).

In 1986 there was a complete re-appraisal of SCRE's role, structure and central purposes. A Forum on Educational Research in Scotland was instituted to bring together teachers, researchers and administrators for the discussion of educational research policy. The proceedings of its meetings are published. Funding from the MSC has made it possible to create a TVEI Student and Teacher Database and a Curriculum Database. The earlier history of SCRE is outlined in a pamphlet by Craigie,J. *The Scottish Council for Research in Education 1928-1972.* SCRE, 1972.

Scottish Educational Research Association (SERA). C/O SCRE, 15 St. John Street, Edinburgh, EH8 8JR.

SERA is an independent organisation. One of its main aims is to promote educational research in Scotland. It holds an important annual conference at St. Andrews 'for the sustained public discussion of policy and practice in Scottish education, informed by perspectives derived from systematic enquiry'. SERA also subsidises the *Scottish Educational Review* (see p.189), 'Scotland's only international educational journal' (if we except the *Times Scottish Education Supplement)*, and publishes a *Newsletter* (3 per annum). SERA was founded in 1974.

Scottish Council for Educational Technology (SCET). Dowanhill, 74 Victoria Road Crescent, Glasgow G12 9JN.

SCET, which is presently undergoing some internal reorganisation, promotes educational technology in its widest sense to all levels of education, industry and commerce. At present there are separate units for Learning Systems (including open learning: see p.74); Research and Development; Microelectronic Software Development; Computer Administration Systems; Media Resources; and Information, Publications and Communications. Its research activity is funded by the Scottish Education Department. SCET produces a wide range of general publications, working papers, guidelines and materiographies.

Details of other organisations, foundations and trusts concerned with educational research in the UK and elsewhere will be found in the:

International Foundation Directory. Latest edn. Europa Publications.

'This directory of international foundations, trusts and other similar non-profit making institutions provides a comprehensive picture of foundation activity on a world scale.' It is well produced and the information is clearly presented. Arrangement is by countries, with indexes of foundations and main activities.

There are several directories which may help you to identify research organisations and institutions and their activities worldwide:

Directory of Educational Research Institutions. 2nd revised edn. IBE: Unesco, 1987.

International Directory of Research Institutions in Higher Education. 2nd revised edn. IBE: Unesco. 1986.

rld Directory of Selected Research and
acher Training Institutions in the Field of
chnical and Vocational Education. **Revised**
n. IBE: Unesco. 1986.

For North America we have the:

search Centers Directory. **Latest edn. Gale**
search Co: USA. 2 vols.

It includes listings of university-related and other
non-profit research organisations in the US and
Canada. Arrangement is by major subjects, with a
detailed subject index containing over 30,000
references. There are also lists of acronyms and
institutions.

26 Records of research

This chapter describes the standard sources for discovering what research has already been done, and what research is currently being carried out in the field of education, mainly in this country but also in American and to a limited extent elsewhere.

All serious researchers will have to consult a number of these works, firstly to establish that their intended topic has not already been researched by someone else, and secondly, to become familiar with the existing literature on the topic finally selected.

The task is now becoming less laborious with the introduction of computerised information retrieval systems (see 26.7) but it will still be necessary to use printed sources. One reason is that the databases accessible online or on CD–ROM are largely American in emphasis and may not include British material that could be very useful to you.

26.1 Handbooks of research

The next two sections are concerned with general surveys of research. They have been divided rather arbitrarily into handbooks and reviews. The distinction is not always definite, and there is an overlap between the two categories. Most of the works in this section have the word 'handbook' in their title. However, the first is a large-scale encyclopaedia which should be known to all researchers:

Encyclopedia of Educational Research. 5th edn., ed. H.E.Mitzel *et al.* Collier-Macmillan: USA, 1982. 4 vols.
> The first edition of this 'classic reference work' was published as long ago as 1941 and the earlier editions are still useful for their periods. There is no comparable work which has succeeded in reviewing and summarising existing research on such an impressive scale. Each article has an

extensive bibliography of items 'available in libraries and/or retrievable from the ERIC Document Reproduction Centre' (see 26.6). Most of the research reported was carried out in the US but its relevance is claimed to be international. Th encyclopaedia is indispensable for anyone who wishes to survey what research has already been done in any area of education.

The encyclopaedia covers education gei erally. There are three substantial han books which are concerned with researc on teaching. They were all produced unde the auspices of the American Education: Research Association.

GAGE, N.L. *Handbook of Research on Teaching* Rand McNally: USA, 1963.
> A well-presented handbook of over 1,200 pages. Th preface states:'In the half-century since research o teaching began, thousands of studies have been made...but no full-dress attempt has yet been mad to do justice to past research on teaching. To summarise, to critically analyse, and to integrate this body of research are major substantive aims o this handbook'. There are four parts: (1) Theoretical orientations; (2) Methodologies in research on teaching; (3) Major variables and area of research on teaching; and (4) Research on teaching various grade levels and subject matters. There are bibliographies at the ends of chapters, and name and subject indexes.

TRAVERS, R.M. *Second Handbook of Research on Teaching.* Rand McNally: USA, 1973.
> This is not a revision of the earlier work but a continuation under a new editor. However, the structure has been altered to take account of significant changes, new approaches, new interests and new technologies. Again there are four parts:(1) Introduction; (2) Methods and techniques of research and development; (3) Research on special problems of teaching; and (4) Research on the teaching of school subjects. There are also chapter bibliographies and name and subject indexes.

WITTROCK, M.C. *Handbook of Research on Teaching: a Project of the American Educational Research Association.* 3rd revised edn. Collier-Macmillan: USA.
> Reflects the progress made in this field over the thirteen years since the previous edition. All the

articles are new and some chapters have no counterpart in the two earlier handbooks. Contributors were asked to summarise and review research findings, assess their significance, evaluate new developments, examine current conflicts and controversies, and link them with work being done in related fields. There are five parts:(1) Theory and method of research in teaching; (2) Research on teaching and teachers; (3) The social and institutional context of teaching; (4) Adapting teaching to differences among learners; and (5) Research on the teaching of subjects and grade levels. There are full chapter references. It is well described as a 'guide to what we know about teachers, teaching, and the learning process'. Together, the handbooks by N.L.Gage, R.M.Travers and M.C.Wittrock represent a very considerable achievement.

Special education is well provided for. he most substantial work is:

ANG, M.C. et al. *Handbook of Special ducation:Research and Practice*. **Pergamon, 987–9. 3 vols.**
ol.1: Learner Characteristics and Adaptive Education. 1987.
ol.2: Mildly Handicapped Conditions. 1988.
ol.3: Low Incidence Conditions. 1989.
Aims to 'review and build upon the past decade of developments and advances in the field of special education in the United States, by examining the state of the art (the research base) and the state of practice, and by identifying specific directions for further research, programme development and policy making'. Topics covered include models, theories, assessment of learning disabilities, research procedures, public policy and implications for future development in the field. The work is intended for educational administrators as well as for academics and teachers. It is likely to become a standard reference source.

Pergamon, the publisher of the above andbook, is using its *International Encyclo- edia of Education* (see p.23) to spawn a umber of separate works, e.g. several one- olume encyclopaedias described in 9.2. There is a research handbook which is derived from the same source:

ORRIS, R.J. and BLATT, B. *Special Education: Research and Trends*. **Pergamon, 1988.**
'Presents in one volume the essence of research literature in special education which has grown exponentially in the past fifteen years. Each

chapter is written by a leading expert in special education or school psychology and takes a critical look at the cutting edge of his or her particular field. The book covers the entire range of handicapping conditions and related topics.' It is designed for courses in special education and for professionals.

An earlier American handbook could still be useful:

KAUFFMAN, J.M. and HALLAHAN, D.P. *Handbook of Special Education*. **Prentice-Hall: USA, 1981.**
Designed as 'a single source of authoritative information for the profession'. It is an original collection of writings on all areas of special education. Coverage includes 'both the theoretical and research underpinning of the field'. After each section there is a detailed bibliography with many references to periodical articles, and there are subject and author indexes.

There are two more Pergamon hand-books on different aspects of education:

PSACHAROPOULOS, G. *Economics of Education: Research and Studies*. **Pergamon, 1987.**
This too is based on the *International Encyclopedia of Education* (see p.23). It aims for 'comprehensive, international coverage of both theoretical and practical aspects of this new and fast-growing field'. The articles are arranged in thematic order, with bibliographies appended to all entries. It was designed as a 'state of the art' survey. There are subject and author indexes.

TITMUS, C.J. *Lifelong Education for Adults: an International Handbook*. **Pergamon, 1988.**
Not strictly speaking a survey of research, but it provides encyclopaedic coverage of the field, with articles by 'specialists from all parts of the world'. Areas covered include theory and principles; the purposes of adult education; participation and recruitment; teaching and learning; the providers of adult education; target groups; systems of adult education; regional and industrial organisation; legislation and finance; and research. 'The problems and initiatives of the developing countries are considered alongside those of advanced countries.'

Finally space must be found for a splendid new handbook which should be extremely useful to a wide variety of readers:

Handbook of Educational Ideas and Practices,
ed. N.Entwistle. Routledge, 1990.
It is aimed at practitioners and students rather
than researchers, but presents a broad conspectus
of contemporary developments which many
researchers would find helpful. Its organisation and
presentation are impressive. There are four main
sections: (A) The nature and function of education;
(B) The management and content of education; (C)
The learning environment; and (D) Individual
development. There are also a great many
chapters, none of which is too long. The authors are
mainly British but 'draw on ideas from the whole
international community' in providing summaries
of the most recent thinking, research findings and
innovatory practices. Commendably they have tried
as far as possible to avoid educational jargon. The
emphasis is on the period of formal schooling, but
there is a separate section on education beyond
school, and another on 'education in contrasting
societies' by foreign educationists. There are short
lists of references at the ends of chapters. This is a
book which was very much needed. It is difficult to
think of anything comparable.

26.2   Reviews of research

There are two older works which should be
mentioned first since they are general
surveys:

BUTCHER, H.J. and PONT, H.B. *Educational
Research in Britain.* University of London
Press. 1968–73. 3 vols.
This is a comprehensive guide, with detailed
bibliographies, to the organisation and practice of
research in Britain. There are full accounts of the
agencies involved and valuable reviews of research
in particular fields. It was intended to be the first of
a continuing series but no further volumes have
appeared. However, the gap has been partly filled
by:

COHEN, L. *Educational Research and
Development in Britain, 1970-1980.* NFER:
Nelson, 1982.
Its aim was to present a current review of research
over a ten-year period. It takes the form of
'comparatively short and accessible accounts of the
more important research studies and development
projects that took place in the major areas of
education in the 1970s'. There are chapters on
topics such as child development, curriculum
theory, home-school relations, games and

simulations, and mixed ability teaching, and othe
on the teaching of particular subjects. Three
separate chapters cover developments in Wales,
Scotland, and Northern Ireland. There is no index

The following works review research
different areas or aspects of education:

ANDERSON, L.W. and BURNS, R.B. *Research in
Classrooms:the Study of Teachers, Teaching ar
Instruction.* Pergamon, 1989.
'The aim of this book is to present a comprehensive
integrated and readable approach to the design,
conduct and interpretation of research on
teaching.' It is included here because it has a usef
chapter on 'Reviewing the research reviews'.

CAVE, C. and MADDISON, F. *A Survey of Recent
Research in Special Education.* NFER, 1978.
Note the date. Undertaken at the instigation of th
Committee of Enquiry into Special Education. Its
aim was 'to review research undertaken in the pas
ten years, either in the United Kingdom or abroac
and to prepare a summary and appraisal of projec
which throw light on the key issues in special
education'. There is a long list of references at the
end.

CLARKE, L. *The Transition from School to Wor.
a Critical Review of Research in the United
Kingdom.* HMSO, 1980.
A short summary of research on this topic. It is on
of a series of three. The other two are concerned
with occupational choice and the practice of
vocational guidance. There is a list of references
and a summary of research methodology used in
previous researches in this area.

*Classroom Teaching Skills: the Research
Findings of the Teacher Education Project,* ed.
E.C. Wragg. Croom Helm, 1984.
The project, based at Nottingham University,
attempted to answer key questions about precisely
what classroom skills trainee teachers need.

GRAHAM, J. *Schools, Disruptive Behaviour and
Delinquency:a Review of Research.* HMSO,
1988. (Home Office research study, no.96.)
Reviews the literature from the viewpoint of those
preventing crime. It suggests what schools can do
do help to prevent children predisposed to
delinquency from embarking on criminal careers.

*International Perspectives on Teacher
Education,* ed. D.K.Sharpes. Routledge, 1988.

Reports on research and practice in teacher
education throughout the world. Includes
specialised studies in areas of social change and
political unrest, e.g. South Africa, Cyprus, Nigeria.

owledge Base for the Beginning Teacher: ed.
C. Reynolds. Pergamon, 1990.
'First in a series of state-of-the-art analyses of
research, theory and practice in the various
domains of teaching' from the American
Association of Colleges for Teacher Education.

cent Advances in Classroom Research, eds
**Bennett and C.Desforges. Scottish
ademic Press, 1985.**
A British Psychological Society monograph. Sections deal with curriculum content—mathematics
and writing, and with context matching and reader
planning.

*search in Learning Disabilities: Issues and
ture Directions,* eds S.Vaughn and C.S.Bos.
ylor & Francis, 1987.
Based on an American research symposium, this
book 'aims to develop an agenda for future
research'. There is an introduction and summaries
of six 'think tank sessions' with a final synthesising
chapter.

search on Motivation in Education, eds
**,and C.Ames. Academic Press, Inc: USA,
84–9.**
l.1: Student Motivation. 1984.
l.2: The Classroom Milieu. 1985.
l.3: Goals and Cognitions. 1989.
A work which originated in the American
Educational Research Association. It attempts to
integrate recent contributions on the subject and to
provide a 'state of the art' summary of research.

*cial Psychology of Education:Current
esearch and Theory,* ed. R.S.Feldman.
ambridge University Press, 1986.
Concerned with the ways in which the theory and
data of social psychology can be applied to teaching,
learning and other experiences in schools. It reviews
the work already done and the work that needs to
be done, with references at the ends of chapters.

ecial Educational Needs Review. **Falmer
ress. Vol.1 1989.**
A projected series of volumes whose aim is to
provide 'a forum for the dissemination of current
thinking and ideas about the education of pupils
with special educational needs'.

*Trends in Distance Higher Education:*eds
**P.Raggatt and K.Harry. Part 1. Open
University Distance Education Group, 1984.**
A short work whose principal objectives are to
illustrate the scale and diversity of distance
education worldwide, and to encourage contact
between individuals and institutions with a view to
exchanging information.

WILSON, J.D. *Student Learning in Higher
Education.* **Croom Helm, 1981.**
Brings together in a concise and readable form
research from Britain, the USA and elsewhere, and
discusses the implications for staff who wish to
assist students to see meaning in their studies.

WRAGG, E.C. *A Review of Research in Teacher
Education.* **NFER-Nelson, 1982.**
Reviews 'the international literature on teacher
education, incorporating a summary of recent
research and new developments, and a full
bibliography and suggestions for further reading'.
It does not pretend to be comprehensive, and its
coverage is limited to the preceding decade. The
author has also excluded many reports which he
felt were 'seriously sub-standard pieces of work'.
Indicates priorities for future enquiry.

There is a useful series of books from the
Falmer Press which are not primarily concerned with reviewing research but do
contain some relevant material, e.g.

New Directions in Educational Evaluation, ed.
E.R.House. Falmer Press, 1986.
'A collection of articles about educational
evaluation by some of the leading international
authorities in the field, summarising current
controversies and future likely trends and
developments.' Several chapters review the
literature on particular aspects, e.g. teacher
evaluation in the organisational context. Most
chapters have notes and references. Other volumes
in the series are:

New Directions in Educational Leadership, ed.
P.Harling, 1984.

New Directions in Educational Psychology.
   **1. Learning and teaching; ed. N.Entwistle,
      1985.**
   **2. Behaviour and motivation in the
      classroom, eds N. Hastings and
      J. Schwieso, 1987.**

New Directions in Primary Education, ed. C. Richards, 1982.
Updated by *Emerging Issues in Primary Education*, ed. M.Clarkson. Falmer, 1988.

New Directions in Religious Education, ed. J. Hull, 1982.

New Directions in Remedial Education, ed. C.J. Smith, 1985.

New Directions in the Study of Reading, ed. M.M. Clark, 1985.

If you are interested in the last of these volumes, see also the *British Register of Reading Research* and *Reading Research*, both published annually by the Reading and Language Information Centre at the University of Reading (see p.187).

It is worth looking out for series or individual volumes with titles such as '*Advances in...*', '*New Developments in...*', '*New Directions in...*', since they may help you to keep up to date with recent research. Examples are:

Advances in Special Education. Jaicon Press: USA. Irregular.

Advances in Teacher Education, eds V. McLelland and V.P. Varma. Routledge, 1989.

Advances in Teacher Education. Ablex: USA, Vol.1 1985.

New Developments in Educational Assessment, eds H.D. Black and W.B. Dockrell. Scottish Academic Press, 1988.

New Directions in Vocational Education, ed. A. Rumney. Routledge, 1989.

Recent Developments in Curriculum Studies, ed. P.A.Taylor. NFER-Nelson, 1986.

There are two long-established American reviews of research which should be familiar to British researchers:

Review of Research in Education. **American Educational Research Association: USA annual.**
The first volume of this important series appeare in 1973. 'The purpose of the review is to survey disciplined inquiry in education through critical and synthesising essays. It will attempt to inform its readers not only what has been, and is being done, but perhaps more importantly, what will be and should be done in educational research. The substantive problems and domains of education w be the primary focus of the review, but it will also report, assess and evaluate technical and methodological developments. In addition, it will alert to theory in other fields, particularly the behavioral sciences: sociology, anthropology, economics, political science.' Each annual volume divided into several sections which are concerned with different areas of interest. The review shoulc be scanned by all serious researchers.

Review of Child Development Research. **Various editors. Chicago University Press: USA, irregular.**
This work has a long history. Volume 1 appeared i 1964, vol.7 in 1985. The volumes are prepared by the Society for Research in Child Development. 'The aim of the series is to increase communicatic and the exchange of ideas and information betwee scientists involved in basic research and individual involved in the application of such knowledge with children and families.' Each volume covers a wide variety of topics.

Committed researchers in special educa tion could consult:

STERNLICHT, M. and M. *Special Education: a Sourcebook.* **Garland: USA, 1987.**
'A select, topically organised, annotated bibliography reviewing the most important research from 1960 to the present, as well as landmark works published before 1960'. It cites books, chapters, articles, dissertations, etc. primarily in English. An appendix lists major journals in the field.

There are two interesting works whic are concerned with research in educatio from an international standpoint:

ALTBACH, P.G. *Comparative Higher Education: Research Trends and Bibliography.* **Mansell, 1979.**
'Consisting of an essay and a bibliography, this volume provides a discussion of the origins and

development of comparative and higher education as a field of study, an interpretation of the key issues of higher education as they affect various countries, and a select list of contributions to the literature of the subject.'

LTBACH, P.G. and **KELLY, D.H.** *Higher Education in International Perspective:a Survey and Bibliography; with an essay by Jan Kluczynski.* **ansell, 1985.**
This handsome volume was produced as the result of a meeting organised by Unesco's European Centre for Higher Education in 1982. It provides a synthesis of the then current state of higher education research in Europe, the USA, Canada and Israel. The main focus is 'a bibliography of 7,000 entries, reflecting the nature and development of the international literature on higher education over the past 20 years'. It includes books, articles, unpublished theses, conference papers and government documents in the major written languages: English, French, German, Russian, and Portuguese. It also includes a brief survey of journals in the field of higher education (pp.22–5) and a list of them is provided (pp.52–3).

So far in this section we have been concerned with research rather than researchers. There is a short survey which may do a little to redress the balance:

DOOLEY, P. et al. *Survey of Educational Researchers in Britain.* **Department of Educational Enquiry, University of Aston in Birmingham. 1981.**
'This differs from most research accounts in that its subject is the research community itself.'
Questionnaires and interviews were used to find out more about those involved in carrying out research activities. There is a bibliography.

26.3 Theses and dissertations

This section and the next are concerned with records of academic theses, dissertations and research projects. An effort has been made to distinguish between completed theses in this section and ongoing research in the next. This has not always been possible since some records contain both. The standard record of completed theses in this country is:

Index to Theses with Abstracts, Accepted for Higher Degrees by the Universities of Great Britain and Ireland and the Council for National Academic Awards. **4 per annum. Aslib.**
The *Aslib Index to Theses*, as it is known, has been appearing regularly since 1950, but there was an important development in 1986 (vol.35 part 1) when an abstract of each thesis was included for the first time. The frequency of publication was also increased from two to four issues per annum. The abstracts are about 500 words long on average. Entries are arranged in broad subject order, e.g. education (B3) which is subdivided into theory and principles: educational psychology and sociology; history; Great Britain and Ireland; comparative education; school administration; teacher training; methods of teaching; curriculum; etc. A note is given on the availability of each thesis. There are author and subject indexes. Online access is planned.
    Aslib also publishes *Abstracts of Theses* on microfiche. Each issue corresponds to an issue of the *Aslib Index to Theses* starting with vol.26 part 1. Photocopies of individual abstracts are available from the Information Centre at Aslib.

Most doctoral theses accepted at British universities are included in *British Reports, Translations and Theses* (BRTT) (see p.133). It is published by the British Library Document Supply Centre, which now has over 40,000 doctoral theses available for loan (see the end of this section).

For earlier coverge, indeed right back to the early eighteenth century when theses first made their appearance, there is a standard general source:

Retrospective Index to Theses of Great Britain and Ireland 1716–1950, eds **R.R.Bilboul** and **F.L. Kent.** ABC-Clio, 1975–7. 5 vols. Vol.1: *Social Sciences and Humanities,* 1975.
'This volume lists the titles of about 13,000 theses in the social sciences' (including education and educational psychology) 'covering all universities in Great Britain and Ireland at which higher degrees were conferred before 1950.' However, 'only one or two universities – London and Oxford – had as many as ten theses each year before the 1920s...the number gradually increased until the Second World War. There was then a peak period in the late 1940s'.
    The main arrangement is by subject. Theses are indexed under specific rather than general terms, with numerous cross-references. Under each

heading titles are arranged alphabetically. For educational theses there are general and miscellaneous headings followed by headings for education in different countries and for types of education, e.g. adult, higher, physical, secondary. There is an author index.

Together the *Aslib Index to Theses* and the *Retrospective Index to Theses* provide continuous coverage of British theses (including educational theses) from 1814 to date.

The most impressive of all general records of theses (or dissertations, as they are known in America) is an American publication. It has the advantage of providing very full summaries of the theses included:

Dissertation Abstracts International. Section A:The humanities and social sciences. Section B: The sciences and engineering. Section C: European abstracts. A and B monthly, C quarterly; with annual cumulation. University Microfilms International: USA.
The theses listed in section A are mainly American and Canadian but there are some from other countries. Section C has abstracts of theses in all disciplines accepted for doctoral and postgraduate degrees at European institutions. The arrangement is by broad subject headings alphabetically, and the abstracts are up to 350 words.

From vol.xxx no.1 there is 'a mechanised keyword title index' which lists the abstracts alphabetically by keywords contained in their titles. The author indexes in each issue cumulate and merge annually. This is an important source for serious researchers. UMI has now introduced *Dissertation Abstracts Ondisc* which gives access to almost a million dissertations written since 1861 on compact disc. Note also:

Comprehensive Dissertation Index. 1861–1972, 37 vols. 1973–1982, 38 vols. Annual supplements in bound volumes and microfiche. University Microfilms International: USA.
Another key source for access to dissertations, from the same publisher, but this time no abstracts are provided. It is intended for those who prefer to use printed sources to conduct their searches although it is also available online from *Dialog*. The arrangement is by broad subject including education, sociology and psychology, and the lack of specific headings makes it less easy to use. Nevertheless it is an important finding aid.

There is a comparatively recent checklist of British theses on education:

British Education Theses Index 1950–1980. 3rd edn. eds by J.R.V. Johnston and J. Marder. Librarians of the Institutes and Schools of Education, 1983. (Microfiche)
BETI, as it is known, lists by subject and by author all theses for degrees in education and related subjects awarded by British and Irish universities which were included in the *Aslib Index to Theses* (see p.183) during the period. It is available only on microfiche, with updates. The terms used in BETI are included in the *British Education Thesaurus* (see p.19).

There is an older standard list of theses on education:

BLACKWELL, A.M. *A List of Researches in Education and Educational Psychology Presented for Higher Degrees in the Universities of the United Kingdom, Northern Ireland and the Irish Republic from 1914–1948, Classified According to a Modification of the Dewey Decimal Classification System.* Newnes for the NFER. 1950.
It includes a subject index. Various supplements were published up to 1968–69.

Two more recent sources may be mentioned briefly.

Web Directory of Masters Level Educational Dissertations, 1976–1987, ed. A.Lewis. Psychological Services (Worcester), 1988.

Web Register of Research Theses in Education, completed and validated on an ongoing basis by the CNAA; ed. A.C.Crocker. Psychological Services (Worcester). No.1 1987—. (The first issue covers theses validated 1970–1986.)

For retrospective coverage of theses from Irish Universities we have:

Register of Theses on Educational Topics in Universities in Ireland; compiled by J.Coolahan et al. Officina Typographica, 1980, annual supplements.
Every effort was made to make the register as comprehensive as possible but 'the inclusion of a thesis title is not a guarantee that the thesis is at present available for consultation'. The arrangement of entries is inconveniently

chronological, and the subject index only gives long lists of the running numbers used.

For British theses on the history of edu-tion there is:

search in the History of Education:a List of ieses for Higher Degrees in British niversities. History of Education Society, nual.

A brief list in pamphlet form which gives titles, authors and supervisors, and degrees awarded. It is arranged by subjects as set out on the contents page and there are indexes of universities, subjects and authors. First published in 1968. Retrospective coverage in this field is provided by:

heses and Dissertations in the History of ducation Presented at British and Irish niversities Between 1900 and 1976, compiled y V.F.Gilbert and C. Holmes. History of ducation Society, 1979.

The aim here is comprehensiveness. It is arranged in a classified sequence with indexes of persons, places, subjects and authors. Note also:

issertations on the History of Education 970–1980, compiled by E.R. Beauchamp. carecrow Press: USA, 1980.

An American list compiled by extracting relevant titles from *Dissertation Abstracts International* (see above). About 2,500 dissertations are included. The arrangement is by country, then by topic, with a subject index.

Other specialised lists include:

egister of Advanced Studies in Further and ligher Education originating in the colleges f education (technical). 3rd edn. Bolton :ollege of Education (Technical), 1987.

A select list of studies submitted for awards within these four institutions: Bolton College, Garnett College, Huddersfield Polytechnic, and Wolverhampton Polytechnic. Entries are arranged by course, then by author, with author and subject indexes.

:HARNLEY, A.H. *Research in Adult Education in he British Isles: Abstracts and Summaries, •rincipally of Master and Doctorate Theses •resented Since 1945*. National Institute of .dult Education, 1974.

The theses and other publications summarised are those available for inter-library loan. They are grouped into eight main sections and subdivided into topic areas. A coding system is used. The

abstracts and summaries are full and helpful. Note the date.

For British theses on comparative educa-tion we have:

PARKER, F. and PARKER, J .P. **Education in other Lands: a Bibliography of 91 British Graduate Theses and Dissertations.** *Educational Studies*, vol.2 no.1, Mar.1976, pp.45–86.

A bibliography by two Americans which brings together theses on comparative education from a variety of sources, but again the date should be noted. Arrangement is by authors' names, but a subject index appeared in the next issue of the journal: vol.2 no.2, June 1976, pp.160–70.

Once you have identified a thesis in which you are interested, your library should be able to borrow it for you, either direct from another library or more usually from the British Library Document Supply Centre, which now acquires about two thirds of the university theses produced in this country. However, there are strict regulations about the use of borrowed theses and they will normally have to be consulted in your library, not at home.

There is a short book which discusses thesis literature in a general way and could provide useful background reading, though a new edition is needed:

DAVINSON, D. *Theses and Dissertations as Information Sources*. Bingley, 1977.

26.4 Current research projects

Details of current educational research projects are included in:

Current Research in Britain. Vol.3: Social Sciences. British Library, annual.

This is part of a four-volume work which gives details of 60,000 projects, a third of which are not included in previous issues. The main arrangement is by institutions. A complete list of these appears at the beginning. There are also indexes of names, study areas, and keywords which help to pinpoint research by individuals, or on particular aspects of education, psychology, and sociology. Before 1986 it was published as *Research in British Universities, Polytechnics and Colleges,* and before 1976 as *Scientific Research in British Universities and Colleges.*

A main source for information about recent (and less recent) educational research projects in this country is the:

Register of Educational Research in the United Kingdom. NFER: Nelson, irregular.
Vol.1: 1973–76.
Vol.2: 1976–77.
Vol.3: 1977–78.
Vol.4: 1978–80.
Vol.5: 1980–82.
Vol.6: 1983–86.
Vol.7: 1987–89.
Note that the volumes cover varying periods. The information is supplied by universities, colleges, government departments, and other organisations and institutions. The majority of entries in each volume are new, the remainder being updated when necessary from the previous volume. Arrangement is by institutions, then by authors' names. There is also a subject index.

The DES is involved in promoting research projects and providing financial support for them. There is a continuing record:

DEPARTMENT OF EDUCATION AND SCIENCE. Current Educational Research Projects Supported by the DES. Annual.
The projects are listed under broad headings, e.g. pupil performance; (a) the Assessment of Performance Unit; (b) the effectiveness of schools; (c) general. Brief summaries of each project are given. There is no author index. There is a corresponding publication for Scotland (see p.187).

For further and higher education in particular there is:

Register of Research into Higher Education:Mainly in the United Kingdom. Society for Research into Higher Education. 2-yearly.
It aims to give complete coverage of the UK. Items listed are mainly from universities but there are some from polytechnics and colleges. A number of

completed theses are included as well as the current ones. A short summary of each thesis is given but since 1974–75 these have been very brie There is a classified arrangement. Fuller information is available from the SRHE (see p.17 There was a companion work for Europe (see below) but only two issues were published.

There is also a *Register of Advanced Stud₄ in Further and Higher Education* originating the Colleges of Education (Technical) (s₄ p.185).

For the most recent information on cu₄ rent research projects we must turn to:

Research into Higher Education Abstracts. 4 per annum. Society for Research into Higher Education.
This is an abstracting periodical. Short summaries of new projects are given in each issue, and coverage of the UK is as complete as possible. About 400 periodicals are scanned for appropriate material, as well as books, reference works and selected theses. The abstracts are arranged in related groups then alphabetically by author. The endlist of periodicals abstracted could be useful to researchers.

For special education we have:

Register of Research in Special Education in the United Kingdom. NFER-Nelson. vol.1:1983–84. 1986. (In progress.)
It aims to include all current research in special education in the UK. The main arrangement is by the name of the institution initiating the research and the entries are numbered consecutively. There is a name index and also a subject index which is based on keywords added to each entry. Note also:

Skill Directory of Research:Young People and Adults with Special Needs, compiled by B.Kent. National Bureau for Students with Disabilities (NBSD) (formerly the National Bureau for Handicapped Students), 1988.
A directory of current and recent research into matters relating to the post-school education and training of young people with disabilities. About 180 projects are listed in nine sections. There is a subject index and an index of authors/researchers. Updates appear from time to time in *Educare*:the journal of the NBSD.

Those who are interested in research an₄

evelopment work in schools, especially in elation to the curriculum, teaching ethods and examinations may have ncountered the *Schools Council Project Files nd Index*. This was a set of information neets on research and development rojects originally funded by the Schools ouncil and the Nuffield Foundation in ngland and Wales. It was updated every wo years, and supplemented in between by bi-monthly news sheet called *Schools ouncil Link*. There was also a termly *ewsletter*. After the demise of the Schools ouncil (see p.174) responsibility for the *roject Files and Index* was taken over by the chool Curriculum Development Commit- ee (see p.174).

On more specific aspects of education here are:

Register of Research and Development in areers Guidance. National Institute for areers Education and Counselling, annual.
The Institute is jointly sponsored by CRAC (see p.79) and Hatfield Polytechnic. The register provides summaries of ongoing research and development projects. Arrangement is by a special classification system, with indexes of researchers and institutions. Each entry has a full page to itself signed by the project director. There are occasional supplements. The *Register* derives from the *CRAC/NFER Register of Research in Educational and Vocational Guidance* published in 1974.

Register of Research on Information Technology n Education. Council for Educational Technology.
'A register of projects held in the CET/DES database using superfile on a Nimbus computer.' It provides descriptions of projects in all areas of education, and gives details of researchers, their addresses, staffing and funding. Information is retrieved using keywords selected from the *Eudised Multilingual Thesaurus* (see p.19).

British Register of Reading Research. Reading and Language Information Centre, University of Reading School of Education, annual.
First published in 1976 this provides two separate lists: one of ongoing research, the other of completed research. They are arranged alphabetically by researchers' surnames. There follows a series of abstracts, then lists of reference

words and keywords to assist identification. There is also an annual *Reading Research* (ed. E.J.Goodacre), from the same source. It provides a general review of the research published during the year, followed by annotated lists of articles and books.

Detailed information on numerous education research projects is included in:

Research Supported by the Economic and Social Research Council. ESRC, annual.
This lists all the research projects in the social sciences funded by the ESRC (see p.174) in progress or completed during the year. There are six main sections, one of which is Education and Human Development. Abstracts of about 200 words are given in 'language that an intelligent layman can understand'. There is a subject index of keywords and an index of investigators. Information about the *ESRC Data Archive* is included.

Scottish educational research projects are covered by several publications:

SCOTTISH COUNCIL FOR RESEARCH IN EDUCATION. *Annual Report*. University of London Press.
The SCRE was described on p.174. Its annual report includes a list of researches in education and educational psychology presented for degrees in Scottish universities. There is a *Newsletter* which provides information on new developments and publications. It was formerly called *Research in Education* (not to be confused with the periodical issued by Manchester University Press with the same title.)

SCOTTISH EDUCATION DEPARTMENT. *Educational Research in 19—: a Register of Current Educational Research Projects Funded by the SED*. Annual.
There is a corresponding publication for England and Wales issued annually by the DES (see p.186) but this gives more detail. The projects listed are based in colleges of education, central institutions, universities, SCRE (see above) and SCET (see p.176).

JOINT COMMITTEE OF COLLEGES OF EDUCATION IN SCOTLAND. *Bulletin of Research:Major and Minor Projects*. C/o Northern College of Education, irregular.
Formerly known as the *NICCER Bulletin*. The National Inter-College Committee for Educational Research was discontinued in 1985 and replaced by a new Steering Committee on Research. Full

information about major projects is given, minor ones are merely listed. The main arrangement is by institution, then by project alphabetically. Number 6 has two articles on educational research in Scotland.

Note that a keyword index to the last three publications (above):the *SCRE Annual Report,* the *SED Register of Research* and the *JCCES Bulletin of Research,* is held at the SCRE library. Coverage is from 1982.

Summaries of recent Scottish educational research projects will be found in each issue of the *Scottish Educational Review* (2 per annum) (formerly *Scottish Educational Studies*). Another useful source is:

Edinburgh University, Centre for Educational Sociology. *Bibliography:Research Conducted by Past and Present Members of the Centre and by Others Associated with it.* **CES, annual.**

'The bibliography is arranged chronologically and the subject matter of each entry is indicated by one or more keywords after the synopsis.' A complete list of these keywords precedes the main text. The CES is also associated with the:

Scottish Education Data Archive. **Edinburgh University, Centre for Educational Sociology. (Database.)**

This is a publicly accessible database on school leavers in Scotland dating back to 1962. The data in the archive are available for analysis under the collaborative research programme to anyone with a serious interest in Scottish education who is able to carry out analyses of computerised data. Those accessing the database, which is on the computing system of the Edinburgh Regional Computing Centre, will make use of the *Collaborative Research Dictionary:*a dictionary of variables from the Scottish School Leavers' Survey held in the SEDA, and the *Collaborative Research Questionnaires* issued in conjunction with the dictionary. A dictionary and questionnaire package are issued after each survey.

Full information about the package and its use are given in parts 1 and 2 of the dictionary. For those who are registered users of the Edinburgh Regional Computing Centre, or who can connect with the Edinburgh computing network, further information and updates are available online.

Since 1981 the SEDA has been operated jointly by the CES and the SED. Practitioners are involved at every stage of the research process, from the

planning of questionnaires through to data analysis and the publication of findings. A *Collaborative Research Newsletter* has appeared irregularly.

For current research projects in Europe there is an abstracting service:

EUDISED R & D Bulletin. **4 per annum. K.G.Saur for the European Documentation and Information System for Education: West Germany.**

R & D stands for research and development. Each issue contains generous extracts of about 250 ongoing and recently completed projects in the field. The details of projects are supplied by the national agencies in each member country of the Council for European Co-operation. The entries for the UK are based on those in the *Register of Educational Research* (see p.186).

The abstracts are in alphabetical order by topics, which are clearly listed at the beginning. Indexing is by descriptors (terms) taken from the *EUDISED Multilingual Thesaurus* (see p.19). The abstracts themselves are in English, French and German. There are author and subject indexes, and a cumulated annual index. Online access to the *EUDISED* database is available.

The SRHE started to publish a projected series of volumes in 1973 but only two appeared:

Register of Research into Higher Education in Western Europe **(excluding the UK). 1973: 1974-77. Society for Research into Higher Education.**

These were pioneering volumes which did not pretend to be comprehensive. Entries are serially numbered, classified into related sections, and as far as possible grouped into topics within sections. Indexes of research workers and institutions are provided.

An international survey of educational research projects has been published by Unesco:

Inventory of Educational Research on Higher Education Projects Undertaken by Higher Education Institutions. **Unesco, 1987. (Preliminary version.)**

Covers projects carried out during the last decade by establishments of higher education. It was prepared in co-operation with the International Associastion of Universities. Responses were received from institutions in 54 countries but coverage is not comprehensive. Only basic information is given. Arrangement is under countries alphabetically then by institutions. Unesco has also produced:

formation on Research in Progress: a 'orldwide Inventory. **2nd edn. Unesco, 1982.** This provides an overview, followed by profiles, of information systems and services on research in progress generally. There is some coverage of education, but the section on the UK is disappointing.

6.5 Periodicals concerned with research

ome periodicals consist entirely of re-
:arch articles and these are obviously a ontinuing source of information for the ducational researcher, but there are not nough of them. A good example is the *eview of Educational Research* (4 per annum. .merican Library Association). It is well 'orth searching its files for relevant mater-il. Before 1970 each issue was devoted to a articular theme.

Again, too few periodicals are involved in ublishing research articles for the prac-ising teacher, and there are gaps here wait-
1g to be filled. The best known British xample is *Educational Research.* (3 per annum. .FER-Nelson), which 'presents new inform-d thinking and empirical evidence on ssues of contemporary concern in edu-ation'. More recently the NFER have tarted *Topic,* a journal in loose-leaf format ontaining reports and leaflets which high-ight the findings of research for teachers.

Some periodicals of more general nterest may include articles of potential alue to the educational researcher or the eacher with a particular interest in re-

search. Good examples of these are the *British Journal of Educational Studies* (3 per annum. Blackwell for the Standing Confe-rence on Studies in Education), and the *Scottish Educational Review* (2 per annum. Scottish Academic Press).

There is a helpful evaluation of journals relevant to educational research in Alt-bach,P.G. and Kelly, D.H. *Higher Education in International Perspective* (see p.182), pp.22–5, with a separate list on pp.52–3. A much fuller list will be found at the end of the latest issue of *Research into Higher Education Abstracts* (see p.186). It includes about 300 titles indexed by the service.

Two periodicals must be singled out here because of the substantial amount of re-search material they contain, and because they are in microfiche format and may consequently be overlooked. The first is a very important source indeed:

CORE **(Collected Original Sources in Education). 3 per annum. Carfax. (Microfiche)**
On its first appearance in 1977 the publisher described *Core* as 'an entirely new concept in educational research'. It makes available research material which because of its sheer size and complexity could not readily be published by conventional means. A very wide range of topics has been covered. The microfiches are contained within a normal journal cover and eye-legible contents and abstracts are provided. Unlimited copying of material from *Core* is permitted as long as the copies are not offered for sale.

The second periodical is narrower in scope but is still a considerable research resource in its own field:

Journal of Sources in Educational History. **3 per annum. Carfax. (Microfiche.)**
'This aims to provide in microfiche form a selection of basic original source material for students and teachers of educational history. The sources selected amount to the equivalent of about 1,200 pages per annual volume of three numbers...They include selections from official records, newspapers,

personal recollections and contemporary texts and photographs.' Unlike *Core* (above) each issue is devoted to a particular theme, e.g.:

The Education of Girls and Women in Industrial England (vol.5 no.2, 1982).
Inspectors' Reports on Elementary Schools (vol.6 no.1, 1983).
The History of Special Needs Education (vol.7 no.3, 1984).
School Ephemera of the 19th and 20th Centuries (vol.8 no.2, 1985).
Equal Pay for Teachers (vol.9 no.1, 1986).
Recent Developments in INSET: a Review (vol.11 no.1, 1987).
Primary Head Teachers and Delegation (vol.12 no.2, 1988).

26.6 Resources in education (ERIC)

This is the only section of this guide which is devoted to one publication. *Resources in Education* has been given this prominence because of its unique character and special importance:

Resources in Education (ERIC). Monthly. Educational Resources Information Center: USA.
ERIC was established by the US Office of Education in 1966. It is a national information system with a network of decentralised documentation centres, which provides one central source for obtaining documents related to education. Its function is to make information on the latest research and developments readily availabe to the people who need it. This it does by collecting, abstracting, indexing, and disseminating all the relevant information on an impressive scale.
It covers not only educational research reports but also conference papers, speeches and addresses, teacher and curriculum guides, and other documents. The scope is avowedly international, but there is a strong emphasis on American documents. Unfortunately there is no comparable British publication.
The main sequence of abstracts is in numerical order by a special code number but there are indexes of subjects, authors and institutions. An annual cumulation is published by Oryx Press in

two volumes. Most of the original documents are available for purchase either in microform or as hard copy. *Resources in Education (RIE)* and another ERIC's publications, the *Current Index to Journals in Education (CIJE)* are also accessible online through Dialog. This has become the normal avenue of approach, but both are now available on CD-ROM which many will prefer if it is provided (see 26.7).
Resources in Education was called *Research in Education* until it changed its title in 1975. For a comprehensive summary of ERIC products and services see *A Pocket Guide to ERIC*. A full list of guides to ERIC will be found in:*Search Aids for Use with Dialog Data Bases* (Latest edn. Dialog Information Services). There is a short chapter on ERIC in the *International Yearbook of Educational and Training Technology* (1990), pp.13–17.

26.7 Using bibliographic data-bases (online and CD-ROM)

Apart from chapter 20 which was concerned with non-book materials, and section 14.17 which was devoted to online educational directories such as *Campus* 2000, this guide has concentrated on printed reference sources (including microforms) and reference to online and other systems has been incidental. However, an increasing number of printed sources are becoming available online through a computer terminal, and on compact disc (CD-ROM).

Despite the higher initial costs to libraries in the acquisition of discs and the purchase of appropriate equipment, CD-ROM is making ground because of its powerful storage and search capabilities and convenient format. Although the information held cannot always be as current as that available online, CD-ROM is more user friendly and much preferred by students and researchers where it is available. After some initial guidance most readers are able to use CD-ROM on their own, and the

ngth of their search is not inhibited by
e cost factor which affects the use of
line.

The *World Book Encyclopedia* (p.22).
Whitaker's Books in Print (p.113) and the
British Education Index (p.156) are just a few
the works already mentioned whose
ontents are retrievable online. The OCLC
eference Service, available to libraries in
the UK, claims to provide access to over 15
million bibliographic records, from the
World Guide to Libraries (p.4) and *Who's Who*
p.99) to the *World of Learning* (p.99) and
the *Research Centers Directory* (p.176) A
surprising number of the works described
in this book are also available on CD-ROM
but their potential usefulness in this form
limited at present by libraries' ability to
afford them.

The entire resources of ERIC (see 26.6),
the bibliographic database most used by
educational researchers, may be tapped
using a computer terminal linked to the
Dialog system in California. However,
ERIC is available on CD-ROM from at least
three different sources – Dialog, OCLC and
SilverPlatter, Inc. (all USA). A brief
description of the last one may be helpful:

**ERIC on CD-ROM: a bibliographic disc
indexing the contents of journals, books and
research documents in the field of education
from 1966 to the present. Discs cover
1966–1975; 1976–1982; 1983 to date, updated
quarterly and annually. Distributed by
Microinfo Ltd, PO Box 3, Omega Park, Alton,
Hampshire GU34 2PG.**

ERIC on CD-ROM consists of two separate
files:*Current Index to Journals in Educations* (see p.157)
and *Resources in Education* (see p.190). They are
accompanied by a quick reference guide 'which
provides advice and guidance for users; enables
them to expand or narrow their search; limit their
search to a specific field; search on another topic;
use a previous search; display the results of their
search; print or transfer to disc the results of their
search'.

Obviously retrieval of bibliographic and
other information either online or via CD-
ROM can be invaluable to educational researchers for a variety of purposes. However, it is important to realise that they are
not a complete substitute for manual searching but an added facility or resource, which
will become more and more useful as
databanks increase in size and depth.

If you are using these systems some skill
and persistence are needed to find the information you require and you will have to
know precisely what you want from them.
In this context you will find the appropriate
educational thesaurus helpful (see 8.4:
Educational thesauri). In the case of ERIC
you will use the *Thesaurus of ERIC Descriptors*
(see p.18). It is a detailed list of the terms
employed by ERIC and from it you will
select those most relevant to your chosen
topic, always making due allowance for the
American terminology. The search will then
be carried out at the terminal, if necessary
with the help of a qualified librarian. An
online search in particular can be time-
consuming and therefore more expensive,
especially for inexperienced users of the
system.

What you retrieve will normally be a
straightforward list, perhaps quite long, of
references or short extracts, mainly American, not all of which may be relevant for
your particular purpose. Once you have
identified those likely to be useful you may
wish to obtain the documents themselves
either in hard copy or on microfiche. This
will normally be done through the inter-
library loan procedure.

It is desirable before embarking on a
search to ensure that you have exploited
the resources of your own library which are
after all readily available to you. In other
words a manual search will probably pre-
cede an online search in the majority of
cases. Nevertheless, an online or CD-ROM

search will often pinpoint articles or items on the library shelves which your manual search has failed to reveal.

Many students will be able to survive without using these systems, and so will some teachers and researchers even if the facilities are readily available. The level, depth, scale and for online searching the possible cost, of an enquiry are factors which will affect your decision about whether to conduct a search or not. If you are simply looking for a few books or articles on mixed ability teaching you will not benefit from a long string of bibliographic references from a sophisticated retrieval system.

But for serious students or researchers who have some acquaintance with the literature of their subject and who feel that they have exhausted the resources of their own library, an online or CD-ROM search offers definite advantages. Those who would like more information about using online systems could consult:

HOUGHTON,B. *Online Information Retrieval:an Introductory Manual to Principles and Practice.* 3rd edn. Bingley, 1989.
   It is designed for those 'seeking to familiarise themselves with the principles and techniques of online access to bibliographic databases'. There is a useful new section on CD-ROM. The same author has a chapter in Higgens,G. (see p.13), which would be a good starting point.

For those who wish to keep up to date with developments in this field, there are several periodicals which could be scanned if they are available in your library:

CD-ROM Librarian. 11 per annum. Meckler: USA.
Online Notes. 10 per annum. Learned Information.
Online Review. 6 per annum. Aslib.
   The first of these has a very interesting review (in vol.5 no.4 Apr.1990, pp.22-9) of the CD-ROM version of the *International Encyclopedia of Education* which is not yet available commercially.

26.8 Lists of databases

There are several publications which could help potential users to identify relevant databases from the rapidly growing number now available in a variety of fields. There is a standard British source:

Online Bibliographic Databases, J.L.Hall and M.Brown. Latest edn. Aslib.
   It describes over 250 databases which 'provide access to 160 million references.' There is a '1,000 reference bibliography' and there are thirty pages of indexes. Pull-out samples are included.

More substantial international lists of databases include the following. The first has a European emphasis:

EUSIDIC Database Guide. Learning Information Ltd, 2-yearly.

Data Base Directory. Knowledge Industry Publications: USA. 2 vols. annual.

Online Database Search Services Directory. Latest edn. Gale Research Co: USA.

There is a list of educational databases:

Directory of Educational Research Information Sources. Latest edn. Foundation for Educational Research in the Netherlands.
   This gives international coverage of bibliographical publications and databases in educational research and related areas. Note also:

EUROPEAN CENTRE FOR THE DEVELOPMENT OF VOCATIONAL TRAINING. *Databases for Education and Training:Conference Report.* European Communities: HMSO, 1989.

There are two important directories of
tabases and publications which are now
ailable on CD-ROM:

●-ROM Directory. Latest edn. TPFL
blishing.
The latest edition (1989) describes almost 400 titles
available or annuounced, an increase of 100% over
the previous year, although it is suggested that the
UK is lagging behind other European countries.
There are useful explanations of CD-ROM, its

advantages and disadvantages compared with
online searching, a hardware section, notes on
relevant books, periodicals, conferences, etc. and a
glossary. An invaluable though expensive
publication.

***CD-ROMs in Print*. Meckler: USA, annual.**
Provides detailed information on all CD-ROMs
currently available, indexing them by subject, title,
product, and company. It includes a glossary of the
most commonly used optical terms.

27 Conclusion

If you have read this far you may be a little discouraged by the sheer number of information sources which are available for 'finding out in education'. However, it is unlikely that any of the libraries you are using has all of these resources. The important thing is that you should be able to make the most effective use of the resources which are available to you.

You must try to identify the type of reference source which is most likely to help you, and then the particular examples of that type which could yield the answers you require. The detailed annotations provided throughout this guide should enable you to make appropriate choices and find your information quickly and efficiently.

It is worth remembering that there is often more than one possible source for a piece of information. For example, lists of HM Inspectorate reports on schools and colleges may be found in a variety of publications. There is no reason to be disappointed, therefore, if your library does not have a particular item.

One quality you must have is peseverance. There is a lot of information tucked away in reference books that does not appear in their lists of contents or their indexes. Tracking down the information you need can be an enjoyable, challenging and rewarding experience. There is something of Sherlock Holmes in all of us. With patience and application, and a little inspiration and luck, perhaps we can be equally successful.

28 Title index

No author index has been provided, but here are separate title and subject indexes. The title index should enable the reader to identify the majority of works mentioned in the book very quickly. However, the titles listed in chapter 5 (Some books on how to study) and in section 17.3 (Open University course readers) have not been included, since these are straightforward lists; nor are annual reports (except for those of the DES and the SED) (see 11.1) or annual conference proceedings (see 11.2).

A word by word arrangement is used for the index. Initials and acronyms are filed as words; hyphenated words are filed as separate words; 'encyclopaedia' and 'encyclopedia' are interfiled, and so are 'year book' and 'yearbook'. Only one page reference is given for each title (though some entries in the text extend over more than a page). Additional, as opposed to main entries for titles are not recorded, but 'see' references are used very frequently throughout the book.

There are a few series entries, e.g. for *Audit Commission Reports* and for the *Rediguides*. There are no entries for mainstream educational periodicals, including the *Times Educational Supplement* and the *Times Higher Education Supplement*, which are referred to in the text on numerous occasions.

Where there are two or more identical titles the subtitle has been added if there is one, and the author's surname given if necessary to avoid confusion. You should check the index under titles beginning with the words `educational research' for the arrangement used in such cases.

Title index

29 Subject index

The title and subject indexes are to some extent complementary, as the title often reveals the subject. This subject index is a selective one. It contains entries for types of information sources, e.g. dictionaries, official publications, subject indexes to periodicals; and for organisations, etc. described in the text, e.g. the National Foundation for Educational Research. It does not, except incidentally, include entries for the subject content of books and other items. As in the title index, a word by word arrangement is used.

Subject index